DISCARDED
JENKS LRC
GORDON COLLEGE

WII
G
Wenham, Mass. 01984

P9-CQN-872

15.50

Effective
Educational and
Behavioral
Programming for
Severely and Profoundly
Handicapped Students

Effective Educational and Behavioral Programming for Severely and Profoundly Handicapped Students

A Manual for Teachers and Aides

by
Dorothy Popovich
Consultant for Psychological Services
Macomb Intermediate School District
Mt. Clemens, Michigan

·P·A·U·L·H·
BROOKES
PUBLISHING C⁰

Baltimore · London

Paul H. Brookes Publishing Co.
Post Office Box 10624
Baltimore, Maryland 21204

Copyright 1981 by Macomb Intermediate School District,
Mt. Clemens, Michigan.
All rights reserved.

Typeset by The Composing Room of Michigan, Inc. (Grand Rapids).
Manufactured in the United States of America by Universal
Lithographers, Inc. (Cockeysville, Maryland).

LB
1570
.P63

Library of Congress Cataloging in Publication Data

Popovich, Dorothy.
    Effective educational and behavioral programming for severely and profoundly hand-
icapped students.

    Bibliography: p.
    Includes index.
    1. Curriculum planning.   2. Classroom management.
I. Title.
LB1570.P63   371.9   80-27706
ISBN 0-933716-14-1

Contents

Preface

There were few provisions for educating severely and profoundly retarded persons before 1974. Since that time, federal law has mandated that these students be educated, yet many of the instructors who become responsible for educating the severely and profoundly retarded have little or no background to prepare them for this task. The purpose of this book is to provide instructors with an introduction to those behavioral principles and techniques that will permit them to effectively educate their students.

The material is presented in nontechnical language whenever possible. It follows a logical sequence that increases in complexity, and its frequent quizzes help you master each section before you move on. In this way, the very principles presented are being used throughout the text. The use of this text will help shape your behavioral skills, and the quizzes will ensure that you successfully master the material. It is hoped that you will find this book useful and that it will help you develop effective, humane, and enduring programs for your students.

Acknowledgments

The assistance and support of several individuals were instrumental in helping this book reach completion. First and foremost, I would like to thank Fred Nowland and Don Thomas for their generous help throughout all stages of the project. They, in turn, were supported by the Macomb Intermediate School District Board of Education, Dr. Robert Lutz, Superintendent, and Dr. Urey Arnold, Deputy Superintendent. I am also grateful to Dr. Sandra Laham and Dr. Ernest Vargas for their comments on the text.

Lastly, I would like to thank the Michigan Department of Education for its financial support of this project, and especially Rich Richardson of the Michigan State Department of Education for all his efforts.

To Pete and Chedo
Jen and Erin

Part I

Creating a Curriculum
and an Appropriate
Learning Environment

Chapter 1

BEHAVIORAL OBJECTIVES

After reading this chapter, you will be able to:

1. List a student's entering behaviors and select an individualized teaching goal.
2. List the three criteria that behavioral objectives must meet.
3. List the three ways to specify the criteria for acceptable performance in a behavioral objective.
4. Select objectives that do not meet the criteria for being behavioral.
5. Write 10 behavioral objectives that meet the following criteria:
   a. Tell what the student does.
   b. Specify measurable behaviors.
   c. Specify the criteria for acceptable performance.

Upon entering a classroom or institution for mentally impaired persons, one of our first observations is likely to be that these individuals are different from our friends or the people with whom we grew up. Retarded persons often *behave differently;* this is obvious to all who have contact with them.

As a teacher or aide, your goal is to help retarded students become as much like their "normal" peers as possible. You will achieve this goal by changing and shaping the behavior of your students. Skills such as toileting, self-feeding, and ambulation are but a few of the many rudimentary behaviors that you must teach your students if they are to begin to approximate a normal existence in our society. Once these skills are mastered, more complex behaviors, such as dressing and personal hygiene skills, can then be taught to further the student's progress toward "normalization."

The question of greatest concern to those who have the responsibility of educating retarded students is, *How can I best teach these students the behaviors they must have?* In this chapter we begin to answer this question.

It is now well established that the most effective techniques for teaching retarded students are derived from the behavioral model or approach. This approach provides us with the tools to be effective teachers, while it helps to simplify the learning process. A few basic facts about the behavioral approach will help you understand the reasons for its effectiveness.

This approach is based on direct observation of a student's behavior, not on opinions about the behavior. When we directly observe a behavior, we can describe it fully by specifying when, where, why, and how often it occurs. Furthermore, a behavioral approach breaks down the educational task into small observable units. This division allows for objective measurement and a way to establish agreement upon what behaviors are or are not occurring. The behavioral approach provides a scientific method for teaching the retarded student new behaviors.

ENTERING BEHAVIORS

In order to select appropriate goals for a student, you must first determine the student's *entering behaviors:*

ENTERING BEHAVIORS ARE THOSE BEHAVIORS THAT THE STUDENT POSSESSES BEFORE INSTRUCTION BEGINS. DATA ON THESE BEHAVIORS TELL YOU WHERE TO BEGIN YOUR INSTRUCTION.

Ask yourself, "What can Jimmy do right now?" You will determine what he can do by: 1) observing and recording his behavior, 2) reading previous reports of his behavior, 3) talking to his parents about what he has accomplished at home, and 4) talking to his previous teachers and aides about his behavior in their classrooms. The most reliable information will be your own direct observations. You will rely foremost on the data you record since others may express opinions rather than reporting the behaviors that have transpired. Once the data have been collected and you know what Jimmy can do, you are ready to select a goal.

Jimmy can hold a spoon in his right hand, and he can scoop the food from his plate onto the spoon. However, Jimmy does not lift the spoon to his mouth. He has excellent reach, grasp, and lip control, so his teacher knows that there is no physiological reason for his reluctance to feed himself. The behavioral goal the teacher selects is "Jimmy will feed himself." The teacher lists Jimmy's entering behaviors as: 1) being able to hold a spoon, and 2) being able to scoop food onto the spoon. The teacher recognizes that Jimmy must learn to lift the spoon and place it in his mouth. Because the teacher analyzed Jimmy's entering behaviors, a realistic goal has been set and Jimmy's instruction is individualized.

When measuring entering behaviors of severely and profoundly retarded students, you should concentrate on areas of self-help, personal hygiene, and language because they are essential for approximating a normal life.

Jenny is an 8-year-old moderately retarded girl who is a new student in Ms. Smith's classroom. During the first week of school, Ms. Smith began assessing Jenny's entering behaviors. Last year's teacher had written in her progress report that Jenny had completed the following objectives: 1) stack blocks, 2) sort two shapes, and 3) point to the colors red and brown. While Ms. Smith was reviewing the progress report, Jenny was playing on a mat nearby. Suddenly, Jenny exclaimed, ''Brown, brown,'' while she pointed to some feces she had deposited on the mat. At that moment, Ms. Smith became acutely aware of the absurdity of educational evaluations that neglect to consider normalization when measuring students' entering behaviors.

Although Jenny's previous teacher had taught her a few skills, she obviously had not had the normalization model in mind when she selected Jenny's educational goals. Shape sorting and stacking blocks were surely secondary goals to the self-help skills that Jenny would need to lead a more normal life. If Jenny's previous teacher had identified Jenny's entering behaviors in the areas of self-help as well as in eye-hand coordination, it would have been clear to her that toilet training Jenny was an important goal.

This example dramatically illustrates what can happen when a teacher or an aide ignores a student's individual assessment of behaviors and instead selects unrealistic goals or arbitrary tasks. There are very few people who would want to sit beside Jenny and teach her to sort shapes if her pants were soiled. Clearly, because toileting herself is not one of Jenny's entering behaviors, toilet training will become one of Ms. Smith's first behavioral objectives for Jenny.

WRITING BEHAVIORAL OBJECTIVES

Once you have selected individualized goals for a student and you are certain that the goals are realistic—that the student can successfully complete them, you are ready to write those goals as behavioral objectives.

A BEHAVIORAL OBJECTIVE IS A DESCRIPTION OF THE BEHAVIOR THE STUDENT MUST EXHIBIT.

Writing behavioral objectives is the first step in the actual behavioral change process. All behavioral objectives must meet *three criteria*.

THE FIRST CRITERION OF A BEHAVIORAL OBJECTIVE IS THAT IT MUST PRECISELY STATE WHAT THE STUDENT IS TO DO.

The behavioral objective tells you what you want the *student* to do, that is, what he or she is to learn. Behavioral objectives emphasize the behavior of the traditionally specified goals. For example, teachers once constructed lesson plans with statements such as:

1. Teach dressing skills to Sam, Lisa, Diane, and Fred.
2. Teach gross motor skills to Jim, John, and Rita.

These lesson plans were stated in terms of what the *teacher* would do and were accompanied by notes listing the materials the teacher would need. However, no specific behavioral measure relating to the student's performance was given. In contrast, behavioral objectives set an individual goal for each student. The objective is written in terms of the *student's* behavior. These individual goals might include:

1. Sam will take off his clothes.
2. Lisa will put on her clothes.
3. Rita will walk across the balance beam.
4. John will roll the ball across the floor.

These goals now fulfill the first criterion of a behavioral objective. Each states *precisely* what the teacher wants the student to do, and there is an individual goal for each student.

To determine if you understand the first criterion of a behavioral objective, check the statements below that express what the *student* must do (i.e., how the student is to behave).

_____ 1. Janice will brush her teeth.
_____ 2. Ms. Jones will teach Billy to walk 10 feet in a saddle walker.
_____ 3. Tina will take off her shirt upon command.
_____ 4. Ms. Jones will give Terry a list of words, and Terry will circle all the nouns.
_____ 5. Bobby will feed himself with a spoon.
_____ 6. Ralph will allow the teacher to use his hands to pick up his pants.
_____ 7. Susan will bathe herself.
_____ 8. Janet will brush her hair while the teacher provides physical assistance.
_____ 9. Kathy will match two squares and two circles.
_____10. Ms. Shelton will draw a circle and ask Lisa to draw one just like it.

Turn to page 13 for the correct answers.

Now, see if you can write five examples of what you want the student to do. In doing so, make sure that the behavior will be performed by the student. Remember, it can be anything your student does or anything you would like the student to do.

Example: Mary will tie her shoe.

1. _____   _____
        (student)   (behavior)
2.
3.
4.
5.

THE SECOND CRITERION OF A BEHAVIORAL OBJEC-
TIVE IS THAT IT MUST BE MEASURABLE.

A behavioral objective must be stated in measurable terms so that two or more independent observers can agree on whether or not the behavior occurs. Usually, an *active verb* will express a behavior that can be seen and measured by two or more people.

The importance of stating an objective in active, measurable terms cannot be overemphasized. If it is not stated in active, measurable terms, there may be some confusion about what the student is doing. For example, when a teacher says that a student is "anxious," we have no clear idea of what behaviors the student is displaying. However, saying the student pulls his hair and screams each time he enters the gym gives you a description of a behavior that is observable by two or more people. When a mother tells you that her son throws tantrums, you do not know whether he cries, screams, kicks, slaps, swears, or displays a combination of these behaviors. The behavior must be defined in observable terms before a behavioral change process can begin.

The following list contains observable behaviors often seen in the classroom. They are all actions that could be a part of any behavioral objective.

Observable Behaviors

Asks	Dresses	Pulls hair	Spins
Assembles	Eats	Pushes	Spits
Bathes	Feeds himself	Puts	Stacks
Bites	Hits	Reads	Strings
Breaks	Holds	Rocks	Swallows
Brushes	Jumps	Runs	Swears
Chews	Kicks	Says	Talks
Circles	Lifts	Scratches	Tears
Climbs	Looks at	Screams	Walks
Combs	Places	Screws	Washes
Cries	Points to	Selects	
Dances	Prints	Sits	
Draws	Pulls	Slaps	

After reading this list, create your own list of *active behaviors*. Think of students in your classroom who are involved in new learning activities or students who have displayed inappropriate behaviors that you would like to eliminate. How would you specify these behaviors? Remember that the behavior can be anything your student does provided that it is an *action* performed by that student.

Compare your list to the list below. If you have written any of the words or phrases on this list, you have written *impressions* of behaviors and *not* the observable *actions* needed to write a behavioral objective. To meet the second criterion, the goal must be measurable so that two or more people can agree on its occurrence. While looking at the list below, think of the multitude of behaviors two or more people could infer from each impression. It will become clear to you why impressions of behavior have no place in the classroom.

Impressions of Behaviors

Abusive to others
Alert
Anxious
Appears
Approachable
Attempts
Aware of
Calm
Concentrates
Cooperates
Demonstrates
Distracted
Engages
Expresses
Flexible
Gets into things
Good knowledge
Happy
Has ability to
Has sense of right and wrong
Hostile
Hyperactive
Inappropriate speech

Indicates
Interacts
Irritable
Knows
Low self-concept
Mad
Misbehaves
Nervous
Poor knowledge
Possesses knowledge of
Respects
Sad
Self-abusive
Self-controlled
Stereotypic behavior
Smelling
Thinking
Throws tantrums
Unaware of
Understands
Unhappy
Withdrawn

To determine if you understand the second criterion of a behavioral objective, check the sentences below that express measurable behaviors.

_____ 1. Steven throws tantrums every afternoon.
_____ 2. Steven kicks his feet and cries.
_____ 3. Christine hits Gary.
_____ 4. David is angry.
_____ 5. Marilyn spits at Ms. Roberts.
_____ 6. Susan is crying.
_____ 7. The baby is unhappy.
_____ 8. Mary experiences difficulty when feeding herself.
_____ 9. John is aware of his extremities.
_____10. Carolyn circles all pictures that are complete.

_____11. Missy points to foods eaten for breakfast.

_____12. Tim has a good knowledge of safety procedures.

Turn to page 13 for the correct answers.

THE THIRD CRITERION OF A BEHAVIORAL OBJEC-
TIVE IS THAT IT SPECIFIES THE CRITERION OR
CRITERIA LEVEL FOR ACCEPTABLE PERFORMANCE.

A behavioral objective should not only specify precisely the student's behavior in measurable terms, but it should also state the criterion or criteria level
for acceptable performance. Your task is to decide which aspects of the student's
behavior indicate that the objective has been met. There are three ways to specify
the criteria for acceptable performance in a behavioral objective.

THE FIRST WAY TO SPECIFY A CRITERION IS TO
SET A TIME LIMIT WITHIN WHICH THE PERFOR-
MANCE MUST OCCUR.

Frances, an aide, was training James to dress himself. The objective she was
working on stated, "James will put his shoes and socks on." Frances gave James
his shoes and socks at 9:30 a.m. and told him to put them on. James played with
the shoes until 11:30 a.m. and then put them on and went to lunch. It took James
2 hours to carry out the task. Has he completed the objective successfully?

According to the way the objective was written, James had indeed completed the objective. However, because the objective did not contain criteria for
acceptable performance, James was allowed an inordinate amount of time to
complete the task. As a result, a great deal of valuable training time was lost. In
this case, an appropriate criterion level of performance for the objective would
have been, "James will put his shoes and socks on within 5 minutes."

THE SECOND WAY TO SPECIFY A CRITERION IS TO
STATE THE NUMBER OF ACCURATE BEHAVIORS
REQUIRED TO COMPLETE THE OBJECTIVE.

In a classroom for emotionally impaired students, John was learning to play
a number lotto game. His teacher's objective stated, "John will match cards in
number lotto." John mismatched one card out of 20, and the teacher said that
John did not know how to play number lotto. The next day a substitute teacher
was in the room, and she read John's number lotto objective. When the substitute
teacher gave John the opportunity to play number lotto, he once again matched
19 cards and mismatched one. The substitute teacher left the regular teacher a
note stating that John had completed the objective. Which teacher was correct?
Neither, because the objective had not stated "how many" cards John had to
match.

To rewrite this objective so that two or more people would agree on whether or not John had met the objective, the following wording could be used: "John will match 90% of the cards in number lotto," or "John will match 9 out of every 10 cards in number lotto." These objectives state specifically how many behaviors the student must accomplish or how accurate the student must be.

THE THIRD WAY TO SPECIFY A CRITERION IS TO STATE THE CONDITIONS UNDER WHICH THE BEHAVIOR IS TO BE DISPLAYED.

Tina, an aide, taught Madalyn to feed herself with a spoon. When Tina said, "Pick up spoon," Madalyn scooped food from her plate onto her spoon. Madalyn then placed the spoon in her mouth, removed it, returned the spoon to her plate, released the spoon, and waited for another command. The behavioral objective written by the teacher stated, "Madalyn will eat with a spoon."

Tina told the teacher that Madalyn had completed the objective and was ready for another one. After observing Madalyn during lunch that day, the teacher said to Tina, "Madalyn has not completed the objective. You still have to remind her to pick up the spoon."

"But she is eating with a spoon, just like the objective says," exclaimed Tina.

"That's not enough, she has to eat with a spoon independently," the teacher explained.

In this case, the objective was poorly written because it did not state the conditions under which the behavior was to occur. The disagreement between Tina and the teacher would not have happened if the teacher had written the following objective: "Madalyn will independently eat with a spoon."

On the basis of Madalyn's behavior and the above objective, Tina and the teacher would have agreed that Madalyn was not yet eating independently. They would have known the *condition* under which Madalyn was to eat with a spoon.

As we have seen, the criteria for an objective that has been written behaviorally can be stated in terms of the following:

1. A time limit
2. Accuracy
3. The conditions under which the behavior is to occur

Remember, when you write a behavioral objective, it must:

1. State precisely what the student is to do
2. Be measurable
3. Specify the criteria and/or acceptable performance by:
   a. Setting a time limit within which the performance must occur

b. Stating the number of accurate behaviors required to complete the objective

c. Stating the conditions under which the behavior is to be displayed

Before continuing through this chapter, check the objectives below that contain a criterion for acceptable performance.

_____ 1. Janice will remove 90% of the pegs in the peg board when given a verbal command.

_____ 2. Susan will feed herself when gestural prompts are provided.

_____ 3. Fred will walk across the porch.

_____ 4. David will tie his shoes independently.

_____ 5. Linda will select all red squares when red and blue squares are presented.

_____ 6. George will answer all questions in Chapter 1 correctly.

_____ 7. Francis will hold a cup in one hand for 5 seconds without spilling any liquid.

_____ 8. John will pour the juice.

_____ 9. Richard will scrub the floor.

_____10. Mary will fly a kite for 10 minutes.

Turn to page 14 for the correct answers.

SUMMARY

The most effective approach for teaching retarded students the behaviors they need to become as normal as possible is the behavioral approach, which relies on direct observation.

When beginning a program, it is imperative that the student's entering behaviors be directly observed and recorded. And in keeping with the concept of normalization, goals should be selected that will help the student lead a more normal life.

Once goals have been established, behavioral objectives can be written. These objectives must: 1) state the student's behavior precisely, 2) state the student's behavior in measurable terms, and 3) specify the criteria for acceptable performance.

REVIEW QUESTIONS

Part 1: On the next page, place a check mark in the appropriate column to indicate which criteria of a behavioral objective are included in each.

Part 2: Rewrite those objectives that do not meet all three criteria for an accurate behavioral objective. (Example: 1. The student will stop upon command 9 times out of 10.)

	Student's behavior	Measurable	Criterion
1. The student will understand the meaning of "stop."			
2. The student will put his pants on when told to 9 out of 10 times.			
3. The student will write the three components of a good behavioral objective.			
4. The student will count from 1 to 10.			
5. The student will independently feed himself with a fork.			
6. The student will dry his hands with a towel each time he is asked.			
7. Given an oral description of all events, the student will know the safety rules for using the pool.			
8. The student will assume responsibility for his own acts.			
9. The student will appreciate his family after watching four 30-minute movies on orphans.			
10. The student will learn self-help skills.			
11. The student will be able to understand the poems of Ezra Pound.			
12. The student will demonstrate a sense of right and wrong.			
13. The student will brush his teeth with 100% accuracy when physical prompts are provided.			
14. Ms. Smith will teach Johnny a unit on spelling.			
15. The student will walk across the 6-foot balance beam within 3 minutes with a teacher holding one of the student's hands.			
16. The student will wash her hair in the basin within 15 minutes after the teacher has measured the shampoo.			
17. Mr. O'Hara will teach Ronnie to sand a piece of oak.			
18. The student will write a definition of friendship after reading four poems on the topic.			
19. The student will be able to sort 25 nuts and bolts after 10 days of training in the workshop.			
20. The student will walk 6 feet in a walker as you provide verbal prompts.			

Turn to page 14 for the correct answers.

Part 3: Write five behavioral objectives. Make sure that they: 1) tell what the student does, 2) specify measurable behavior, and 3) specify the criteria for acceptable performance.

1.

2.

3.

4.

5.

Review Chapter 1 to correct your answers.

SUGGESTED READINGS

Bloom, B. S. *Taxonomy of educational objectives.* New York: Longmans, Green, 1956.

Ebel, R. L. Behavioral objectives: A close look. *Educational Technology,* November 1979, *19,* 171–173.

Kapfer, P. G. Behavioral objectives and the curriculum process. *Educational Technology,* May 1970, *5,* 14–17.

Mager, R. F. *Preparing instructional objectives.* Palo Alto, CA: Fearon, 1962.

Mager, R. F. *Developing attitude toward learning.* Palo Alto, CA: Fearon, 1968.

Papham, W. J. The instructional objectives exchange: New support for criterion-referenced instruction. *Educational Technology,* November 1970, *10,* 174–175.

Vargas, J. S. *Writing worthwhile behavioral objectives.* New York: Harper & Row, 1972.

ANSWERS TO CHAPTER QUESTIONS

Answers to Questions on Page 6

__✓__ 1. Janice will perform the behavior of brushing her teeth.

_____ 2. This statement is not expressed in terms of the student's behavior. It tells what the teacher will do.

__✓__ 3. Tina is performing the behavior of taking off her shirt.

__✓__ 4. Terry is performing the behavior of circling all nouns.

__✓__ 5. Bobby will perform the behavior of feeding himself.

__✓__ 6. Ralph is performing the behavior of letting the teacher use his hands. The behavior we can see is the teacher's hands on Ralph's hands.

__✓__ 7. Susan is performing the behavior of bathing herself.

__✓__ 8. Janet is performing the behavior of brushing her hair.

__✓__ 9. Kathy is performing the behavior of matching.

_____10. This statement is not expressed in terms of the student's behavior. It tells what the teacher will do.

Answers to Questions on Page 9

_____ 1. This sentence does not express a measurable behavior. One person may infer that a tantrum is screaming, another may infer that it is lying on the floor, and still another may infer that it is none of these.

✓ 2. The words *kicks* and *cries* express a measurable behavior. Two or more people could agree on what a kick and a cry are, and they could measure the number of times a child kicks and cries.

✓ 3. A hit is measurable. Two or more people could measure the number of times Christine *hits* Gary.

___ 4. Anger is not a measurable behavior. Two or more people could not agree on anger.

✓ 5. Spitting is a measurable behavior. The number of times someone spits can be recorded.

✓ 6. Crying is a measurable behavior. The number of times Susan cries in a day or in an hour, for example, can be counted.

___ 7. Unhappiness is not measurable. Two or more people could not necessarily agree on what unhappiness is. One person may infer that the baby is hungry, another that he is wet, and still another may infer that he is thirsty.

___ 8. This sentence does not express a measurable behavior. Two or more people could not agree on what behaviors indicate that Mary is experiencing difficulty.

___ 9. The word *aware* is not measurable. Two or more people could not agree on the behaviors they are observing.

✓ 10. This sentence expresses a measurable behavior. Two or more people can count the number of pictures that are circled.

✓ 11. This sentence expresses a measurable behavior. Two or more people can measure the number of times Missy points to particular foods.

___ 12. This sentence does not express a measurable behavior. Two or more people could not agree on or measure what constitutes "good knowledge."

Answers to Questions on Page 11

✓ 1. This objective states the accuracy (90%) and the condition (a verbal command).

✓ 2. This objective states the condition (a gestural prompt) under which Susan will feed herself.

___ 3. This objective does not contain a criterion for acceptable performance.

✓ 4. This objective states the condition (independently) under which David will tie his shoes.

___ 5. This objective does not contain a criterion for acceptable performance.

✓ 6. This objective states the accuracy (all questions correct) of answering the questions.

✓ 7. This objective states the time limit (5 seconds) and the accuracy (without spilling any liquid).

___ 8. This objective does not contain a criterion for acceptable performance.

___ 9. This objective does not contain a criterion for acceptable performance.

___ 10. This objective states the time (10 minutes).

Answers to Review Questions on Pages 11–12

Part 1

✓	✓	✓

Part 2

1. The student will stop upon command nine times out of 10.
2. Meets the criteria.
3. The student will *correctly* write three components of a good behavioral objective.
4. The student will count from 1 to 10 when verbally prompted.

√	√	√
√	√	√
√	√	√
√	√	√
√	√	√
√	√	√
√	√	√
√	√	√

5. Meets the criteria.
6. Meets the criteria.
7. Upon command, the student will point to pictures illustrating pool safety with 90% accuracy.
8. The student will throw away his milk carton after lunch each day.
9. The student will list at least five disadvantages of being an orphan after watching four 30-minute movies.
10. The student will be able to independently dress himself each morning.
11. Given 25 minutes, the student will write a synopsis of one of Ezra Pound's poems.
12. Given two pictures of withdrawing money from the bank, the student will circle the right way.
13. Meets the criteria.
14. Johnny will spell the five words on page 292 in his spelling book with 100% accuracy.
15. Meets the criteria.
16. Meets the criteria.
17. Ronnie will sand a 2' × 2' piece of oak until a piece of nylon will slide across it without snagging.
18. Meets the criteria.
19. Meets the criteria.
20. Meets the criteria.

Chapter 2

TASK ANALYSIS

After reading this chapter, you will be able to:

1. Define the two methods to analyze the steps of a task analysis.
2. Given a situation and behavioral objective to teach, determine the appropriate method to analyze the steps of the task.
3. Know how to determine the appropriate method to analyze a task.
4. List the three steps involved in writing a task analysis.
5. Given a behavioral objective, write a task analysis.

You have learned that writing a behavioral objective is the first step toward effective teaching. The behavioral objective designates the task the student is to learn. Once the student's behavioral objective has been specified, the steps or behaviors the student must learn must be determined. To analyze this behavior you ask, *What steps (behaviors) must the student perform in order to attain that objective?* The careful analysis of the behaviors required to learn the behavior is a task analysis. This is the second step in the effective teaching model.

WRITING A TASK ANALYSIS

A TASK ANALYSIS IS A DETAILED DESCRIPTION OF EACH BEHAVIOR NEEDED TO ACCOMPLISH AN OBJECTIVE.

A task analysis describes the chain or sequence of behaviors needed to accomplish a behavior. (Response or behavior chains are described in detail in Chapter 8.) The analysis of the behaviors and the sequence in which they are taught are essential components of a good task analysis. Each step in the chain must specify the exact behaviors the student must perform to attain the stated behavioral

---

Step 1:   Place gear shift in the position marked P for "park."

Step 2:   Place the car key in the ignition.

Step 3:   Place right foot on accelerator.

Step 4:   Turn the car key.

Step 5:   Apply slight pressure on the accelerator.
↓
BEHAVIORAL OBJECTIVE
The student will be able to start car with an automatic transmission.

Figure 1.   Task analysis of starting a car.

objective. These steps must be sequenced or *ordered* to ensure that the student will master the behavioral objective.

A task analysis can be conducted for any one of the myriad tasks that we perform each day. For example, an important task many of us perform daily is starting a car. You may recall that when you first learned to drive, your driving instructor described a sequence of steps for you to follow in starting the car. Although your instructor probably did not state that he had performed a task analysis of starting a car, in fact, that was exactly what had been done. After you had reliably met the instructor's car-starting objective, the instructor then began teaching you the chain of behaviors related to driving the car.

Let's assume that your behavioral objective is to teach someone to start a car with an automatic transmission. You plan to have the student sitting in the driver's seat with the car keys in hand. Your task analysis has indicated that the behavior chain that leads to car starting consists of: 1) placing the shift lever in the position marked P for park, 2) placing the key in the ignition, 3) placing the right foot on the accelerator, 4) turning the car key, and 5) applying slight pressure to the accelerator.

Attaining the objective of starting a car was accomplished only after all five steps, or behaviors, in the task analysis were completed. As you look at the task analysis of starting a car shown in Figure 1, two points will become immediately obvious. First, the objective cannot be completed if any behavior in the chain has been omitted. Second, the completion of one behavior in the chain serves as a signal to perform the following behavior. These two points convincingly illustrate why it is *so* important that each behavior in the chain be included in the task analysis.

Almost everyone learns to start a car with little difficulty after the behavior chain involved has been described or demonstrated to them. With required skills, simple behaviors can be learned within a few trials: The learner either performs what he or she was told or shown or logically determines the behavioral sequence independently. As educators of retarded students, however, we are teaching individuals who often have limited skills and who cannot always figure out the next step. We may have to spend many trials teaching the student just one of the steps. For these students, accurate sequencing of educational tasks is crucial. A task analysis outlines each step in its proper sequence, thus making it possible for students to master their educational objectives. For the teacher, the task analysis is as important as, if not more important than, it is for the student because 1) it provides the guidelines for helping students reach their educational objectives, and 2) it identifies learning problems. You can use task analyses to record students' progress as they meet their educational objectives. The steps accomplished can be cited for parent reports and at meetings of individualized education program (IEP) planning committees. You can identify learning problems by recording the student's progress on each step within the task analysis. If a student has completed one or more steps but is currently having difficulty on the next step, you can stop the training and examine your task analysis step. You will most likely find that the task analysis step is too difficult and needs to be broken down into smaller, less complex steps.

DETERMINING THE STEPS IN A TASK ANALYSIS

There are two ways to determine the steps in a task analysis. One way is to rely on your memory as you list the sequence of behaviors. The other way is to physically perform each behavior in the sequence and write each step down as you perform it, or have someone else perform the behavior as you record the steps.

Writing a task analysis from memory has both advantages and disadvantages. The advantages are:

1. Little time is required.
2. The analysis can be accomplished in any environment.
3. No special equipment is required.

For example, a task analysis of toothbrushing is easier to do from memory than going to the bathroom and listing each behavior involved in brushing your teeth. And this task analysis can be written without having a toothbrush, toothpaste, and a sink.

The disadvantage of writing a task analysis from memory is that some steps may be forgotten. Many complex activities contain steps that are often overlooked. For example, when writing a task analysis for toothbrushing, it is easy to forget the step that specifies that the toothbrush is held with the bristles facing upward when the toothpaste is applied. This can be a difficult discrimination for some retarded students, yet it would be obvious to a normal individual. When a step or behavior is omitted in a task analysis, valuable instructional time is lost because the objective cannot be completed unless all behaviors (steps) are included. Consider the amount of time that would be lost in teaching toothbrushing if the step of teaching the student to hold the toothbrush with the bristles upright were omitted.

Physically performing each behavior is the second method of conducting and writing a task analysis. The advantage of this method is that you will be more likely to include all the steps and thereby spend less time rewriting the task analysis.

The disadvantages are:

1. You may have to perform the task analysis outside your classroom because many tasks you wish to teach do not occur there (e.g., toothbrushing).
2. Special equipment may be needed to perform the task analysis.

The advantage associated with physically performing each behavior in the task analysis outweighs the disadvantages. For example, it may be inconvenient to write a task analysis before or after school because you need a specially equipped area. However, the time you save and the frustrations you avoid by not omitting a step will be well worth your extra efforts.

To decide which of the two methods is best for writing any particular task analysis, ask yourself the following questions:

1. Are you familiar with the objective (i.e., do you perform the task regularly)?
2. Is there a likelihood that you might omit a step?
3. Is special equipment needed?
4. Is a specially equipped area needed?

If your answer to the first question is yes and you answered no to the others, then using your memory would probably suffice. If the first question was answered no and the remaining three questions were answered yes, then it would be best for you to physically perform the task. In cases where you are not familiar with the objective and you do not have the special equipment or area necessary, you may want to watch someone else perform the task (i.e., another teacher or therapist who does have the equipment and/or area readily available) and you can record the steps as they are performed. Actual observation is the recommended method of writing a task analysis because it is scientific and therefore preferable to "memory." However, there will always be circumstances where observation is not possible and you will be forced to rely on your own experiences. When this occurs, be especially careful to include each and every step.

Before continuing this chapter, answer the following questions.

1. Mr. Pierce is attempting to write a task analysis for the following objective: "James will float on his back for 3 minutes when he is in 6 feet of water." It is winter and the school pool is temporarily closed. Which method of writing a task analysis should Mr. Pierce use?

2. Mr. Quinn is attempting to write a task analysis for toothbrushing. Mr. Quinn wears dentures and cleans them in a machine. Which method of writing a task analysis should he use?
3. Aunt Bertha was asked by her niece for the recipe for her special cinnamon rolls. Bertha answered that she never followed a recipe but would write one the next time she made the rolls. Which method will Aunt Bertha be using to task analyze the objective of "making cinnamon rolls"?
4. Ms. Evans would like to write a task analysis for jumping on a trampoline since her students have access to it when they are with the gym teacher. She also would like to record the students' progress. The trampoline is kept in the gym and Ms. Evans cannot leave her classroom during the school day. By the time she is free to leave her room at the end of the day, the gym door has been locked. Which method will Ms. Evans have to use if she is to write a task analysis for jumping on a trampoline?
5. The drivers education teacher would like to write a task analysis for starting a car. Which method of writing a task analysis would he use?
6. The drivers education teacher would like to write a task analysis for hemming a skirt. He has never hemmed a skirt before. Which method of writing a task analysis would he use?
7. Andy has taught kindergarten for 20 years and now he would like to write a task analysis for teaching the matching of colors. Which method would he use?

Turn to page 27 for the correct answers.

SEQUENCING THE STEPS IN A TASK ANALYSIS

Whether you rely on your memory or physically perform each behavior when writing a task analysis, you must follow the three steps listed below in order to ensure that your task analysis is complete.

1. *Specify the objective.* The behavioral objective must be stated in terms of the task the student is to learn. As outlined in Chapter 1, the behavioral objective will: 1) specify what the student will accomplish, 2) specify the criteria for acceptable performance, and 3) define the behavior in observable, measurable terms.
2. *Specify the student's entering behaviors.* To determine the student's entering behaviors, present the student with the opportunity to complete the objective. As the student engages in the task, list those behaviors that the student can perform. These behaviors, then, are the student's entering behaviors because they can be performed when the student begins, or enters, the new objective. If the student does nothing, that, too, is observed and recorded.

When specifying the entering behaviors, you are asking, *What can the student do* **now**?

3. *Sequence the steps (behaviors) that lie between the objective and the entering behavior.* As you may have guessed, it is critical to generate a list of all the behaviors between the student's entering behaviors and the objective. This can easily be done as follows: 1) list the objective at the bottom of a sheet of paper, and 2) list the student's entering behaviors in their proper sequence at the top of the sheet. You are now ready to list the sequence of steps needed to complete the objective.

The following example illustrates how these three steps are used to construct a task analysis. (The following objective and task analysis were used in a prevocational setting where students were being taught simple discrimination to prepare them for sorting exercises in a closed workshop. Students working on this type of activity should have acquired expertise in the areas of self-help and independent living.)

Behavioral Objective: The student will insert a circle in the shape-sorting box after attaining five consecutive positive responses on each step of the task analysis.

Step 1: Specify the objective.
The student will insert a circle in the shape-sorting box.

Step 2: Specify the student's entering behaviors.
The teacher gives the student an opportunity to perform the objective so that she can determine what he can do now. She observes that the student can lift the circle and take it to the box. These behaviors are the student's entering behaviors.

Step 3: Sequence the steps that lie between the objective and the entering behaviors.
The goal is for the student to insert a circle in a shape-sorting box, and his entering behaviors are lifting the circle and taking it to the box. With the beginning and end of the task defined, the question is, *What steps lie between these two points?* The teacher performs the task to ensure that no step is omitted from the task analysis. The teacher then lists each step after she performs it. This performance of the task shows that if the student can already lift the circle and take it to the box, he must then:

1. Place the circle on top of the shape-sorting box.
2. Place the circle over or next to the appropriate inset.
3. Push the circle through the inset and into the box.

The steps in the task analysis are small and they are sequenced so that the easy steps occur before the more difficult ones. Even smaller steps could be inserted in this task analysis, depending on the student's entering behaviors. If an evaluation of the student's entering behaviors indicated that the student could only pick up the circle, the basic sequence of steps would be as follows. The student will:

1. Pick up the circle.
2. Take the circle to the shape-sorting box.
3. Place the circle on top of the shape-sorting box.
4. Place the circle over or next to the appropriate inset.
5. Push the circle through the inset and into the box.
6. Release the circle.

Task analysis must be individualized for each student. You will begin writing the task analysis after you have determined the student's operant level. You will ask, *Where within the task is this student now?* and *What are the steps he must learn to complete the objective?* The number of task analysis steps will differ with each student. In the preceding example, a student who could identify the shape of the circle could proceed from step 1 to step 5 with little or no difficulty. However, the student unable to discriminate between the insets would encounter great difficulty proceeding from step 3 to step 4. The teacher would have to break down task analysis step 4 to teach the student the skills needed to accomplish that step. *Each task analysis that you write will differ*.

Critical information has been omitted from the following task analysis. Fill in the missing information and then turn to page 27 to check your answers.

Behavioral Objective: The student will pull his pants to the waist from his ankles on three out of five trials when instructed to do so.

Step 1: Specify the objective.

The student will _____

Step 2: Specify the student's entering behaviors.

Provide the student with an opportunity to perform the objective so that you can determine his entering behaviors. Assume that his entering behaviors are at step 1 and then list all the steps for the entire task.

Step 3: Sequence the steps that lie between the objective and the entering behaviors.

The student will:

1. Reach for the waistband of his pants.
2. Grasp his pants at the waistband.
3. Pull his pants to his calves.
4.
5.
6.
7. Pull his pants to his waist.

SUMMARY

A task analysis breaks the teaching or behavioral objective into small, easy-to-teach behaviors. The task analysis should be written *after* the objective has been stated and it should include all behaviors needed to accomplish the objective. You can write a task analysis by relying on your memory to list the behaviors, or you or someone else can physically perform each behavior and list the behaviors as they are performed. A task analysis is written according to the following three steps: 1) specify the objective, 2) specify the student's entering behaviors, and 3) sequence the steps that lie between the objective and the entering behaviors.

Not only will a task analysis provide a starting point for the development of lesson plans, but it will also help you guide the student through those behaviors needed to attain the individually selected objectives. Lesson plans result in activities that help the student realize each behavioral objective. When you carry out lesson plans, you are guiding the student through those behaviors needed to attain the individually selected objectives. Task analysis will help you present effective and expedient instruction for your students.

REVIEW EXERCISE

Fill in the missing information. Then turn to page 28 to check your answers.

Behavioral Objective: The student will take his pants off on three out of five trials when instructed to do so.

Step 1:   Specify the objective.

The student will _____

Step 2:   Specify the student's entering behaviors.

Give the student an opportunity to perform the objective so that you can determine his entering behaviors. Assume that the task is being written for general use, and thus the student's entering behaviors will be at step 1.

Step 3:   Sequence the steps that lie between the objective and the entering behaviors.

The student will:

1. Pull his pants down from his waist to his hips.
2.
3.
4.
5.
6. Pull his pants down to his ankles.
7. Remove one foot from his pants.
8.

REVIEW QUESTIONS

Part 1. Please complete the following statements.

1. A detailed description of each behavior needed to accomplish an objective is a _____ _____.
2. The student cannot attain the objective if a _____ in the task analysis has been omitted.
3. Writing a task analysis can be accomplished by two methods:
   a.
   b.
4. The three advantages of relying on your memory to write a task analysis are:
   a.
   b.
   c.
5. The disadvantage of relying on your memory to write a task analysis is:
   _____
6. The advantage of performing each behavior and listing it when you write a task analysis is: _____
7. The two disadvantages of performing each behavior and listing each step in the task analysis are:
   a.
   b.
8. What are the steps in writing a task analysis?
   a.
   b.
   c.
9. Describe how a student's entering behavior is determined.

10. A task analysis should be written before the behavioral objective is written. True of false.

Turn to page 28 for the correct answers.

Part 2. Read the following objectives and corresponding task analyses. Then place a check mark next to each task analysis that is complete.

_____ *Task Analysis 1:* When instructed, the student will fold her socks within 1 minute.

The student will:
   1. Place one sock on top of the other, heel on heel, toe on toe.

    2. Roll the socks from the toes to the tops.

    3. Spread open the end of the sock that is on the outside roll.

_____ *Task Analysis 2:* When instructed, the student will shampoo her hair when given the shampoo within 10 minutes.

The student will:

    1. Wet her hair.

    2. Apply shampoo to her hair.

    3. Rinse her hair.

_____ *Task Analysis 3:* When instructed, the student will clap his hands upon verbal command.

The student will:

    1. Let you hold his hands.

    2. Move his hands forward when instructed.

    3. Allow you to clap his hands together when told, "Clap."

    4. Clap his hands together as you physically guide him from the wrist.

    5. Clap his hands together when instructed.

_____ *Task Analysis 4:* When instructed, the student will snap a snap closed on three out of four trials.

The student will:

    1. Grasp the right side of the waistband with the right thumb behind the snap and the right forefinger near the outside of the snap.

    2. Grasp the left side of the waistband with the left forefinger over the outside of the snap and the left thumb behind the waistband and near the snap.

    3. Bring the snaps together so that the top of the snap is resting on the bottom of the snap.

_____ *Task Analysis 5:* The student will wet his toothbrush when instructed within 30 seconds.

The student will:

    1. Turn on the water.

    2. Place the toothbrush under the water.

    3. Turn off the water.

Turn to page 28 for the correct answers.

SUGGESTED READINGS

Ackerman, J. M. Operant conditioning techniques for the classroom teacher. (6th ed.) Albany, OR: Linn County Mental Health Clinic, 1969.

Anderson, R. C., Faust, G. W., Roderick, M. C., Cunningham, D. J., & Andre, T. (eds.). Section V. Reinforcement and feedback. In: *Current research on instruction.* Englewood Cliffs, NJ: Prentice-Hall, 1969.

Giradeau, F. L. The systematic use of behavior principles in training and teaching developmentally young children. In: B. Stevens (ed.), *Training the developmentally young.* New York: John Day, 1971.

Hall, R. V., & Broden, M. Behavior changes in brain-injured children through social reinforcement. *Journal of Experimental Child Psychology*, 1967, *4*, 463–479.

Kuhlen, R. G. (ed.). Section 9, Methods of providing reinforcement in the schools. *Studies in Educational Psychology.* Waltham, MA: Blaisdell, 1968.

Mager, R. F. *Analyzing performance problems; or you really oughta wanna.* Belmont, CA: Fearon, 1970.

Mechner, F. Science education and behavioral technology. In: R. Glaser (ed.), *Teaching machines and programmed learning.* Washington, D.C.: National Education Association, 1965.

ANSWERS TO CHAPTER QUESTIONS

Answers to Questions on Pages 20–21

1. Mr. Pierce will have to rely on his memory since the school pool is closed. However, if it is likely that he may omit a step, he should physically perform the behavior in another pool to ensure that the task analysis is complete. Or, if possible, he could wait until the school pool is re-opened before instructing James.
2. Even though he wears dentures, Mr. Quinn can still physically perform the movements required to brush his teeth. He can do this in his classroom without using any special equipment.
3. Aunt Bertha will physically perform the task of making cinnamon rolls and list the ingredients and steps.
4. Ms. Evans will have to rely on her memory since she does not have access to the trampoline. However, if at all possible, Ms. Evans should obtain some release time so that she can check her task analysis by performing the task herself.
5. The drivers education teacher could rely on his memory to write the task analysis because it is a sequence of steps he teaches every day.
6. In order to write a complete task analysis, the drivers education teacher would have to physically perform the task of hemming a skirt and list all of the behaviors involved. He would do this because he is not familiar with the task. It also would be helpful if he would have the home economics teacher show him the steps involved in hemming a skirt.
7. Andy can rely on his memory to write a task analysis since he has taught the components of this task for many years.

Answers to Questions on Page 23

Step 1: Specify the objective.
The student will pull his pants up from his ankles when instructed to do so.

Step 3: Sequence the steps that lie between the objective and the entering behaviors. Since you are assuming that the student cannot accomplish any of the steps in pulling up his pants, you will ask yourself, *What are all the steps involved in pulling up pants?* You may want to perform the task so that you will not omit any steps.

4. Pull his pants up to his knees.
5. Pull his pants up to his thighs.
6. Pull his pants over his buttocks.

Answers to Review Exercise on Page 24

Step 1: Specify the objective.
The student will take off his pants when instructed to do so.
Step 3: Sequence the steps that lie between the objective and the entering behaviors.
Once you have determined the student's entering behaviors, you will ask, *What behaviors lie between the entering behaviors and the goal?* You will actually perform the task or construct it from memory.

2. Pull his pants down from his waist to the top of his thighs.
3. Pull his pants down from his waist to the middle of his thighs.
4. Pull his pants down from his waist to his knees.
5. Pull his pants down from his waist to his calves.
8. Remove the other foot from his pants.

Answers to Review Questions, Part 1, on Pages 24–25

1. task analysis
2. step
3. a. By relying on memory.
   b. By physically performing the behavior.
4. a. Little time is required.
   b. The analysis can be accomplished in any environment.
   c. No special equipment is required.
5. Some steps may be forgotten.
6. You will be more likely to include all the steps and thereby spend less time later rewriting the task analysis.
7. a. You may have to perform the task analysis outside your classroom because many tasks you wish to teach do not occur there (e.g., washing hair, bathing).
   b. Special equipment may be needed to perform the task analysis.
8. a. Specify the objective.
   b. Specify the student's entering behaviors.
   c. Sequence the steps that lie between the objective and the entering behaviors.
9. The teacher gives the student an opportunity to perform the objective so that he or she can determine what the student can do now.
10. false

Answers to Review Questions, Part 2, on Pages 25–26

_____ *Task Analysis 1:* This is not a complete task analysis. The student can spread open the end of the sock that is on the outside roll, but unless she tucks the roll into the open end, the socks will not be properly rolled. This fourth and final step is needed.

_____ *Task Analysis 2:* This is not a complete task analysis. The student must rub the shampoo into her hair and work it into a lather before it is rinsed if she is to shampoo her hair effectively and appropriately. A step was omitted between Steps 2 and 3.

√ **Task Analysis 3:** This is a complete task analysis. There are sufficient steps to enable most students to learn to clap their hands.

___ **Task Analysis 4:** This is not a complete task analysis. A fourth step should be included to teach the student to apply pressure to the snaps in order to close them.

√ **Task Analysis 5:** This is a complete task analysis.

Chapter 3

STRUCTURING THE LEARNING ENVIRONMENT AND DETERMINING THE OPERANT LEVEL

After reading this chapter, you will be able to:

1. List characteristics of a distraction-free, structured learning environment.

2. Select examples of classroom situations that permit adaptation.

3. Define and determine an operant level.

4. Define a baseline condition using two different methods.

5. List the two questions you ask to determine when to stop collecting baseline data.

6. Evaluate the adequacy of baseline data according to the questions.

You have selected the student's behavioral objectives and have written a task analysis. The behavioral objectives specify what the student will learn; the criteria set for the objectives determine when the student acquires the skill; and the task analysis outlines the steps the student will take to attain the desired objective. The data you collect tell you when you have arrived.

In this chapter, you will learn how to structure your classroom and how to determine your students' progress. Three main points are considered: 1) creating a distraction-free, structured learning environment, 2) permitting the student to adapt to this environment, and 3) determining the student's operant (entering) level of behavior via a baseline condition.

31

CREATING A DISTRACTION-FREE LEARNING ENVIRONMENT

Students, especially severely and profoundly retarded students, are easily distracted and this distractibility can cause difficulties when you attempt to teach them a new behavior. To provide the optimal learning environment, you must structure the environment so distractions are kept to a minimum. The teacher, the student, and the teaching materials should be the only objects (stimuli) in the area. Anything that might create a distraction must be eliminated.

RETARDED STUDENTS ARE EASILY DISTRACTED, SO INSTRUCTION SHOULD OCCUR IN A DISTRACTION-FREE ENVIRONMENT.

Students are different, and you will find that various students are distracted by different things. Some common distractions are extraneous noises, bright colors, bright clothing worn by the teacher, toys or equipment other than those the student is working with, other students or instructors, and, especially, new adults.

To minimize or eliminate the many and varied distractions in your classroom, use an empty room that is devoid of distractions or create an area in your classroom that is free of distraction.

A distraction-free classroom area can be created by sectioning off a portion of the room with a screen or a partition. If you have a screen or a partition, make sure that the student faces the corner with his or her back to the classroom. Regardless of how you choose to separate this area from the rest of the room, it should 1) have no windows, 2) have nothing on the walls, 3) contain only the materials needed for instruction, 4) be as far away from other students and instructors as possible, and 5) be as far away from extraneous noises as possible.

Creating the initial appropriate learning environment for severely and profoundly retarded students requires a one-to-one instructional situation with only the student and a teacher or aide present, and only the learning material that is necessary during the training session. If more than one type of learning material is used, it is important to keep it in a closed cabinet in the learning area or in another room. The only learning material in the child's view must be the object with which the student is currently working. For example, if a classroom contains 12 students, one teacher and two aides, two staff members would be teaching one-to-one in distraction-free areas. The other staff member then watches over the remaining 10 students as they play with toys, lie on air mattresses, or take naps. As each child finishes his one-to-one session, his instructor returns him to the classroom area. The instructor is then ready to take another child out of the classroom and into an effective learning environment. This ensures that each student receives the maximum quality instruction each day. Generally, each one-to-one session lasts approximately 15 minutes. The exception is when a complex behavior such as toileting or feeding is being taught.

The learning materials can be transported with the student, but under no circumstances should the room have an array of learning materials available to the student. When the children are in the play area, they can have a limited variety of toys to play with. The toys in the play area should be rotated daily.

Those students who are not involved in one-to-one instruction should receive as much stimulation and as many activities as possible while they wait for their one-to-one instruction. Because the emphasis here is on stimulating the students, a variety of interesting stimuli are not only permissible but highly desirable. The stimulation should be varied as much as possible.

This brief description of the classroom makes it apparent that grouping severely and profoundly retarded students around a desk or table for instruction, as is commonly done, is certainly not advocated. It would create a chaotic situation with students looking at each other, rather than the instructional materials, and engaging in inappropriate behaviors to entertain each other or get attention from the teaching staff. To avoid this situation, the one-to-one model is used until the students are prepared to be taught in a group situation. When that time arrives, you will have taken a giant stride toward normalization.

At this point, answer the following questions. (Answers can be found on page 46.)

1. A classroom for severely and profoundly retarded students is devoid of any pictures on the walls or toys to play with. Is this classroom an example of a distraction-free structured learning environment?
   a. Yes
   b. No
2. The following diagrams are of classrooms for severely and profoundly retarded students. Which diagram is an example of the best distraction-free learning environment?
   ○, student; □, paraprofessional; △, teacher; |, partition; X, toys/equipment.

a.

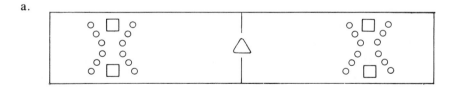

b.

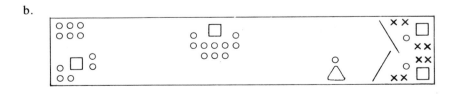

c.

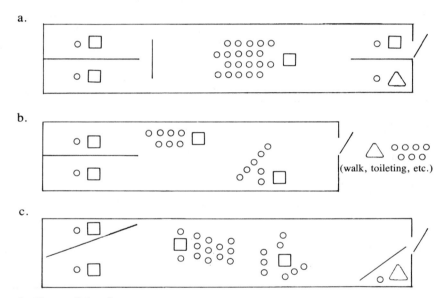

d. None of the above

3. The following diagrams are of classrooms for severely and profoundly retarded students. Which diagram is an example of the best distraction-free
   learning environment?

   ○, student; □, paraprofessional; △, teacher; |, partition; **X**, toys/equipment.

a.

b.

c.

d. None of the above

4. Ms. Werner has a classroom of 24 severely retarded students. She has four
   paraprofessionals to help her provide instruction for these students. The diagram below depicts the current structure of her classroom. Draw another
   diagram, using the rectangle at the top of the next page, that creates a more
   distraction-free environment for instruction.

   ○, student; □, paraprofessional; △, teacher; |, partition.

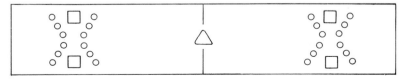

```
┌─────────────────────────────────────────────────────────┐
│                                                         │
│                                                         │
│                                                         │
│                                                         │
│                                                         │
│                                                         │
└─────────────────────────────────────────────────────────┘
```

PERMITTING ADAPTATION TO THE LEARNING ENVIRONMENT

Once you have created a distraction-free, structured learning environment, the student must be given the opportunity to adapt to this new situation. When the student has adapted, instruction can take place.

How do you behave when you enter a room filled with people you don't know? You probably remain silent and listen to the various conversations. After a period of time, you may join in one of the conversations. When you bring a new puppy home, how does it behave during the first few days? The new puppy will probably hide under the furniture or behind a door until it begins to explore its new environment. If a student is transferred to a new school in mid-year, what behaviors does he or she exhibit in the classroom? The student will probably watch other students for a while and then very gradually join them in various activities.

Feeling comfortable in a new situation is important because we must adapt to new environments before we will begin to engage in appropriate behaviors. Retarded students are no different. They must have the opportunity to explore any new environment or situation before they are expected to pay attention and learn. To help make your retarded students feel comfortable in the learning situation, arrange for them to spend some time there before you begin your instruction.

> STUDENTS MUST HAVE AN OPPORTUNITY TO ADAPT TO THEIR LEARNING ENVIRONMENT.

Remember, if you do not permit the student to adapt, he or she may be distracted by some of the stimuli in the new environment and all your instructional efforts will be frustrated. The following example dramatically illustrates the importance of allowing students to adapt to the teaching/training situation.

Mr. Johnson had begun training three of his students. Each student was sitting on a toilet, which contained a plastic bowl that made a musical sound when a student urinated in it. The musical tune was a cue to the teacher. Upon hearing the tune the teacher would reinforce the student for urinating in the toilet. During this process the music would also become a reinforcer for the student because he would begin to pair the musical sound with teacher reinforcement. The first time one of the students urinated, the sound of the music startled all three students. The student who had urinated reacted by ceasing to urinate, the second student began to cry, and the third student jumped off the toilet and ran around the room attempting to find the source of the musical sound. Mr. Johnson realized that he had not permitted the students to adapt to the sound. He immediately suspended the training and began activating the musical tunes repeatedly, independent of any behavior by the students. Eventually, the students demonstrated that they had adapted to the sound of the music because they no longer acted startled whenever it sounded. At this point, Mr. Johnson resumed the toilet training program.

Remember, never begin instruction until the students have adapted to the new learning environment. The students' behavior will tell you when they have adapted.

STUDENTS HAVE ADAPTED TO A NEW ENVIRONMENT OR SITUATION WHEN THEY BEGIN TO DISPLAY BEHAVIORS THAT ARE COMMON FOR THEM IN THEIR OLD ENVIRONMENT.

Before continuing this chapter, check what you have learned thus far by answering the following questions.

1. William is toilet trained and has used a portable potty in his room for 6 months. William's instructor would like to teach him to use the bathroom across the hall. How can the instructor help William adapt to the new learning environment?
2. Ruth is a 10-year-old profoundly retarded child. In order to teach her to walk, she needs to wear a leg brace. How could Ruth be helped to adapt to the leg brace?
3. Jeffrey arrived in your classroom today. He had lived in an institution for 8 of his 9 years and had been in a foster home for 1 month. You are instructing your students in self-help skills. How can you help Jeffrey adapt to his new learning environment?
4. Today is your first day at your new job as an aide in a classroom for profoundly retarded students. You walk into a classroom of 12 students, one teacher, and one other aide. How will you adapt to your new environment?

Suggested answers are on page 47.

DETERMINING THE OPERANT LEVEL AND CONDUCTING A BASELINE CONDITION

Once you have created a distraction-free structured environment and permitted adaptation, you will need to determine the operant level of the behavior you wish to change (see Chapter 2).

THE OPERANT LEVEL DESCRIBES THE FREQUENCY OF THE ENTERING BEHAVIOR.

Knowing the operant level provides information on how often the behavior occurs before you attempt to increase or decrease that behavior. For instance, Ms. Sec would like to reduce Denise's toileting accidents. Before beginning a toilet training program, Ms. Sec must determine how many times Denise wets her pants each day.

Ms. Sec will use this information to plan a toilet training program. The period of time (or days) during which the behavior is measured before the training is called the baseline period.

A BASELINE IS THE PERIOD OF TIME DURING WHICH A BEHAVIOR IS OBSERVED AND MEASURED WITHOUT ANY THERAPEUTIC OR INSTRUCTIONAL INTERVENTION.

Determining the operant level during a baseline condition helps the instructor evaluate the effectiveness of a program and provides an objective measurement of the behavior's occurrence. It is extremely important that we know how often the behavior occurs under natural conditions so that we can make intelligent decisions about what we wish to do concerning the behavior. Otherwise, we find ourselves using impressions or guesses concerning the student's behavior, rather than using a scientifically based teaching model. The following example will help you understand the importance of determining the operant level via a baseline condition.

Oftentimes it will appear that a behavior occurs more often than it really does. For example, Dr. Hankin, the consulting psychologist, was disturbed because every time he saw Gordon, Gordon was picking his gums. Dr. Hankin wanted to eliminate this behavior so he asked Gordon's teacher to conduct a baseline in order to determine Gordon's operant level of gum picking. After the baseline was taken, however, Dr. Hankin discovered that Gordon only picked his gums once every 2 weeks, and these occurrences corresponded with Dr. Hankin's visits to the classroom. Measuring the occurrence of the behavior (operant level) during a baseline demonstrated to Dr. Hankin that Gordon's gum picking was not the problem he had thought it was. Furthermore, it told Dr. Hankin that he should analyze his own actions in order to determine why Gordon only picked his gums when Dr. Hankin was present.

The next example illustrates how determining the operant level during treatment helps us to establish whether or not our intervention has been effective.

Mr. Edward's behavioral objective was to train Brian to pull his pants up. When he tallied Brian's operant level of pulling up his pants, he found that Brian could pull his pants up from his knees and would do so only twice during each 15-minute training session. Mr. Edwards would give Brian 18 trials during each 15-minute training session. Brian would only respond twice within each training session. Two weeks after giving Brian daily instructions in pulling on his pants, Mr. Edward's data revealed that Brian could still only pull his pants up from his knees and would do so only twice during each session. Brian's pants raising behavior had not increased during intervention nor had he learned any more of the behavior chain of pants raising (i.e., pulling his pants up from his ankles). As a result, Mr. Edwards knew he needed to reevaluate his training techniques as well as his task analysis before attempting any further training with Brian.

Determining an operant level of behavior can be accomplished in a variety of ways depending on the particular behavior you wish to measure. The first and most general method is to simply *tally the number of times the behavior occurs during a specified period of time*. Each time the behavior occurs, simply place a check mark on a sheet of paper. For example, you may wish to determine how often your student, Mary Oatly, independently feeds herself during lunch.

Name: Mary Oatly
Behavior to be counted: Number of times Mary independently carries the spoon from the plate to her mouth at lunch.

Date	Number of times behavior occurs	Recorder
8/1/80	✓ ✓ ✓	Janet Spear
8/2/80	✓ ✓	Janet Spear
8/3/80	✓ ✓ ✓ ✓	Janet Spear
8/4/80	✓ ✓ ✓	Hilary Essex
8/5/80	✓ ✓ ✓	Janet Spear

Our baseline record reveals that Mary's operant level of self-feeding ranges from two to four times per lunch and the average is three times. Note that the recording was conducted for 5 days. The number of days was not chosen arbitrarily. Rather, the baseline was conducted until the operant level appeared to be stable.

How do you know when you have a stable baseline? To determine stability make sure that the baseline adequately shows the range (variability) of the behavior.

Let's consider these points in regard to the above example.

1. Does the baseline adequately show the range of behavior? In other words, was the baseline conducted over a long enough period of time to ensure that no drastic changes in the operant level occurred? Mary's operant level of self-feeding showed no drastic changes—she did not feed herself once at lunch one day and 12 times the following day. Thus, the answer to the first question would be, "Yes, the baseline accurately shows the range of behavior."
2. Is the final baseline number as low or lower than the previous session or day? Mary fed herself with a spoon three times on the last day, three times on the previous day, and the average was three times. Thus, the answer to the second question is also, "Yes."

Since the answer to both questions is yes, baseline data need no longer be recorded, and it is appropriate to begin the program to teach self-feeding. If the answer to either question had been no, baseline data would continue to be collected until an affirmative answer could be given to both questions.

When you look at baseline data, you want to look for trends in the frequency of behavior. If the behavior is increasing and one *wants* it to increase, an instructional program is not necessary. If the behavior is stable or increasing and you want it to decrease, then you would plan on intervention to decrease the frequency of the behavior. In this way you can decide if it is appropriate to intervene when behaviors are not changing over time. If trends in data are not consistent, contingencies are changing. It is important to find out what these contingencies are and then control them to produce the goal behavior.

For example, a major error would have been made if the teacher had decided to begin a program to increase Mary's self-feeding after the third day of recording. Mary had increased her self-feeding from two responses on August 2, to four responses on August 3. Had the intervention increased her self-feeding responses to seven on August 4, the argument could be made that Mary was already beginning to increase her self-feeding independent of the intervention. As a result, the teacher would never know whether the intervention was successful in increasing self-feeding or whether it simply coincided with the same day that Mary had increased her self-feeding. Because of this dilemma, the teacher would not be likely to use the intervention to teach self-feeding to other students.

The problem caused by prematurely terminating a baseline can also occur when you are attempting to decrease an inappropriate behavior. Let's consider Mary Oatly again. Suppose that Mary throws food at lunch. Our baseline record of her operant level of food throwing revealed the following:

Name: Mary Oatly
Behavior to be counted: Number of times Mary throws food at lunch.

Date	Number of times behavior occurs	Recorded by
8/1/80	√ √ √	Janet Spear
8/2/80	√ √	Janet Spear
8/3/80	√ √ √	Hilary Essex
8/4/80	√	Hilary Essex
8/5/80	√ √ √ √ √	Hilary Essex

Suppose we had begun the treatment after August 4 and had reduced Mary's food throwing to zero within 2 days. The argument could be made that Mary was giving up her food throwing anyway since it had decreased to one time during 8/4/80. Perhaps Mary had simply grown tired of throwing her food. We would never know for sure if the treatment had started on August 5. However, since we did not end the baseline until the last baseline recording on August 5, which was higher than the previous day's recording, we can confidently attribute the elimination of Mary's food throwing to our treatment procedure. Remember, *the student's behavior during the baseline will tell you when to end the baseline recording.*

A second common method of determining the operant level is to use *time sampling.* In time sampling, you simply observe the student at fixed intervals (e.g., every 5 minutes) for a specified period of time (e.g., 30 seconds) and then record whether or not the behavior occurred. The behavior can then be expressed as a percentage (i.e., the number of instances in which the behavior was observed, divided by the number of observations, times 100).

$$\frac{\text{number of instances}}{\substack{\text{number of possible}\\\text{instances}}} \times 100$$

Thus, rather than counting each instance of the behavior, you simply determine the percentage of time the behavior occurs. Time sampling is especially useful when the operant level of the behavior is very high (e.g., self-stimulatory behavior). The following example illustrates the time sampling method of recording.

Billy Shears appears to rock continuously throughout the day and his instructors have decided to determine his operant level of rocking. The time sampling record showed that Billy's operant level of August 1 was rocking in 76.9% of the observed intervals. A baseline for Billy's rocking could be obtained by continuing to observe him each day until his baseline percentage of rocking was stable. The way you would determine whether or not an adequate baseline had been taken, of course, would be to ask the questions listed earlier in the chapter (the same questions asked concerning Mary Oatly's baseline, page 38).

A more comprehensive discussion of the issues related to recording behavior is presented in Chapter 9.

Name: Billy Shears

Behavior to be measured: Rocking will be observed every 5 minutes for 15 seconds during a 1-hour period. A check mark indicates that he rocked at some time during the observation interval. A zero indicates that rocking did not occur during the observation interval.

Date: August 1, 1980   Recorded by: Ed Jones

Time	Rocking occurred ($\sqrt{}$)	No rocking (0)
9:00	$\sqrt{}$	
9:05	$\sqrt{}$	

Time	Rocking occurred ($\checkmark$)	No rocking (0)
9:10	$\checkmark$	
9:15	$\checkmark$	
9:20	$\checkmark$	
9:25		0
9:30	$\checkmark$	
9:35	$\checkmark$	
9:40		0
9:45		0
9:50	$\checkmark$	
9:55	$\checkmark$	
10:00	$\checkmark$	
Total	10	

Percentage of time rocking 76.9 (10 $\div$ 13 $\times$ 100)

At this point, answer the following questions on determining the operant level of a behavior. The answers are on page 47. Reread the preceding section if you have any difficulties with the questions.

1.

Name: Susan Brown
Behavior to be counted: Number of times Susan independently sits down in her seat upon command.

Date	Number of times behavior occurs	Recorded by
7/16/80	$\checkmark$ $\checkmark$ $\checkmark$ $\checkmark$	Linda Shelton
7/17/80	$\checkmark$ $\checkmark$ $\checkmark$	Linda Shelton
7/18/80	$\checkmark$ $\checkmark$ $\checkmark$ $\checkmark$	Craig Stevens
7/19/80	$\checkmark$ $\checkmark$ $\checkmark$	Craig Stevens
7/20/80	$\checkmark$ $\checkmark$ $\checkmark$ $\checkmark$	Linda Shelton

a. The baseline record revealed that Susan's operant level of sitting upon command ranged from _____ to _____ times per day and averaged _____ times per day.
b. Was the baseline conducted long enough to ensure that no drastic changes in the operant level occurred?
c. Was the final baseline number as low or lower than the previous session or day?
d. Are more baseline data required? Why or why not?

2.

| | Number of times | |
Date	behavior occurs	Recorded by

Name: Ross Hall
Behavior to be counted: Number of times Ross walks to an instructor when requested to do so.

Date	Number of times behavior occurs	Recorded by
9/3/80	√ √	Patti Ansel
9/4/80	√ √	Judy Kohrs
9/5/80	0	Judy Kohrs
9/6/80	√	Judy Kohrs
9/7/80	√ √	Susan Springer
9/8/80	√	Judy Kohrs

a. The baseline record revealed that Ross's operant level of walking to his instructor ranged from ＿＿ to ＿＿ times per day and averaged ＿＿ times per day.
b. Was the baseline conducted long enough to ensure that no drastic changes in the operant level occurred?
c. Was the final baseline number as low or lower than the previous session or day?
d. Are more baseline data required? Why or why not?

3.

Name: Jane Woods
Behavior to be counted: Number of times Jane throws her cup at lunch.

Date	Number of times behavior occurs	Recorded by
7/16/80	√ √	Jeff Miller
7/17/80	√	Paul Franks
7/18/80	√ √ √ √	Jeff Miller
7/20/80	√ √ √	Jeff Miller
7/23/80	√ √ √ √	Paul Franks
7/24/80	√ √ √ √	Paul Franks
7/25/80	√ √ √	Jeff Miller
7/26/80	√ √ √ √	Jeff Miller
7/27/80	√ √ √ √	Jeff Miller
7/30/80	√ √ √ √ √	Jeff Miller

a. The baseline record revealed that Jane's operant level of cup throwing ranged from ＿＿ to ＿＿ times per day and averaged ＿＿ times per day.
b. Was the baseline conducted long enough to ensure that no drastic changes in the operant level occurred?

c. Was the final baseline number as high or higher than the previous session or day?

d. Are more baseline data required? Why or why not?

4.

Name: Eric Ronge

Behavior to be measured: Eric's staying in his chair. Eric will be observed for 5 seconds every 5 minutes during a 1-hour period. A check mark indicates that he was in his chair during the 5-second observation interval. A zero indicates that Eric was out of his seat during the 5-second observation interval.

Date: September 6, 1980   Recorded by: Crystal Peters

Time	In seat	Out of seat
1:00	√	
1:05		0
1:10	√	
1:15	√	
1:20	√	
1:25		0
1:30		0
1:35		0
1:40		0
1:45		0
1:50	√	
1:55		0
Total	5	7

What percentage of the time was Eric in his seat?

5.

Name: Phil Ames

Behavior to be measured: Percentage of time Phil stays on task. The task is finger painting. Phil will be observed for 5 seconds every minute during the 15-minute finger painting session each day.

Date	Percentage on task	Recorded by
9/8/80	30	Sandy Barnes
9/9/80	35	Sandy Barnes
9/12/80	27	Alice Bornstein
9/13/80	30	Sandy Barnes
9/14/80	24	Alice Bornstein

a. The baseline record revealed that Phil's operant level of on-task behavior ranged from _____ % to _____ % per day and averaged _____ %.

    b. Was the baseline conducted long enough to ensure that no drastic changes in the operant level occurred?

    c. Was the final baseline session percentage as high or higher than the previous session?

    d. Are more baseline data required? Why or why not?

6.
_____

Name: Pat Secours

Behavior to be measured: The percentage of time Pat is out of his seat. Pat will be observed for 10 seconds every 5 minutes throughout the 6-hour school day and his percentage of out-of-seat behavior will be calculated for each hourly session.

Date: 8/11/80

Session number	Percentage of time out of seat	Recorded by
1	40	Harvey Smithwick
2	37	Harvey Smithwick
3	68	Lisa Littlejohn
4	41	Lisa Littlejohn
5	53	Ed Rambo
6	57	Lisa Littlejohn

    a. The baseline record revealed that Pat's percentage of out-of-seat behavior ranged from ____% to ____% per session and averaged ____%.

    b. Was the baseline conducted long enough to ensure that no drastic changes in the operant level occurred?

    c. Was the final baseline session percentage as high or higher than the previous session?

    d. Are more baseline data required? Why or why not?

APPLICATION PROJECT

In the first three chapters of this text you have learned to prepare for behavioral change. You have: 1) written a behavioral objective, 2) written a task analysis, 3) determined the student's entering behaviors, and 4) determined the operant level via baseline data. The following application project involves using this information.

    Perform the following: 1) write an objective for one student in your class, 2) write a task analysis for that objective (assume that the student will begin on step 1), 3) determine the student's entering behaviors within the task analysis (which behaviors necessary for completing this objective does the student bring with him to the task?), and 4) determine the operant level (the frequency of the entering behavior) via a baseline. Collect the baseline data for 5 days and comment on the trends of your data; that is, based on your data collection, is a program necessary?

SUMMARY

Before instruction can begin, students must be placed in a distraction-free, structured environment. Once a distraction-free environment has been established, students should be given time to adapt to the learning environment. A student has adapted to a new environment when he or she begins to display behaviors that were commonly seen in the old environment. When the student has adapted, instruction can take place. This initial learning environment consists of one-to-one instruction with only the student and instructor present.

The operant level describes the frequency of occurrence of the entering behavior before instruction begins. It is determined via a baseline, which is the period of time during which a behavior is observed and measured prior to any therapeutic or instructional intervention. Determining the operant level during a baseline condition helps the instructor evaluate the effectiveness of an intervention and allows the objective measurement of the occurrence of a behavior.

To determine whether or not an adequate baseline has been established, consider the following questions: 1) Does the baseline adequately show the range (variability) of the behavior? 2) How does the occurrence of the behavior on the proposed final day or session compare to the previous days or sessions? If the intervention is to increase the behavior, then the final baseline data point should be the same or lower than the ones for the previous sessions or days. Conversely, if the intervention is to decrease the behavior, then the final baseline data point should be the same or higher than the ones for the previous sessions or days. When sufficient baseline data have been collected, intervention can begin.

Two methods of determining an operant level are by tallying the number of times the behavior occurs during a specified period of time and by time sampling in which you record whether or not the behavior occurred during a specified period.

REVIEW QUESTIONS

1. Retarded students are easily _____; therefore, instruction should take place in a _____-_____ environment.
2. Creating a _____-_____ environment for retarded students requires _____ to _____ instruction.
3. Students must have an opportunity to _____ to the learning environment before instruction begins.
4. The occurrence of the behavior before instruction or intervention begins is described by the _____ _____.

5. The period of time during which a behavior is observed and measured before instruction begins is the _____.

6. Determining the operant level via a baseline allows the objective measurement of a behavior's occurrence and _____ _____.

7. The two questions you must ask to determine whether you have collected sufficient baseline data, i.e., established a stable baseline, are 1) Does the baseline adequately show the r_____ (variability) of the behavior, and 2) How does the final baseline d_____ p_____ compare to the previous d_____ or session's data point?

8. When you look at the baseline data, you want to look for trends in the _____.

9. If the behavior is increasing and one wants it to increase, an instructional program is _____.

10. One method of determining an operant level is to _____ the number of times the behavior occurs.

11. Another method of determining an operant level is _____ _____, in which you record whether or not the behavior occurred during a specified period.

Answers are on page 48.

SUGGESTED READINGS

Craighead, W. E., Kazdin, A. E., & Mahoney, M. J. *Behavior modification: Principles, issues and applications.* Boston: Houghton-Mifflin, 1976.

Gambrill, E. D. (ed.). *Behavior modification: Handbook of assessment, intervention and evaluation.* San Francisco: Jossey-Bass, 1977.

Neisworth, J. T., & Smith, R. M. *Modifying retarded behavior.* Boston: Houghton-Mifflin, 1973.

Thompson, T. I., & Grabowski, J. (eds.). *Behavior modification of the mentally retarded.* New York: Oxford University Press, 1972.

ANSWERS TO CHAPTER QUESTIONS

Answers to Questions on Page 33

1. No. To create a distraction-free, structured learning environment, you must have learning areas that are devoid of distractors. The classroom, however, must be an exciting, stimulating place.

2. The correct answer is diagram C. Two students are receiving one-to-one instruction in a distraction-free environment while the remaining students are working in groups. There is no one-to-one instruction in classroom A. Classroom B has too much equipment in the one-to-one training area, and one student is receiving one-to-one instruction from the teacher out in the classroom.

3. The correct answer is diagram B. Two students are receiving one-to-one instruction in distraction-free areas, while three groups of seven students are being supervised by one instructor each and the doorway is not blocked. In classroom A there are far too many students left to be supervised effectively by one instructor and the doorway is blocked. Also, a partition does not separate the students receiving one-to-one instruction from their classmates. In classroom C two instructors are left to randomly control 21 students and the partitions do not adequately separate the students receiving one-to-one instruction from their classmates.

4. Either of these diagrams would be appropriate:

Answers to Questions on Page 36

1. William should be taken to the bathroom, shown the toilet, and then placed on it before he expresses the desire to use the toilet. He should be taken to that bathroom several times throughout the day and placed on the toilet for 1 or 2 minutes. After a day or so, William should adapt to the new environment.
2. Ruth should have the opportunity to play with the leg brace and then wear it for short periods of time.
3. Jeffrey should not receive instruction until he has had an opportunity to play in the classroom and interact with the students and instructors. Although we are not sure of Jeffrey's degree of retardation, the rule of adaptation before instruction still holds.
4. Before instructing the students, you will play with them and help the teacher and aide attend to the students' physical needs. In this fashion, you will learn about the students, your co-workers, and the classroom routine.

Answers to Questions on Pages 41–44

1. a. 3 to 5, 3.8
   b. Yes.
   c. No.
   d. Yes. The baseline should be continued until the last baseline data point is the same or lower than the previous day's data point. This is necessary because the purpose of the intervention is to increase the number of times that Susan will sit in her seat when requested to do so.
2. a. 0 to 2, 1.33
   b. Yes.
   c. Yes.
   d. No. The baseline is sufficient because the purpose of the intervention is to increase the number of times that Ross walks to his instructors on command.

3. a. 1 to 5, 3.4
   b. Yes.
   c. Yes.
   d. No. The baseline is sufficient because the purpose of the intervention is to decrease the number of times Jane throws her cup at lunch.
4. 41.6% (5 ÷ 12 × 100)
5. a. 24% to 35%, 29.2%
   b. Yes.
   c. Yes.
   d. No. The baseline is sufficient because the purpose of the intervention is to increase Phil's percentage of on-task behavior during finger painting.
6. a. 37% to 68%, 49.3%
   b. Yes.
   c. Yes.
   d. No. The baseline is sufficient because the purpose of the intervention is to decrease Pat's percentage of out-of-seat behavior.

Answers to Review Questions on Pages 45–46

1. distracted
   distraction-free
2. distraction-free
   one-to-one
3. adapt
4. operant level
5. baseline
6. helps the instructor determine or evaluate the effectiveness after the intervention begins
7. range, data point, day's
8. frequency of behavior
9. not necessary
10. tally
11. time sampling

Chapter 4

THE INSTRUCTIONAL CYCLE

After reading this chapter, you will be able to:

1. Define and select an example of a stimulus.

2. Define and select an example of a response.

3. Define and select an example of a consequence.

4. Define and select a reinforcing consequence.

5. Define and select a punishing consequence.

So far, you have learned to write behavioral objectives, write a task analysis, structure the learning environment, and determine the operant level of behavior. You are now ready to use all of this information to increase your student's skills using individualized program objectives. Individualized objectives are those objectives written to meet the particular needs of each student.

In order for your students to attain the objectives you have set for them, you must understand *the instructional cycle*. There are three elements in the instructional cycle: a stimulus, a response, and a consequence. (The instructional cycle is also referred to as the *three-term contingency*.) In this chapter, you will learn about these three elements and how they relate to one another in forming a blueprint for instruction. Furthermore, when you finish this chapter, you will understand the prediction and management of behavior.

THE STIMULUS

A STIMULUS IS ANY OBJECT, PERSON, OR EVENT
IN THE ENVIRONMENT THAT SETS THE OCCASION
FOR A RESPONSE TO OCCUR.

The first element in the instructional cycle is the stimulus, which sets the occasion for the response to occur by preceding it. A stimulus can be any object, person, or event in the environment. A few of the numerous stimuli in your classroom are toys, tables, teacher's aides, a verbal command, and a demonstration. Your students are stimulated by the consequences of interacting with a toy or a person.

If a mobile hangs above a child's bed and the child touches it, the mobile will turn, a pleasant melody will be heard and the baby will smile. The mobile has served as a stimulus. The child is stimulated by the consequences of the pleasant melody and the movement of the mobile.

The importance of any particular stimulus is that it will usually cue a particular response. When you are driving a car and you approach a traffic light that turns red and you stop, you and the car are not hit by other cars. The traffic light is a stimulus to the response of stopping the car, which is followed by the consequence of safety. You, in turn, are stimulated (rewarded for stopping) by the consequence (safety) of obeying the traffic light.

You may have encountered students who react to stimuli in inappropriate ways because they are reinforced with attention. For example, Richard, a large profoundly retarded boy reaches into his pants for a piece of feces and then smears it across the dining room table. The teacher and three aides run to Richard and take him to the bathroom to change and shower him. The presence of the feces was the stimulus for smearing the feces. The consequence of smearing the feces was attention and a warm bath and a change of clothing. Richard was stimulated by the consequences of feces smearing.

Listed below are examples of various stimuli that you might find in your classroom and the responses they are likely to cue. Remember, stimuli can be objects, people, events, or commands, and the students are stimulated by the consequences of interacting with the goldfish, table, feces, other students, or your instructions.

Stimulus	Response
1. Goldfish in a fishbowl	Alice sticks her hand in the fishbowl.
2. Food on table	Sam throws food.
3. Feces in diaper	Debbie smears feces.
4. Rocking chair	Brian rocks in the rocking chair.
5. Refrigerator	Cathy opens the refrigerator door to hunt for food.
6. "Steven, sit down."	Steven sits in his chair.
7. Open classroom door	Donna runs out of the classroom.
8. Aide brings in lunch trays	Children go to the table.

THE RESPONSE

A RESPONSE IS THE ACTIVITY OR BEHAVIOR THE STUDENT PERFORMS IN THE PRESENCE OF A PARTICULAR STIMULUS.

The second element in the instructional cycle is the response, which is the activity or behavior the student performs in the presence of a stimulus. Some common responses include sitting, walking, crying, talking, grasping a ball, biting, and tearing. The importance of the relation between a stimulus and a response cannot be overstressed. When you understand this relation, you can design programs to either increase or decrease a response. The following two examples demonstrate the wide variety of stimulus-response relations.

Mr. Wolf has a student, Jeff, who was taught to dress *before* he ate breakfast each day. At the institution where Jeff lived previously, each student had to be dressed before he or she ate breakfast. Jeff's behavior of dressing was stimulated by the consequence of eating breakfast. In the new institution, students are required to eat breakfast before they dress. Mr. Wolf simply says that Jeff will have to build new habits. However, if Mr. Wolf were aware of the relation between the stimulus response and consequence, he would be able to alter the consequence (breakfast), thus causing Jeff to respond differently when he wakes up each morning.

Listed below are examples of various stimuli and the responses that are likely to be performed in relation to these stimuli. As you continue reading through this chapter you will learn that it is the consequence that maintains these behaviors (responses).

Stimulus	Response
1. Presence of shape-sorting box	Erma sorts two shapes.
2. Glass of milk	Jimmy drinks milk.
3. Paste on table	Sarah eats paste.
4. Children outside playing	Bruce looks through window and watches children play outside.
5. Paper	Shelly tears the paper.
6. Roll of toilet paper	Jessica unrolls the toilet paper.
7. Dog wagging its tail	Tammy grabs the dog's tail.

Before continuing this chapter, read each of the statements below and determine the stimulus and response for each situation.

1. Judy began to cry as the dog entered the play yard.
   Stimulus:
   Response:
2. Adam threw a ball through the window when Ms. Kelly told him to return to his seat.
   Adam's stimulus:
   Adam's response:
3. Mary twisted Ted's arm when he threw her doll in the toilet.
   Mary's stimulus:
   Mary's response:

4. Ned had not had anything to drink for 6 hours. When he was in the bathroom, he began to drink from the toilet.
   Ned's stimulus:
   Ned's response:

Answers are on page 59.

THE CONSEQUENCE

THE CONSEQUENCE IS THE ENVIRONMENTAL CHANGE THAT FOLLOWS THE OCCURRENCE OF THE BEHAVIOR.

The third element in the instructional cycle is the consequence, which is an event that follows the response. In other words, the consequence is what happens to the student after he or she has responded.

Sometimes the consequence is a natural event. For example, Dennis sees a bright red burner on the stove and is attracted to it. He edges toward the stove and when no one is looking, he reaches up and touches the red hot coils of the burner. He burns his finger and begins to cry. The stimulus in this situation was the bright red burner. The response to seeing the burner was touching it, and the consequence was the pain from touching the coil which resulted in the burn. This consequence was a natural event because it was produced by the environment. Such natural consequences, whether negative or positive, are a part of our everyday world. As such, they have an effect on the way we behave.

There is another type of consequence that plays an even greater part in determining how we behave each day. These consequences are the ones that other people in the environment deliberately arrange to follow our behavior. They do so because they want to have an effect on our future behavior. Any intervention program that you design, whether it is to increase or decrease a behavior, must primarily concentrate on the development of consequences that will produce the desired effect in the behavior.

The issue of developing programmatic consequences is discussed below, but first read each of the situations below and see if you can identify the stimulus, response, and consequence for each situation.

1. Cindy runs to the bulletin board and tears the papers off. The instructor grabs Cindy's hands to prevent her from tearing any more papers.
   Cindy's stimulus:
   Cindy's response:
   Cindy's consequence:
2. Daniel picks up all his toys and places them in a toy box after his mother says, "Pick up your toys." His mother gives him a big hug and tells him he is a good boy.

Daniel's stimulus:

Daniel's response:

Daniel's consequence:

3. Hector picks the scab on his hand so often that it does not have time to heal. Each time the instructor sees him pick the scab, she takes him to the infirmary to see his favorite nurse who cleanses the wound.

Hector's stimulus:

Hector's response:

Hector's consequence:

4. Madeline flings paper clips at the instructor during craft class. Each day the instructor becomes angry and tells Madeline to leave the room. Madeline leaves the room and takes a nap in the hall.

Madeline's stimulus:

Madeline's response:

Madeline's consequence:

5. Jeffrey eats the paste placed on the table for art projects. Each time the instructor catches him eating paste, she rinses his mouth with cherry-flavored mouthwash.

Jeffrey's stimulus:

Jeffrey's response:

Jeffrey's consequence:

Turn to page 59 for the correct answers.

Now, let us look at two situations in which the stimulus and the response are identical although the consequences are distinctly different.

The instructor places a ping pong ball on Judy's desk. Judy bends down, purses her lips, and blows the ball toward her instructor who is seated across from her. The instructor says, "Good, Judy, good blowing the ball," and gives her a bite of an Oreo cookie.

The instructor places a ping pong ball on Brian's desk. Brian bends down, purses his lips, and blows the ball toward the instructor who is seated across from him. The instructor says, "No, Brian, don't blow the ball," and then turns away from Brian for 2 minutes.

In these two situations, the stimuli were the same (the ping pong ball) and the responses were the same (blowing the ball), but the consequences were very different. The consequences that Judy received were praise and a bite of her favorite cookie. The instructor wanted Judy to receive a pleasant consequence because she was supposed to blow the ping pong ball. By doing so, she was strengthening her mouth and throat muscles, which is very important. According to her physical threapist, Judy drools because her mouth and throat muscles are weak.

The consequences that Brian received were a reprimand and being ignored by his instructor. The instructor wanted Brian to receive an unpleasant consequence because he was supposed to hand the ball to the teacher rather than blow it. It was important for the instructor to dissuade Brian because Brian often misbehaved in instructional sessions by blowing lightweight objects at his instructor.

These two situations illustrate an extremely important point: The type of consequence that is delivered following a behavior is determined by what effect the instructor wants to have on the future occurrence of the behavior. If the instructor wants the behavior to increase or continue, then he or she arranges for a pleasant consequence to follow the behavior. Regardless of which choice the instructor makes, the future behavior will be affected by the consequence. This is why we say that *behavior is a function of its consequences.*

As you may have surmised, there are two basic types of consequences, *reinforcing* consequences and *punishing* consequences. When a *reinforcing* consequence follows a response or behavior, that response will *increase* in frequency; that is, it will occur more often in the future. When a *punishing* consequence follows a response, that response will *decrease* in frequency; that is, it will occur less often in the future.

In the above examples, Judy's blowing response was followed by reinforcing consequences, praise and a bite of her favorite cookie, whereas Brian's blowing response was followed by punishing consequences, being reprimanded and ignored. We refer to the relation between Judy's behavior and the reinforcing consequences as reinforcement and the reinforcing consequences as reinforcers because they strengthen a behavior. We refer to the relation between Brian's behavior and the punishing consequences as punishment and the punishing consequences as punishers because they weaken a behavior.

Through the use of reinforcers or punishers, you can manage your students' future responses. Because you can manage your students' future responses, you can predict what these responses will be. This is why you can understand how to predict and manage behavior once you have learned about the instructional cycle.

Reinforcing Consequences (Reinforcers)

A REINFORCER IS ANY EVENT THAT MAINTAINS OR INCREASES THE PROBABILITY OF THE RESPONSE IT FOLLOWS.

If an event is to be a reinforcer, it must be something the student likes and something for which the student will behave or respond. Thus, just what the reinforcing consequences are is determined by the student's behavior even though the choices may not seem like something positive or pleasant as far as the teacher is concerned.

Punishing Consequences (Punishers)

A PUNISHER IS ANY EVENT THAT DECREASES THE
PROBABILITY OF THE RESPONSE THAT IT FOLLOWS.

If an event is to be a punisher, it must reduce the behavior. As with reinforcers, the selection of punishers must be based on the student's behavior even though the punishers may not seem to the teacher to be unpleasant events. To determine whether or not a consequence is punishing, you must note whether occurrence of the response it follows decreases. If the response decreases, the consequence is a punisher.

Before continuing this chapter, check the situations below where a punishing consequence occurs. Consider each situation from the standpoint of what most students would find punishing.

_____ 1. Alice dips her hand into the play dough and begins eating it. Her teacher, Ms. Brooks, tells Alice to stop eating the play dough and spit it out. Alice responds by swallowing and then grabbing more play dough. Ms. Brooks walks over to Alice, tells her that it is wrong to eat play dough, and then brushes Alice's teeth with mouthwash. Alice cries throughout the toothbrushing. The consumption of play dough by Alice decreases from 15 times a day to 5 times a day.

_____ 2. Ms. MacNulty is placing food on the table as she calls her family to the kitchen for dinner. Her son, Patrick, runs into the kitchen and throws the mashed potatoes on the floor. Ms. MacNulty makes Patrick clean the mashed potatoes off the floor and then scrub the floor while the rest of the family eats dinner. The number of times Patrick was throwing mashed potatoes during each meal increased from 10 times to 20 times per meal after this.

_____ 3. Karen was asked to put her bike in the garage and was given a popsicle. She sat in front of her house next to the bike and watched the popsicle melt upon the ground.

Turn to page 60 for the correct answers.

THE INSTRUCTIONAL CYCLE

How you can use the three elements in the instructional cycle—the stimulus, the response, and the consequence—to effectively instruct your students is examined below. But, first, let's summarize briefly: The *stimulus* is any physical object or occurrence in the environment that sets the occasion for the response to occur. A stimulus can be an object, a command, an event, or a person. The *response* is the activity or behavior the student performs in the presence of the stimulus. The *consequence* is what happens to the student after his or her response.

You are ready to begin instructing your students. Assume that you want to teach a student the following objective: "Jim will pull his pants up from his hips." The response you want Jim to make is "pulling his pants up from his hips." To help Jim do this, you must provide a consequence for this response. You have observed that Jim likes you so you decide to give him a hug. You have also observed that he likes graham crackers so you decide to pair the hug with a graham cracker and with praise, "good boy," each and every time Jim raises his pants. You also decide to provide a cue to stimulate the behaviors. The cue involves placing Jim's pants at his hips, positioning his thumbs inside the waistband and his other fingers outside the waistband, and giving the verbal command, "Jim, pants up." When Jim responds and pulls his pants up to his waist, you give him reinforcing consequences—the praise, a hug, and a bite of cracker.

Because you used reinforcing consequences, the data show that Jim's behavior of pulling his pants up from his hips has increased.

Whenever you want to teach a new behavior or increase an old behavior you must:

1. Look at the behavioral objective in terms of the response you want the student to make,
2. Select a stimulus (or stimuli) that will serve as a cue(s) for the student to respond, and
3. Select a reinforcing consequence(s) to increase the probability that the desired response will occur again.

You should make careful observations during any training or teaching situation so that you can pinpoint any problems in the instructional cycle. Observing the response provides information concerning the effectiveness of the stimulus. For example, if Jim could not raise his pants from the hips because the pants were too tight, then the stimulus could be changed, e.g., Jim could be given a looser pair of pants. Similarly, if Jim did not respond to the verbal instruction, then a gesture by the instructor, such as raising her hand, could accompany the command, "Jim, pants up."

Observing the response also provides information regarding the choice of the behavioral objective. For example, an objective that is either too easy or too difficult may have been selected. For instance, it may be too difficult for Jim to raise his pants without any instruction or without physical guidance of his hands. If this occurs, the instructor can select another objective that is more appropriate, e.g., "Jim will pull his pants up from his hips when physical guidance of his hands is provided."

Sometimes the stimulus and response are appropriate, yet the student does not appear to be progressing. He or she may respond correctly on some days and incorrectly on others. If this occurs, the consequence is probably not very reinforcing, and another reinforcing consequence should be selected.

Remember, observing the response and the consequence helps you pinpoint problems in the instructional cycle. Your data will tell you how successful your program is, and they will tell you when to rewrite your program.

Before continuing this chapter, read the objectives below and write the response the student should make and the stimulus you would select to serve as a cue for that response. Write a sentence to indicate that the consequence you have selected for your student will be reinforcing (e.g., Sally loves Oreo cookies (the reinforcing consequence will be a bite of an Oreo cookie)).

1. Sally will turn the dial on the surprise busy box.
   Stimulus:
   Response:
   Reinforcing consequence:
2. Jeffrey will pull his pants up from the hips.
   Stimulus:
   Response:
   Reinforcing consequence:
3. Beverly will brush the front surface of her teeth.
   Stimulus:
   Response:
   Reinforcing consequence:
4. Richard will walk 6 feet in his saddle walker.
   Stimulus:
   Response:
   Reinforcing consequence:
5. Sandy will raise a two-handled cup to her mouth and drink.
   Stimulus:
   Response:
   Reinforcing consequence:

Answers are on page 60.

SUMMARY

The instructional cycle includes a *stimulus*, a *response*, and a *consequence*. The stimulus is any object, person, or event in the environment that sets the occasion for the response to occur. In effect, the stimulus serves to cue the response. A response is the behavior or activity the student performs in the presence of the stimulus. The consequence is what happens to the student after the response occurs.

There are two types of consequences: reinforcing consequences, and punishing consequences. Reinforcing consequences increase the response they follow because they are pleasant events. Reinforcing consequences are called reinforcers because they strengthen the response and increase the probability that it will occur again. The relation between the response and reinforcer is called reinforcement. Punishing consequences decrease the response they follow because they are unpleasant events. Punishing consequences are called punishers because they weaken the response and decrease the probability that it will be repeated. The relation between the response and punisher is called punishment. In light of this, we say that behavior is a function of its consequences.

Whenever you teach a new behavior or increase an old one, you must: 1) look at your individualized behavioral objectives in terms of the response you want the student to make, 2) select a stimulus (or stimuli) that will serve as a cue(s) for the student to respond, and 3) select a reinforcing consequence(s) to increase the probability that the desired response will occur again. You can pinpoint any problems in the instructional cycle by making careful observations of the response and the effects the reinforcing consequence has on the response.

REVIEW QUESTIONS

1. The instructional cycle is comprised of a _____, a _____, and a _____.
2. Any object, person, or event in the environment that sets the occasion for the response to occur is a _____.
3. The behavior, or activity, the student performs in the presence of the stimulus is a _____.
4. What happens to the student after the behavior occurs is called a _____.
5. There are two types of consequences: _____ and _____.
6. Reinforcing consequences _____ the occurrence of the response they follow.
7. Any event that maintains or increases the probability of the response it follows is a _____.
8. The relation between the response and the reinforcer is called _____.
9. Any event that decreases the probability of the response it follows is a _____.
10. The relation between the response and the punisher is called _____.
11. Observing the response provides information on the effectiveness of the _____ and the choice of the _____.
12. If the _____ is not reinforcing, the student will not progress.

Answers are on page 61.

SUGGESTED READINGS

Ashem, B. A., & Poser, E. G. (eds.). *Adaptive learning: Behavior modification with children.* New York: Pergamon Press, 1973.

Graziano, A. M. (ed.). *Behavior therapy with children.* Chicago: Aldine-Atherton, 1971, 1975. (2 vols.)

Hollis, J. H. Effects of reinforcement shifts on bent wire performance of severely retarded children. *American Journal of Mental Deficiency*, 1965, *69*, 531–535.

Lovaas, I. O., & Bucher, B. D. (eds.). *Perspectives in behavior modification with deviant children.* Englewood Cliffs, NJ: Prentice-Hall, 1974.

MacCubrey, J. Verbal operant conditioning with young institutionalized Down's syndrome children. *American Journal of Mental Deficiency*, 1971, *75*, 696–701.

Martin, G. L., McDonald, S., & Omichinski, M. An operant analysis of response interactions during meals with severely retarded girls. *American Journal of Mental Deficiency*, 1971, *76*, 68–75.

O'Leary, K. D., & O'Leary, S. G. *Classroom management: The successful use of behavior modification.* New York: Pergamon Press, 1972.

Schroeder, S. R. Parametric effects of reinforcement frequency, amount of reinforcement, and required response force on sheltered workshop behavior. *Journal of Applied Behavior Analysis,* 1972, *5*, 431–441.

Thompson, T., & Grabowski, J. (eds.). *Behavior modification of the mentally retarded.* New York: Oxford University Press, 1972.

Whitman, T. L., Zakaras, M., & Chardos, S. Effects of reinforcement and guidance procedures on instruction-following behavior of severely retarded children. *Journal of Applied Behavior Analysis*, 1971, *4*, 823.

ANSWERS TO CHAPTER QUESTIONS

Answers to Questions on Pages 51–52

1. Stimulus: The presence of the dog.
   Response: Judy's *crying*.
2. Stimulus: Ms. Kelly telling Adam to return to his seat.
   Response: Adam's *throwing* the ball through the window.
3. Stimulus: Ted's throwing the doll in the toilet.
   Response: Mary's *twisting* Ted's arm.
4. Stimulus: The water in the toilet.
   Response: Ned's *drinking* from the toilet.

Answers to Questions on Pages 52–53

1. Stimulus: Papers on the bulletin board.
   Response: Cindy's *tearing* the papers.
   Consequence: Cindy's hands being held by the instructor.
2. Stimulus: Toys on the floor.
   Response: Daniel's *picking up* toys and placing them in a toy box.
   Consequence: Mother's hugging Daniel and telling him he is a good boy.
3. Stimulus: The scab on Hector's hand.
   Response: Hector's *picking* the scab.
   Consequence: Hector's seeing his favorite nurse and having her cleanse the wound.

4. Stimulus: The presence of the instructor and the presence of paper clips.
   Response: Madeline's *flinging* paper clips at the instructor.
   Consequence: Madeline's taking a nap in the hall.
5. Stimulus: The presence of the paste.
   Response: Jeffrey's *eating* the paste.
   Consequence: Jeffrey's rinsing out his mouth with cherry-flavored mouthwash.

Answers to Questions on Page 55

_V_ 1. The consequence in this situation is punishing. Ms. Brooks brushed Alice's teeth with mouthwash and Alice responded by crying.
___ 2. The consequence in this situation is not punishing. Patrick's behavior increased even though he had to clean up the potatoes and scrub the floor. If the consequence were punishing, the behavior would have decreased.
___ 3. The popsicle was given to Karen before she put the bike away. Not only was the popsicle not a consequence, but it was also not reinforcing because Karen did not like popsicles. If Karen did like popsicles, the behavior of keeping her bike outside would have been reinforced.

Answers to Questions on Page 57

1. Stimulus: A surprise busy box, a verbal command, a gesture if necessary.
   Response: Sally will turn the dial on the box.
   Reinforcing consequence: This statement must establish an object, edible, event, person, or anything else that the student likes and finds reinforcing. This item can then be used as a reinforcing consequence. For example, Sally will be reinforced for turning the dial on the box by receiving her favorite toy.
2. Stimulus: Loose fitting pants positioned on Jeffrey at his hips, a verbal command, a gesture if necessary, or Jeffrey's hands positioned if necessary.
   Response: Jeffrey will raise his pants.
   Reinforcing consequence: This statement must establish an object, edible, event, person, or anything else that the student likes and finds reinforcing. This item can then be used as a reinforcing consequence.
3. Stimulus: Toothbrush, pleasant tasting toothpaste, a verbal command, a gesture if necessary, or placement of toothbrush on Beverly's teeth if necessary.
   Response: Beverly will brush the front surface of her teeth.
   Reinforcing consequence: This statement must establish an object, edible, event, person, or anything else that the student likes and finds reinforcing. This item can then be used as a reinforcing consequence.
4. Stimulus: Someone sitting 6 feet away from Richard, holding his favorite toy or treat, a verbal command, or a gesture if necessary.
   Response: Richard will walk 6 feet.
   Reinforcing consequence: This statement must establish an object, edible, event, person, or anything else that the student likes and finds reinforcing. This item can then be used as a reinforcing consequence.
5. Stimulus: A two-handled cup, a verbal command, placement of Sandy's hands on the cup if necessary, or a gesture if necessary.
   Response: Sandy will drink from a two-handled cup.
   Reinforcing consequence: This statement must establish an object, edible, event, person, or anything else that the student likes and finds reinforcing. This item can then be used as a reinforcing consequence.

Answers to Review Questions on Page 58

1. stimulus, response, consequence
2. stimulus
3. response
4. consequence
5. reinforcers, punishers
6. increase
7. reinforcer
8. reinforcement
9. punisher
10. punishment
11. stimulus, objective
12. consequence

Chapter 5

DISCOVERING AND USING REINFORCERS

After reading this chapter, you will be able to:

1. List the three main types of reinforcers used in classrooms for severely and profoundly retarded students and give an example of each.

2. Define satiation.

3. Define deprivation.

4. Differentiate between a reinforcer and a potential reinforcer.

5. List the five ways to discover reinforcers and give an example of each.

6. List potential edible, social, and physical reinforcers for students in your class.

7. Discover reinforcers for five students in your class.

A reinforcer is the third element in the instructional cycle. As discussed in the previous chapter, a reinforcer is an event that increases the probability that the response it follows will occur again.

Reinforcers are objects or events that students like and for which they will work. It is crucial that you discover a large number of powerful reinforcers for each of your students because the instructional cycle cannot take place without an adequate supply of effective reinforcers.

Discovering reinforcers for severely and profoundly retarded students is an arduous and sometimes difficult task. Unlike normal individuals, retarded persons typically have very few reinforcers. There are two reasons for this. First, their particular learning deficits have prevented them from engaging in a variety of potentially reinforcing activities. Second, they have not been exposed to many potentially reinforcing objects or events.

This chapter shows you how to overcome these problems by using the three main types of reinforcers for severely and profoundly retarded students. You will also learn five ways to discover reinforcers for your students.

TYPES OF REINFORCERS

The three main types of reinforcers that are used in classrooms for severely and profoundly retarded students are:

1. Edible reinforcers
2. Physical reinforcers
3. Social reinforcers

In addition, there are some other types of reinforcers which you will learn about in later chapters.

Edible Reinforcers

EDIBLE REINFORCERS ARE THE FOODS PREFERRED BY A STUDENT.

Edible reinforcers are the foods the student enjoys eating. They are the most powerful of the three types of reinforcers because all organisms must have food in order to survive. If an edible is reinforcing to a student, it will increase the behavior. Because your students are accustomed to edible reinforcers, we use them when we begin teaching a new behavior to a student or begin working with a new student. The goal is to learn how to increase the number of edibles the student will work for and to eventually switch the student to other types of reinforcers (discussed below).

There are two kinds of edible reinforcers: solids and liquids. You can choose to use one or a combination of both, or to switch from one to the other. For example, if you are using potato chips as a reinforcer during a teaching session, you may decide to also use Kool-Aid or another type of liquid reinforcer later in the session. Your decision is based on the biological fact that after the student has been receiving potato chips for a while, he or she will probably become thirsty and a liquid reinforcer will become very effective.

Whichever kind(s) of edible reinforcer you choose to use, *you must provide a large variety*. Otherwise, the student will quickly tire of the same old fare and stop responding. For example, a student may work for Fruit Loops or squirts of grape juice for a few hours, but he or she will soon tire of these foods if they are used all day and every day. When the student stops responding for an edible, we know that it is no longer reinforcing because the student will not work for it. We refer to this phenomenon as *satiation*.

SATIATION OCCURS WHEN A REINFORCER HAS BEEN PRESENTED SO OFTEN THAT IT IS NO LONGER EFFECTIVE IN PRODUCING OR MAINTAINING A BEHAVIOR.

You should have no difficulty remembering to avoid the problem of satiation if you consider that it would be comparable to your being given nothing to eat each day but hamburgers. How long do you think it would take before you could not stand the sight of another hamburger? Satiation is usually a temporary state and usually occurs after a high rate of reinforcement when you are using the same reinforcer.

Remember, you must always provide a variety of edible reinforcers for your students, and when a student does not respond or work for a particular edible, satiation has occurred and the edible is no longer reinforcing.

Providing a variety of edibles allows us to take advantage of the effects of another behavioral principle, *deprivation*.

DEPRIVATION OCCURS WHEN A REINFORCER HAS NOT BEEN PRESENTED FOR A WHILE. AS A RESULT, THE STUDENT USUALLY WILL RESPOND EAGERLY TO OBTAIN THAT REINFORCER.

The more edible reinforcers we use, the more likely it is that the student will be in a state of deprivation for one or more of these reinforcers. As a result, the student will be more likely to keep responding in the training environment. You have experienced the effects of deprivation many times throughout your life. Remember the last time you had a craving for some specific food such as pizza? You probably craved pizza because you do not have it every day. If you use a wide variety of edibles for your students, you will ensure that deprivation, rather than satiation, occurs.

To determine which edibles are reinforcing you will select small, readily available items of food and then let the student sample them. As the students try the various edibles you can keep a record of those they like and those they reject. Some edibles that are small, readily available, and have been effective with other students are:

Liquids	Solids
Grape juice	Popcorn
Orange juice	Potato chips
Milk	Raisins
Apple juice	Corn chips
Water	Pretzels
Kool-Aid	Fruits
Lemonade	Vegetables
Orangeade	Candy
Soda	Gum
Colas	Bread sticks

As with all reinforcers, edible reinforcers must be presented to the student immediately after the correct or appropriate response. To ensure that you can deliver edibles immediately, you should wear an apron whenever you are with your students.[1] The apron should have numerous pockets to accommodate the variety of edibles you will be using. Liquid reinforcers should be placed in squirt bottles, such as catsup dispensers, that fit easily into the apron pockets. At least two different types of liquids should be used. Squirt bottles eliminate hygiene problems since you can give a student a squirt of liquid without having the tip of the bottle touch the student's lips.

Remember, every staff person *must* be wearing an apron that contains several pockets filled with squirt bottles and a variety of solid edible reinforcers so that the edible reinforcers can be delivered immediately.

Physical Reinforcers

PHYSICAL REINFORCERS ARE BODILY CONTACT THAT THE STUDENT LIKES OR ENJOYS. A PHYSICAL REINFORCER WILL INCREASE THE STUDENT'S BEHAVIOR.

There are two kinds of physical reinforcers:

1. Tactile reinforcers
2. Vibratory reinforcers

A tactile reinforcer is any type of physical skin-to-skin contact between you and the student that is delivered in a positive way and for which the student will work or respond. A tactile reinforcer can be a touch, a hug, or a caress on the cheek. As you undoubtedly know, most students find these events to be very reinforcing.

The second type of physical reinforcer, vibratory stimulation, is also a very powerful reinforcer. Vibratory stimulation can be given to a student in two ways. One way is to rub or massage the student in an appropriate area, for example, his back or neck. The other way is to use a vibrator and apply it to the student's neck, arms, hands, or legs. Vibratory stimulation can be an extremely powerful and effective reinforcer for severely retarded students and especially for multiply handicapped students. The vibrator should be carried in an apron pocket along with the edible and liquid reinforcers.

---

[1]There are two potential problems associated with the use of aprons in the classroom. The first is that some students will reach into the pockets when you are not looking and take the reinforcers. To solve this problem, line each pocket with velcro tape so that it stays closed until you wish to open it. The second problem is that some male instructors object to wearing an apron. To solve this problem, furnish those male staff members with a carpenter's apron. It is unimportant what the aprons look like, as long as they perform their intended function.

While vibratory stimulation is a powerful reinforcer, it may not be appropriate for a few of your students. Some students are tactilely defensive; that is, they intensely dislike being touched either physically or via vibration. If you have such a student, you are probably aware of the problem. To overcome the problem, you can begin a shaping program (see Chapter 7) to adapt the student to the tactile and vibratory stimulation. It is a good idea to enlist the aid of your physical or occupational therapist in such a program.

A more serious problem can occur with some multiply handicapped students who suffer from cerebral palsy. *Under no circumstances should you use a vibrator until the student has been examined by a physical therapist and you have been given the okay to use vibration.* Otherwise, you run the risk of causing the student physical harm. There is no problem, however, if you simply wish to use your touch as a reinforcer with these students.

Social Reinforcers

SOCIAL REINFORCERS ARE PRAISE, SMILES, ATTENTION, OR FRIENDLY REMARKS THAT A STUDENT LIKES OR ENJOYS. THE SOCIAL REINFORCER WILL INCREASE THE BEHAVIOR.

The third and *most important* type of reinforcer is social. Many of the behaviors we engage in every day are maintained by social reinforcers. We praise each other, smile at each other, nod our heads at each other. In short, we give some indication to other people that we are pleased with them or that we like them. There is simply no question that praise or attention from someone important to us is very desirable and that we will work hard to obtain it.

Yet, we were not born with a desire for social reinforcers. We learned to enjoy praise, attention, and all the various social reinforcers. As infants we received edible and physical reinforcers from our parents and we eventually paired our parents and their attention with these reinforcing events. Over time, our parents' attention became, in most cases, more important than the very basic reinforcers we enjoyed as infants. Later, we learned that praise had power, and that it often not only led to pleasant social interactions with people but to other powerful reinforcers as well, such as money, prestige, or sex. Perhaps most importantly, we learned that the praise and attention from others made us feel better about ourselves—it increased our self-esteem.

Because food is basic and sustains life, your students will initially find edibles more reinforcing than praise. However, if they are to learn that praise is a powerful reinforcer and thereby progress toward normalization, you *must* deliver a social reinforcer each and every time an edible reinforcer is given. This pairing will take your students through the same types of experiences that made social reinforcers important to you. The rule, then, is: *Always pair a social reinforcer with the delivery of any reinforcer*. An excellent example of how this pairing should be done follows.

Ms. Daniels was teaching Mary to take off her T-shirt. After Mary removed her T-shirt, Ms. Daniels immediately squirted Kool-Aid into Mary's mouth and said, "Good, Mary, good taking off your shirt." Ms. Daniels had paired the edible reinforcer (Kool-Aid) with the social reinforcer of praise ("Good, Mary").

By pairing your attention with edible reinforcers, your students will eventually begin to behave appropriately just for your attention. Using social reinforcers to develop a positive relationship with your students is crucial. You cannot expect a student who does not know you, or who has had infrequent nonreinforcing interactions with you, to find you very reinforcing until you have established a pattern of reinforcing that student. If you do not deliver attention for a student's positive behaviors, that student will seek your attention through negative or inappropriate behaviors. And, most importantly, social reinforcers are the one type of reinforcer that you can be sure will be delivered to the student outside the classroom. Your task is to ensure that the student has a history of receiving social reinforcers for appropriate behaviors. Remember, *you are, or can be, an extremely powerful social reinforcer for your students*, and you should learn to think of yourself as such. You always have a touch, a smile, a glance, and a soft word with you, and these do not cost anything, cause cavities, contain calories, or require an apron.

Before continuing through the chapter, answer the following questions.

1. The foods preferred by a student can be potential _____ reinforcers.
2. There are two types of edible reinforcers: _____ and _____ .
3. When a reinforcer has been presented so often that it is no longer effective in producing or maintaining a behavior, _____ has occurred.
4. When a reinforcer has not been presented for a while and the student will respond eagerly for that reinforcer, _____ has occurred.
5. Bodily contact can be used as a potential _____ reinforcer if it increases the behavior.
6. The two kinds of physical reinforcers are _____ and _____ .
7. Praise, attention, and friendly remarks, when they increase the behavior they follow, are _____ reinforcers.
8. Mr. Foreman was training Megan to point to a picture of a toilet. During the 10:00 a.m. to 10:15 a.m. training session, he asked Megan to point to a picture of a toilet and she did so nine times out of 10. Each time Megan made the correct response, Mr. Foreman reinforced her with a piece of a pretzel. At 10:30 a.m. Mr. Castro began training Megan to move her wheelchair 10 feet forward. Megan responded correctly during her first trial, and

Mr. Castro reinforced her with a pretzel. Mr. Castro again asked Megan to move her wheelchair forward. Megan did not move the wheelchair but pointed at the water fountain and cried.

    a. Were pieces of pretzel a reinforcer for Megan at 10:00 a.m.?

    b. Was the piece of pretzel a reinforcer for Megan at 10:30 a.m.?

    c. What would have been a good reinforcer for Megan at 10:30 a.m.?

9. Ms. Evans, the physical therapist, has decided to train Erin to use a saddle walker. Ms. Evans has never worked with Erin before. She believes that a good reinforcer for Erin would be to say, "Good girl," each time Erin stands in the walker. When the training began, Ms. Evans placed Erin in the walker and each time Erin's feet touched the floor, Ms. Evans said, "Good girl." After 3 days, Erin had not stood in the walker, but rather had merely touched her feet to the floor in a random fashion.

    a. What type of reinforcer was Ms. Evans using?

    b. Is there another type of reinforcer that should be used with, or instead of, the reinforcer "Good girl"?

    c. What would you do to reinforce Erin if it was the first time you ever worked with her?

10. Ms. Quince was training Brian, a child with cerebral palsy, to attend to visual stimuli. She held up a teddy bear and said, "Brian, look." Each time Brian looked at the teddy bear, Ms. Quince reinforced him by lightly caressing his cheek for 5 seconds.

    a. What type of reinforcer was Ms. Quince using?

    b. Should Ms. Quince consult a physical therapist before she touches Brian?

    c. Suppose Ms. Quince decided to use a vibrator to reinforce Brian's looking. Should she consult a physical therapist before using the vibrator?

Answers are on page 76.

DISCOVERING REINFORCERS

Now that you have learned about the three main types of reinforcers, it is important to learn how to discover reinforcers for your students. Since an event is not a reinforcer for someone until it has been shown to increase a behavior, we cannot simply say that chocolate candy, for instance, is a reinforcer for a student, although we know that, in general, most students like chocolate candy. Thus, it remains for us to give the student a piece of chocolate candy following a behavior, and then to observe whether or not that behavior occurs again when it is followed by the candy. If so, then we have established that chocolate candy is indeed a reinforcer for that student. You can avoid a lot of problems by *not* *assuming* what reinforces a student. Rather, regard things that we normally consider to be reinforcers as potential reinforcers until they have been shown to increase a behavior. Once a reinforcer has been established, you should periodically determine that it, in fact, continues to be a reinforcer because students' preferences will change over time.

Remember, each student is unique and has a unique set of reinforcers established by his or her own learning history. Your task as an instructor is to discover, establish, and increase each student's reinforcers.

There are five ways to discover reinforcers for your students:

1. Ask the student.
2. Observe the student.
3. Observe similar types of students.
4. Use the Premack principle.
5. Use reinforcer sampling.

Asking the Student

> THE FIRST WAY TO DISCOVER REINFORCERS FOR STUDENTS IS TO ASK THEM.

The simplest way of determining what is reinforcing for students who have language is to ask them what they would like to have as a reinforcer. Your question might be, "What would you like?" "What would make you happy?" or "What can I do to make you happy?" Most verbal students will appreciate the opportunity to pick their reinforcers and will tell you what they would like. It is amazing how often instructors fail to ask their students what reinforces them. This simple effort can save a great deal of time and trouble.

Many of your students may be nonverbal and therefore unable to tell you what is reinforcing for them. And some verbal students may not be sure of what they find reinforcing. However, these students can still tell you what is reinforcing for them. They will do this when you use the second way of discovering reinforcers.

Observing the Student

> THE SECOND WAY TO DISCOVER REINFORCERS FOR STUDENTS IS TO OBSERVE THEM.

How does the student spend his or her time? Confucius said that if you watch someone, you will know him. Perhaps Confucius was the first behaviorist, because behaviorally oriented educators say that if you observe a student's behavior, you will know your student. The behaviors your students engage in are the behaviors that they find reinforcing or that lead to a reinforcer. For example, if a student sits and rocks all day, we can say with assurance that rocking is a reinforcer. Similarly, it would be safe to say that a student whose frequent misbehavior is followed by staff attention finds that attention reinforcing. So, if you observe your students, you will learn what their reinforcers are.

Occasionally, you will observe a severely or profoundly retarded student who displays so few behaviors that it is difficult to determine what is reinforcing. In this situation, you should use the third way to discover a reinforcer for a student. (You should also try reinforcer sampling, discussed below.)

Observing Other Students Who Are Similar

> THE THIRD WAY TO DISCOVER REINFORCERS FOR STUDENTS IS TO OBSERVE SIMILAR TYPES OF STUDENTS.

Because severely retarded students often share similar deficits, experiences, and backgrounds (for example, living in an institution or nursing home), they often have similar learning histories in terms of the way they behave and the kinds of reinforcers that have been available to them. As a result, you can learn a lot about a student by observing similar types of students. What do other severely and profoundly retarded students in the class like to do? What do they find reinforcing? The answers to these questions will suggest potential reinforcers for the student who does not appear to have any reinforcers. After observing these other students, make a list of potential reinforcers. You may have to try several of these "potential reinforcers" before you find one that is reinforcing for your student.

Using the Premack Principle

> THE FOURTH WAY TO DISCOVER REINFORCERS FOR STUDENTS IS TO USE THE PREMACK PRINCIPLE.

The Premack principle (which is named for David Premack) states that a behavior that a student performs frequently can be used to reinforce a behavior the student seldom performs. For example, Jimmy loves to ride the Big Wheel at school. Each day when Jimmy comes to school, he takes his jacket off, throws it on the floor, and rushes over to ride the Big Wheel. Jimmy's teacher would like him to hang his jacket up when he comes in the classroom; however, Jimmy rarely, if ever, does so. Having just learned about the Premack principle, Jimmy's teacher decides to try it. She tells Jimmy, "You must hang up your jacket before you can ride the Big Wheel." To her surprise and delight, Jimmy dutifully begins to hang his jacket up every day. Jimmy's teacher successfully used the Premack principle: She took a behavior Jimmy frequently performed (riding the Big Wheel) and used it to reinforce hanging up his jacket, a behavior he seldom performed.

Jimmy's mother has the same problem with him. Every day when he comes home from school, he removes his jacket, throws it on the floor, and rushes outside to ride his Big Wheel. One day she says, "I want you to pick up your jacket.'' Jimmy answers, ''Ride my Big Wheel.'' His mother responds, ''I want you to hang up your jacket.'' Jimmy sulks and says, ''Ride Big Wheel now; hang my jacket later.'' Jimmy's mother smiles and says, ''Okay, you can go out now, but when you come back in, you have to hang up your jacket.'' Do you think Jimmy will hang up his jacket when he comes in the house? He probably will not. The reinforcer, going outside and riding the Big Wheel, has already been delivered, and therefore Jimmy's mother has nothing to use as a reinforcer for Jimmy to hang up his jacket. She certainly did not use the Premack principle correctly.

Remember, when using the Premack principle, the low probability behavior, that is, the behavior that is performed infrequently, is followed by the high probability behavior. This high probability behavior serves as a reinforcer for the low probability behavior.

Perhaps you have encountered a student who cannot tell you what he wants as a reinforcer, and you cannot find any particular reinforcer preferences during your classroom observations. He does not respond to the reinforcers of similar types of students, and he does not perform any one behavior frequently enough for you to use the Premack principle. For such a student, you would use a reinforcer sampling procedure.

Using Reinforcer Sampling

THE FIFTH WAY OF DISCOVERING REINFORCERS
FOR STUDENTS IS TO USE REINFORCER SAMPLING.

Reinforcer sampling is a procedure whereby you have the student try a variety of potential reinforcers. Thus, reinforcer sampling offers you an opportunity to determine whether or not the student will like the potential reinforcer. In essence, you are saying to the student, ''Try it; maybe you'll like it.''

If you recall some of your own experiences, you will realize that many of your own current reinforcers were established as such through reinforcer sampling. For example, many of us have had the experience of dining with a friend who says, ''Why don't you try one of my raw oysters? Really they are quite good, especially with a little fresh lemon juice squeezed on them.'' You answer, ''No thanks. I couldn't possibly think of eating one of those slimy things.'' ''Oh, just try one, just try a taste,'' your friend replies. ''No, I couldn't.'' Your friend urges you again, ''Aw, go on, just a taste.'' You take a taste and find, to your surprise, that raw oysters really are good. In fact, you decide right then to order a half dozen for yourself. You may not have been aware of it at the time, but you had just demonstrated the effectiveness of reinforcer sampling.

Reinforcer sampling is a very powerful way of discovering and establishing reinforcers. It is especially helpful with severely and profoundly retarded students who have not had much exposure to a wide variety of potential reinforcers. By using reinforcer sampling, you are expanding the number of reinforcers that you can use to motivate your students to learn.

Before continuing this chapter, answer the following questions.

1. David is an 18-year-old mildly retarded student who attends a work activity center. David is verbal and engages in a variety of activities at the center. His instructor would like to discover some new reinforcers for him. What would be the most expedient method of determining some new reinforcers for David?

2. Mr. Douglas wanted to discover reinforcers for Clara, a multiply handicapped nonverbal student. Mr. Douglas observed Clara for 5 days and discovered that she sat in a relaxation chair and did next to nothing. Since observing Clara did not prove to be an effective method of determining a reinforcer for her, what method should Mr. Douglas try next?

3. William enjoys continually rocking whenever possible. His instructor, Ms. George, would like to teach William to make a peanut butter sandwich. How could Ms. George use the Premack principle to teach William to make a peanut butter sandwich?

4. List five ways to discover reinforcers for a student.
   a. _____ the student.
   b. _____ the student.
   c. _____ similar kinds of students.
   d. Use the _____ principle.
   3. Use _____ sampling.

5. We cannot say that popcorn is a _____ for Trudy until one of Trudy's behaviors has been increased after it has been followed by popcorn on several occasions. Until that occurs, we would refer to the popcorn as a p_____ _____ for Trudy.

Answers are on page 77.

SUMMARY

Students will not be motivated to learn unless we have a variety of reinforcers for them. The three main types of reinforcers that are used in classrooms for severely and profoundly retarded students are: 1) edible reinforcers, 2) physical reinforcers, and 3) social reinforcers.

Edible reinforcers are either solid or liquid foods and are used when we begin instructing new students or teaching new or difficult tasks. Physical reinforcers involve either touching the student yourself or touching the student with various forms of vibratory stimulation. You should always consult a physical therapist before using a vibrator with a student who has cerebral palsy.

In order to deliver edible and physical reinforcers immediately, all instructors should wear aprons with pockets that contain a variety of edibles, two squirt bottles of liquids, and a vibrator.

Social reinforcers are the most important of the three types of reinforcers since the normal world operates, in large part, on the principle of social reinforcement. Initially, social reinforcers should be paired with edibles until the instructor becomes a social reinforcer for the student, at which time the edibles can be eliminated.

We cannot say that an event is a reinforcer for a student until that event increases one of the student's behaviors. Until the event has increased a behavior and thereby become a reinforcer, we must regard it as a potential reinforcer.

If the same reinforcer is continually presented, satiation will take place, that is, the student will cease responding for the reinforcer. The opposite of satiation is deprivation which occurs when a particular reinforcer has not been presented for a while and the student responds eagerly to obtain that reinforcer.

There are five ways of discovering reinforcers for students: 1) ask the student, 2) observe the student, 3) observe similar kinds of students, 4) use the Premack principle, and 5) use reinforcer sampling.

When working with a verbal student, the most expedient way to discover a reinforcer is simply to ask the student what he or she likes. If the student is nonverbal, you should observe the student and make a list of activities, toys, or foods that he or she enjoys. If a student does not demonstrate reinforcer preferences in any areas, you should observe similar students or try reinforcer sampling by introducing the student to various types of potential reinforcers. The final method of discovering reinforcers is to use the Premack principle in which you use a behavior a student frequently performs to reinforce a behavior the student seldom performs.

Each student has different reinforcer preferences and these vary from hour to hour, day to day, and week to week. To use reinforcers effectively, you must use a variety of reinforcers, reinforce immediately, and remember to determine the reinforcer preferences of each of your students on a regular basis. Without effective reinforcers, students will not be motivated to learn.

REVIEW QUESTIONS

Part 1. Complete the following sentences. Then check your answers on page 77.

1. The foods a student enjoys eating are _____ reinforcers.
2. Two types of edible reinforcers are _____ and _____.
3. When using edible reinforcers, you want to deliver the reinforcer immediately. To help do this you can wear an _____.

4. For reinforcers to be effective, they must be delivered _____.
5. The two types of physical reinforcers are _____ and _____.
6. A reinforcer applied to the student's neck, arms, hands, or legs is a _____ reinforcer.
7. Praise, attention, and friendly remarks preferred by a student are _____ reinforcers.
8. When a reinforcer has been presented so often that it is no longer effective in producing or maintaining a behavior, we can say that _____ has occurred.
9. When a reinforcer has not been presented to a student for a long enough time to make the student eager to obtain the reinforcer, a state of _____ occurs.
10. An event that has not yet been shown to increase a specific behavior is a _____ reinforcer.
11. The first way to discover a reinforcer for a verbal student is to _____ him.
12. You will know what a student's reinforcers are if you _____ the student.
13. Occasionally you will observe a student who displays few behaviors. If this occurs, you should observe _____ kinds of students.
14. A behavior the student performs frequently can be used to reinforce a behavior the student seldom performs. This is the _____ principle.
15. A method whereby the student tries potential reinforcers is called _____ _____.

Part 2. Group the following potential reinforcers according to their type: edible, physical, or social. Answers are on page 77.

A hug
M&M
Vibration to neck
Stroking student's face with your hand
Kool-Aid
Bouncing student on your knee
Water
A kiss
Ham

Swinging on a swing
A smile
Rubbing student's hand with cold cloth
A glance
Rubbing student's feet with your hand
Popcorn
A nod
Milk
A pat on the back

Edible	Physical	Social

SUGGESTED READINGS

Bailey, J., & Meyerson, L. Vibration as a reinforcer with a profoundly retarded child. *Journal of Applied Behavior Analysis,* 1969, *2*, 135-137.

Bijou, S. W. A functional analysis of retarded development. In: N. R. Ellis (ed.), *International review of research in mental retardation* (Vol. 1). New York: Academic Press, 1966.

Bijou, S. W. Behavior modification in the retarded: Application of operant conditioning principles. *Pediatric Clinics of North America*, 1968, *15*, 969-987.

Bijou, S. W., & Sturges, P. T. Positive reinforcers for experimental studies with children—consumables and manipulatables. *Child Development*, 1958, *30*, 151-170.

Gardner, W. I. *Behavior modification: Applications in mental retardation.* Chicago: Adline-Atherton, 1971.

Krumboltz, J. D., & Krumboltz, H. B. *Changing children's behavior.* Englewood Cliffs, NJ: Prentice-Hall, 1972.

Larsen, L. A., & Bricker, W. A. *A manual for parents and teachers of severely and profoundly retarded children.* Nashville, TN: IMRID Papers and Reports, Vol. V, No. 22, 1968.

Madsen, C. H., Jr., & Madsen, C. K. *Teaching/discipline: A positive approach for educational development* (2nd ed.). Boston: Allyn & Bacon, 1974.

Patterson, G. R. *Living with children.* Champaign, IL: Research Press, 1976.

Rynders, J. E., & Friedlander, B. Z. Preferences in institutionalized severely retarded children for selected visual stimulus material presented as operant reinforcement. *American Journal of Mental Deficiency,* 1972, *76*, 568-573.

ANSWERS TO CHAPTER QUESTIONS

Answers to Questions on Pages 68–69

1. edible
2. solid, liquid
3. satiation
4. deprivation
5. physical
6. tactile, vibratory
7. social
8. a. Yes.
   b. No.
   c. Megan was probably thirsty from the nine bits of pretzels she had received a half hour earlier. An appropriate reinforcer at 10:30 a.m. would have been a liquid reinforcer.
9. a. A social reinforcer.
   b. Yes. Ms. Evans should pair an edible reinforcer with the social reinforcer. Also, Ms. Evans should name the behavior she is reinforcing, e.g., "Good girl, you are standing in the walker."
   c. When working with a new student, the student should receive an edible and a social reinforcer simultaneously, because a new instructor is unlikely to be socially reinforcing for a student.
10 a. A physical reinforcer.
   b. No. A physical touch is not harmful. Furthermore, if Brian had been tactually defensive, Ms. Quince would have known immediately by his behavior.

c. Yes. Ms. Quince should consult a physical therapist because she intends to use vibratory stimulation and it is not appropriate for some students with certain physical problems, such as some forms of cerebral palsy.

Answers to Questions on Page 73

1. Since David is verbal, the instructor should begin by asking David what he would like to have as reinforcers.
2. Mr. Douglas should observe students who are very similar to Clara. If that is not successful, he may want to try reinforcer sampling.
3. Ms. George would use the behavior that William performs frequently to reinforce the behavior that occurs infrequently. Thus, Ms. George would reinforce William by allowing him to rock each time he makes a peanut butter sandwich.
4. a. Ask
   b. Observe
   c. Observe
   d. Premack
   e. reinforcer
5. reinforcer, potential reinforcer

Answers to Review Questions, Part 1, on Pages 74–75

1. edible
2. edible, liquids
3. apron
4. immediately
5. tactile, vibratory
6. physical
7. social
8. satiation
9. deprivation
10. potential
11. ask
12. observe
13. similar
14. Premack
15. reinforcer sampling

Answers to Review Questions, Part 2, on Page 75

Edibles	Physical	Social
M&M	Vibration to neck	A hug
Kool-Aid	Stroking student's	A kiss
Water	face with your hand	A smile
Ham	Bouncing student on your knee	A glance
Popcorn	Swinging on a swing	A nod
Milk	Rubbing student's hand with cold cloth	
	Rubbing student's feet with your hand	
	A pat on the back	

Chapter 6

SCHEDULES OF REINFORCEMENT

After reading this chapter, you will be able to:

1. Define and give an example of noncontingent reinforcement.
2. Define and give an example of contingent reinforcement.
3. Define and give an example of continuous reinforcement.
4. Discriminate between the appropriate uses of continuous and intermittent reinforcement.
5. Define and give an example of intermittent reinforcement.
6. Define and give an example of a ratio schedule of reinforcement.
7. Define and give an example of an interval schedule of reinforcement.

In this chapter, you will learn about *contingent* and *noncontingent* reinforcement as well as *continuous* and *intermittent* reinforcement. You will also learn how all of these types of reinforcement are best used in the classroom.

NONCONTINGENT REINFORCEMENT

> NONCONTINGENT REINFORCEMENT IS REINFORCE-
> MENT THAT IS NOT RELATED TO ANY SPECIFIC
> BEHAVIOR.

Before you begin using the various schedules of reinforcement, you must first establish yourself as reinforcing and the classroom as a reinforcing place. You will want to raise the density of reinforcement in your classroom so that students regard the classroom and you as reinforcing. To do so, use noncontingent reinforcement at least one week before you begin using behavioral objectives (for example, the first week of the new school year and/or with any new students). Noncontingent reinforcement can occur often and at any time because it is not related to the student's behavior. It is simply the presentation of positive, pleasurable events. For example, during the first week of school, every student in Mr. Bird's room receives milk and cookies at 11:00 a.m. Mr. Bird is using noncontingent reinforcement because *everyone* receives milk and cookies at 11:00 a.m. regardless of their behavior.

Mr. Bird used noncontingent reinforcement during the first week of school because he wanted the classroom and himself to acquire reinforcing properties for his students. (He is paired with the presentation of the reinforcing events.) Mr. Bird knows that students must find you and the classroom reinforcing before they will perform the behaviors you attempt to teach them. It is important to make the environment reinforcing instead of punishing so that students will not engage in inappropriate behaviors. Initially, many students engage in inappropriate behavior to gain attention. Noncontingent reinforcement helps deter this type of problem.

The use of noncontingent reinforcement is not limited to the classroom. Think of times in your own life when reinforcers were delivered noncontingently or independent of your behavior. When a new market opens, it often offers a free sample of food. The establishment is encouraging you to frequent its facility by offering noncontingent reinforcement. Once you have sampled the facility and have been reinforced, the proprietors then begin to fade out the free samples and the food becomes contingent upon your purchasing it. (The discriminative stimuli presented by the market was to cue the behavior of purchasing food. When food is given away, it is a noncontingent reinforcer.)

Another example of the initial use of noncontingent reinforcement to "hook" someone on the available reinforcers is courtship. During courtship, reinforcing compliments are delivered noncontingently by your suitor. You do not have to display any specific behaviors to receive these adulations; you simply receive them because you are you. However, once the courtship ends in marriage, your spouse's reinforcing compliments generally become dependent on specific behaviors. Your hair has to look extraordinary for you to receive a compliment, or you may have to lose 10 pounds before you are told that you are handsome or pretty. Prior to marriage, you received the compliments regardless of your hair style or how much you weighed. Noncontingent reinforcement was used by your suitor to get you "hooked" on him or her as a major source of reinforcement.

You will use noncontingent reinforcement to "hook" your students in the same way. When you deliver social and edible reinforcers independent of any behavior, your students will pair you with the reinforcers you deliver, thereby establishing you as a reinforcer. Once you become a reinforcer (usually after about a week), you will dispense with all forms of noncontingent reinforcement and require specific appropriate forms of behavior from your students in order for them to be reinforced. At that point, all reinforcers would be delivered contingently.

Before continuing this chapter, check the following statements that demonstrate the use of noncontingent reinforcement.

_____1. Mr. Fez passed out lollipops to all children who were seated.
_____2. Ms. White gave every student a pretzel stick after lunch.
_____3. Mr. Thomas reads to Earl for 10 minutes every night at 8:00.
_____4. After Brian hung up his pajamas, Gwynn pushed him on the swing.
_____5. Grandma gave all her quiet grandchildren glasses of lemonade.

Answers are on page 95.

CONTINGENT REINFORCEMENT

> CONTINGENT REINFORCEMENT IS REINFORCEMENT
> THAT DEPENDS UPON A SPECIFIC RESPONSE.

Contingent reinforcement is the opposite of noncontingent reinforcement because it is given only following a specified response. For example, Ms. Brooks gives cookies and milk to everyone who is seated and quiet at 11:00 a.m. Ms. Brooks delivers the reinforcers of milk and cookies contingent on the students' behavior of being seated and quiet. Thus, only those students who are in their seats and quiet will receive the milk and cookies.

Contingent reinforcement is used to strengthen or maintain a behavior. For example, each time your student points to the sink to indicate that he wants water, you say, "Say water." As soon as the student responds correctly by saying "water," you reinforce him by giving him the water. If you continue reinforcing the response of saying "water," you will maintain and strengthen this behavior so that it will occur in the future.

Our everyday behaviors are strengthened and maintained in the same way. That is why we enjoy repeating the things we do well. We are reinforced when we do things well, and this reinforcement builds and maintains our interest. If you play tennis once a week for 6 months and become an accomplished tennis player, you receive reinforcing comments ("Good game"; "Your backhand has really improved") from your friends and opponents. As a result, it is likely that you will continue to play tennis and improve your tennis game. However, if you have been bowling for 6 months and have not improved your bowling average appreciably, friends may lose interest in playing with you and then you are likely to lose interest and give up the sport. Your only consolation may have been a friend's wishing you, "Better luck next time," and such comments are hardly reinforcing or likely to strengthen and maintain your bowling behavior. Thus, when we compare these two activities, it becomes obvious that you continued playing the sport for which you received reinforcement while you gave up the sport for which there was little, if any, reinforcement.

To maintain or strengthen a response, always use contingent reinforcement and reinforce the response each and every time it occurs. Over time, the student will perform the desired response more often in order to receive more reinforcement, thereby strengthening and maintaining the desired response.

Contingent reinforcement will strengthen the behaviors of your severely and profoundly retarded students. For example, Billy is a 14-year-old multiply handicapped boy who has lived in an institution for 12 of his 14 years. When Billy entered his current nursing home, his instructor wanted him to indicate when he had to use the toilet. Billy had no expressive language, but his receptive language was excellent. Accordingly, the instructor trained Billy to point to a picture of a toilet that was taped to the arm of his wheelchair. During the training of this behavior, the instructor spent most of the day with Billy. To maintain and strengthen the behavior, the instructor gave Billy a transistor radio for 5 minutes after each time Billy signaled that he needed to use the toilet. The reinforcer of listening to the radio was made contingent on Billy indicating his need to use the toilet.

Before continuing through this chapter, check the following statements that demonstrate the use of contingent reinforcement.

_____1. Mr. Smith gave each of his children 25 cents on Friday.
_____2. Susan gave peanut butter cookies to all the children who helped her clean the yard.
_____3. Each time a student used the toilet, Ms. Johnson gave him 10 points.
_____4. A bag of potato chips was given to each child who went swimming.
_____5. Popsicles were given to all students.

Answers are on page 96.

The effectiveness of your instructional program depends on the proper use of the various types of contingent reinforcement. Two types of contingent reinforcement are continuous reinforcement and intermittent reinforcement; both types will play a crucial role in your classroom.

CONTINUOUS REINFORCEMENT

> CONTINUOUS REINFORCEMENT IS WHEN A REINFORCER IS DELIVERED EACH TIME THE DESIRED BEHAVIOR OCCURS.

Continuous reinforcement is used when you begin to teach a new response (behavior) because it strengthens a new or weak behavior better than any other schedule of reinforcement. With this schedule of reinforcement, the specified behavior is reinforced every time it occurs. For example, when teaching Sally eye contact, you would use continuous reinforcement by saying, "Good girl, you looked at me," and giving Sally an edible reinforcer each and every time she looks at you. Every time Sally makes eye contact with you she would be rein-forced.

Continuous reinforcement is the only type of reinforcement you should use when beginning to teach a new behavior. However, it is not the schedule of reinforcement you would use to maintain a behavior because behaviors disappear rapidly, that is, they are extinguished (see Chapter 11), when continuous rein-forcement ceases. No doubt, you have encountered this situation yourself. For example, turning on a light switch is a behavior that is typically reinforced every time you do it. If the light does not go on, you do not stand there flipping the switch; after a few flips, you give up and change the light bulb. Or, how long do you continue to put money in a vending machine that does not work? Even if you have received soda from the machine every day for a year, you stop placing coins in the machine very quickly once you have determined that it does not work. This same process occurs in the classroom.

Janice has been tube fed for 10 of her 11 years. A tube was connected to her nose and a nourishing substance was fed into her body. When Janice first began to eat a liquid diet, her instructor reinforced her with ''Good girl, Janice,'' and stroked her hand each time she swallowed a spoonful of liquid. Soon the instruc-tor found that it was taking Janice approximately 1½ hours to eat each meal because of the continuous delivery of reinforcement. The instructor had also grown tired of reinforcing each of Janice's responses and had very little time to spend with the other students during mealtime. Since Janice now ate her liquid meals three times a day, her instructor stopped all reinforcement. Within a day, Janice was spitting out the liquid and had stopped swallowing her food.

In this example, we see the major disadvantage of continuous reinforcement: when the reinforcement stops, the behavior stops. Furthermore, it is quite un-natural to go through life reinforcing a student for every single appropriate response; to do so would result in very little progress in the student's overall behavior. Since it is not realistic to continue to reinforce every appropriate response and because there is always the danger that the behavior will disappear if a few reinforcers are skipped, we must use another reinforcement technique—intermittent reinforcement—to maintain the student's newly learned behaviors. Intermittent reinforcement is discussed in the next section.

Before continuing through this chapter, check the situations below that are examples of continuous reinforcement.

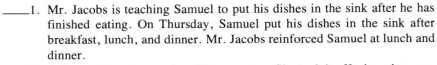

_____1. Mr. Jacobs is teaching Samuel to put his dishes in the sink after he has finished eating. On Thursday, Samuel put his dishes in the sink after breakfast, lunch, and dinner. Mr. Jacobs reinforced Samuel at lunch and dinner.

_____2. Sally was learning to take off her sweater. She took it off when she came into the room in the morning and her teacher gave her a hug. She took it off after recess and was given a tootsie roll.

_____3. Richie picked his clothes up off the floor and his mom let him stay up to watch television for an extra 30 minutes on Monday. On Tuesday, Richie picked up his clothes and his dad took him for an ice cream cone.

_____4. Marilyn was learning to feed herself. The first week she fed herself every day and the aide took her for a walk outside every day. The second week, she fed herself on Monday and Tuesday, but she did not go for walks.

_____5. Jacques was learning to sit up. Jacques sat up on the mat and his therapist gave him a squirt of Kool-Aid. Later that day, he sat up on a mat in the classroom and the teacher gave him a drink of juice.

Answers are on page 96.

INTERMITTENT REINFORCEMENT

INTERMITTENT REINFORCEMENT IS WHEN SOME, BUT NOT ALL, OF THE SPECIFIC RESPONSES ARE REINFORCED.

Many of your behaviors are not reinforced each time they occur; they are only reinforced some of the time, that is, on an intermittent basis. You do not always reach the party you dialed on the telephone. Turning on the radio does not always result in hearing one of your favorite songs. Yet, you continue to use the phone and the radio. These behaviors do not disappear after one or two nonreinforced occurrences. In fact, the more intermittent the reinforcement, the more likely you are to persist in performing the behavior.

Once your student has learned a new behavior and has been on a schedule of continuous reinforcement, you will be ready to use a schedule of intermittent reinforcement. Intermittent reinforcement does *not* follow each response; rather, it follows only *some* responses.

The importance of changing from continuous to intermittent reinforcement cannot be overemphasized because the use of intermittent schedules eliminates the disadvantages associated with the use of continuous reinforcement:

1. Continuous reinforcement can result in *satiation*. Consumable reinforcers can lose their effectiveness and performance may drop dramatically as a result of the satiation that is occurring. For example, a student who is continuously reinforced with edibles all morning long is hardly hungry in the afternoon and therefore may not be motivated to respond for the edibles then.
2. If continuous reinforcement is used and then terminated abruptly, the behavior you are trying to maintain or strengthen will disappear rapidly.
3. Continuous reinforcement "wears out" the person who has to deliver the reinforcement.

4. Continuous reinforcement uses up reinforcers faster. If you have a limited number of reinforcers for a student, they will be used up quickly and the student will become satiated.

One way to avoid reinforcing every response is to deliver fewer reinforcers for the same number of responses. For example, if you want to teach a student to hang up his jacket when he enters the classroom, begin by reinforcing him for hanging up his jacket every day. Then, when your records show the student will reliably hang up his jacket every day, switch to an intermittent reinforcement. To do so, simply reinforce the student for hanging up his jacket on 3 days out of the week instead of 5. You will find to your delight that there will be no decrease in the behavior; the student will continue to hang up his jacket every day.

Let's return to Janice for a moment. Janice was tube fed for years and she is now on a liquid diet. She is on continuous reinforcement because she is reinforced each and every time she swallows. However, it has become time consuming and tiring for the instructor to reinforce Janice continually, so the instructor switches Janice to an intermittent schedule of reinforcement. Now Janice receives praise, "Good girl, Janice," and her hand is stroked after every two or three spoonfuls rather than after each spoonful. Eventually, the instructor will space out the delivery of the reinforcers to a point where Janice only needs to be reinforced for swallowing after every tenth spoonful. Thus, the use of an intermittent schedule will save the instructor time, allow her more time with the other students at mealtime, and start Janice on the road to independent eating.

Remember, intermittent reinforcement should be used to maintain and strengthen the new behavior after you have first established it by using continuous reinforcement. The two primary advantages of using intermittent reinforcement are:

1. It will not cause satiation problems.
2. The newly learned behavior will persist when the intermittent schedule is reduced or ended.

Before continuing through this chapter, check the situations below that describe the use of intermittent reinforcement.

_____1. Each time Joshua looked at his teacher, she placed a spoonful of pudding in his mouth.
_____2. Barbara received a piece of candy bar after every fourth correct response when playing lotto.
_____3. Steven was playing in the sandbox. Every 10 minutes his mother told him he was a good boy for playing.
_____4. Nicholas was given a kiss each day when he returned from school.
_____5. Elizabeth cleaned her room every day for a week. She was reinforced with an ice cream cone on Tuesday, a quarter on Thursday, and a new magazine on Saturday.

Answers are on page 96.

SPECIFIC SCHEDULES OF REINFORCEMENT

Intermittent reinforcement is used to maintain and increase appropriate behaviors once they have been established through continuous reinforcement. The specification of when the reinforcer is to be delivered on an intermittent schedule is called a *schedule of reinforcement*. There are two basic types of intermittent schedules of reinforcement. One, the *ratio schedule*, is based on the number of responses that are performed. As a result, we say that ratio schedules are response dependent. The other, the *interval schedule*, is based upon the passage of an interval of time and a response. As a result, we say that interval schedules are both time dependent and response dependent. The importance of understanding these schedules is that they determine many things about the behavior being reinforced, for example, whether it will disappear rapidly or be persistent, whether it will occur at high rates or very slowly, and when it is likely to occur.

RATIO SCHEDULES

When reinforcement is contingent upon a specified number of responses occurring before the reinforcer is given, the behavior or response is on a ratio schedule of reinforcement. There are two types of ratio schedules of reinforcement: the fixed ratio (FR), and the variable ratio (VR).

Fixed Ratio Schedules

IN USING A FIXED RATIO SCHEDULE, THE REINFORCER FOLLOWS A PREDETERMINED NUMBER OF RESPONSES.

A fixed ratio schedule is one in which a prespecified number of responses must occur before the response is reinforced. For example, if Sandra is reinforced with vibration after every three spoonfuls of food she eats, then Sandra is on a fixed ratio three (FR 3) schedule. FR 3 indicates that every third response is to be contingently reinforced.

Another example of fixed ratio schedules is when Mr. Lox teaches two of his students, Stewart and Mike, to work a 16-piece puzzle. Mr. Lox gives Stewart a pat on the back and an edible each time he correctly places four of the 16 puzzle pieces. Thus, Stewart is on an FR 4 (fixed ratio four) schedule of reinforcement. Mr. Lox gives Mike a pat and edible each time he correctly places two puzzle pieces. Thus, Mike is on an FR 2 (fixed ratio two) schedule of reinforcement, which means that every two responses are reinforced. Once

Stewart successfully completes this puzzle on FR 4 for 2 to 3 days, Mr. Lox will change the fixed ratio schedule so that Stewart is reinforced after he places seven pieces correctly. As a result, Mr. Lox is requiring more responses (seven instead of four) for the same amount of reinforcement because he has moved Stewart to an FR 7 schedule of reinforcement. Eventually, Mr. Lox plans to require Stewart and Mike to work the entire 16-piece puzzle (FR 16) before they receive a reinforcer.

Students on fixed ratios usually respond in two characteristic ways. First, they tend to respond very rapidly until the number of responses needed for reinforcement is achieved. Second, they tend to pause or rest after they have received the reinforcer. Knowing about these characteristics is important because they illustrate two disadvantages of using a fixed ratio schedule:

1. A very high FR schedule (for example, FR 100) can produce an exhausted and overworked student who will cease responding. (Remember, the student will respond rapidly until the number of required responses is achieved.) As a result, you should keep the schedule reasonable.
2. The pause that occurs after the reinforcer is delivered can be a problem when you want the student to display a steady flow of behavior. You do not have steady behavior using fixed ratio schedules because the student stops for a while each time he or she is reinforced before beginning to respond again. The student knows that no additional reinforcement will be forthcoming until he or she again performs the specified number of responses.

The rules for using a fixed ratio schedule are: 1) determine the student's present level of performance, 2) initially select an easy ratio schedule, and 3) then gradually increase the number of responses required for reinforcement. The advantage of an FR schedule is that it is simple to use; you need only reinforce X number of responses.

Before continuing through this chapter, answer the questions below.

1. Jessica is on a fixed ratio four (FR 4) schedule for hanging up her coat. When will Jessica be reinforced?
2. Alfred is on a fixed ratio five (FR 5) schedule for building a 10-block tower. When will Alfred be reinforced?
3. Thomas puts three pegs in a pegboard and Ms. Brown reinforces him with a candy corn. He places three more pegs in the board and is reinforced once again. Thomas is on a fixed ratio _____ schedule.
4. Marilyn dries eight dishes and Mr. Owens tells her that she is a good girl. She dries eight more dishes, and Mr. Owens again tells her that she is good and that she is doing a great job. Marilyn is on a fixed ratio _____ schedule.
5. Write an example of a student on a fixed ratio two (FR 2) schedule.

Answers are on page 96.

Variable Ratio Schedules

IN A VARIABLE RATIO SCHEDULE, THE REIN-
FORCER FOLLOWS A DIFFERENT NUMBER OF RE-
SPONSES EACH TIME, SUCH THAT, OVER TIME, A
SPECIFIC AVERAGE NUMBER OF RESPONSES IS
REINFORCED.

The other type of ratio schedule is the variable ratio schedule in which the number of responses necessary to receive a reinforcer varies. As a result, students cannot predict how many responses they must make before they will be reinforced. This, of course, is in contrast to the fixed ratio schedule where students can easily predict when they will be reinforced since it is always after the same number of responses. It is therefore best to switch a student from a fixed ratio schedule to a variable ratio schedule whenever possible.

There are many examples of the variable ratio schedule operating in our lives. People who gamble are on variable ratio schedules. They sometimes win and sometimes lose but cannot predict when.

Now let's see how to determine and use a variable ratio schedule in the classroom. Remember Sandra, the student who received vibration after every third bite of food she took (FR 3). Her instructor, Mr. Otis, would now like to use a variable ratio schedule to reinforce Sandra's eating. Mr. Otis decides to reinforce Sandra on a variable ratio four (VR 4) schedule. Accordingly, he will reinforce Sandra after two spoonfuls, six spoonfuls, three spoonfuls, and five spoonfuls of food. The reinforcement schedule is indeed variable, ranging from reinforcing after two to six spoonfuls, but Sandra is reinforced on the *average* of every fourth response ($2 + 6 + 3 + 5 = 16 \div 4 = 4$ responses on the average). Hence, we say Sandra is reinforced on a variable ratio four (VR 4) schedule.

When using a variable ratio schedule, you must determine the ratio before instruction begins. Variable ratio does *not* suggest random reinforcement. For example, Mr. Bennett was teaching Harry to walk using a saddle walker. Mr. Bennett had reinforced Harry on an FR 6 (fixed ratio six) schedule for several weeks. Harry had to take six steps in succession in order to receive a reinforcer. Now, Mr. Bennett intends to reinforce Harry on a VR 6 (variable ratio six) schedule. Harry will be reinforced on the average after every six steps he takes. The first time Mr. Bennett used this schedule, he reinforced Harry for taking two steps; then the reinforcer came after five steps, then after nine steps, six steps, and finally after eight steps. Harry took a total of 30 steps and he was reinforced five times, or he was reinforced on the average after every six steps he took (VR 6).

The advantage of a variable ratio schedule is that the delivery of the reinforcer is not predictable so the student will usually not pause after receiving a reinforcer. As a result, a VR schedule produces very steady patterns of behavior and is thus an excellent schedule for the long term maintenance of a behavior or skill.

The disadvantages are:

1. It is time consuming because the teacher must determine the ratio schedule before instruction and data must be taken to do this. However, without data you do not know when to reinforce or cannot see the behavior changing.
2. It requires some expertise on the part of the teacher. Therefore, we do not advise you to use this schedule unless you have developed a good deal of behavioral expertise.

Before continuing through this chapter, answer the following questions.

1. Grant is on a variable ratio schedule. He is putting together felt tip pens and he is being reinforced for every three pens, six pens, four pens, three pens. He is on a VR _____ schedule.
2. Samantha is on a variable ratio schedule. Her housemother reinforces her for making beds. She is being reinforced for every eight beds, three beds, seven beds, two beds. Samantha is on a VR _____ schedule.
3. Howard is learning to dry dishes. Mr. Adams is reinforcing Howard on a VR 5 schedule. Give an example of how often Mr. Owens would reinforce Howard.
4. Janet is reinforcing Billy on a VR 9 schedule for swallowing his saliva. Give an example of how often Janet would reinforce Billy.
5. Give an example of how you would use a variable ratio schedule with one of your students.

Answers are on page 96.

INTERVAL SCHEDULES

An interval schedule of reinforcement occurs for responding after an interval of time following the last reinforced response. There are two types of interval schedules of reinforcement: the fixed interval (FI), and the variable interval (VI).

Fixed Interval Schedules

IN A FIXED INTERVAL SCHEDULE, THE REIN-FORCER FOLLOWS THE FIRST PRESPECIFIED RE-SPONSE THAT OCCURS AFTER A SPECIFIED AMOUNT OF TIME HAS ELAPSED.

In a fixed interval schedule, the first response is reinforced after a prespecified period of time has elapsed. Thus, on a fixed interval 1 minute (FI 1) schedule, the first response that occurs after 1 minute has passed would be reinforced.

As an example of the classroom use of fixed interval schedules, let's return to the self-feeding program for Sandra. You have trained Sandra to feed herself and now want to maintain and strengthen her self-feeding behaviors. To do so, you put Sandra on a fixed interval 2 minute (FI 2) schedule of reinforcement. At the beginning of the meal, you would set a timer to ring in 2 minutes. After the timer rings, you would reinforce Sandra with vibration (a vibrator placed on her arm for 15 seconds) following the first prespecified self-feeding behavior that occurs (e.g., placing the spoon in her mouth).

The advantage of using a fixed interval schedule is that you do not have to count responses; rather, all you must do is set a timer and then reinforce the first response that occurs after the timer rings. As a result, the fixed interval schedule is quite easy to use. However, there is a major disadvantage to using a fixed interval schedule. Like fixed ratio schedules, fixed interval schedules do not produce steady rates of behavior. The student becomes accustomed to the interval and will pause after being reinforced, thus delaying the performance of subsequent behaviors. For example, if Sandra were on an FI 7 minute schedule for self-feeding, she would quickly learn that after she receives reinforcement, 7 minutes will elapse before that reinforcement is available again. Therefore, she can pause for almost 7 minutes before continuing to feed herself. In effect, the student needs to do very little during the interval as long as she responds after the interval has elapsed. To sum up, you should not expect a fixed interval schedule to produce many responses or behaviors.

Before continuing through this chapter, check the situations below that are examples of fixed interval schedules of reinforcement.

_____ 1. Alex was given 10 points at the end of every 5 minutes if he was reading his history book.
_____ 2. Melissa was given a Froot Loop at the end of every 10-second period if she was speaking softly.
_____ 3. John receives a candy bar after he has stacked six blocks.
_____ 4. Gregory was reinforced for every five milk cartons he threw in the garbage.
_____ 5. Marilyn received an M&M every 10 minutes if she was still playing in her backyard.

Answers are on page 97.

Variable Interval Schedules

IN A VARIABLE INTERVAL SCHEDULE, THE REIN-
FORCER FOLLOWS THE FIRST SPECIFIED RESPONSE
AFTER DIFFERENT AMOUNTS OF TIME HAVE
PASSED.

The second type of interval schedule is the variable interval (VI) schedule of reinforcement in which the time requirement is not held constant but is a specified average. The variable interval is the most desirable of all reinforcement schedules that you will use in the classroom. The following example illustrates why.

Earlier, we left Ms. Jamison teaching two of her students to walk with a saddle walker by using a fixed interval schedule of reinforcement. Although things had gone well for a few days, the major disadvantage of the fixed interval schedule had emerged and was causing problems. Both students, Donald and Jenny, had quickly become accustomed to the fixed intervals, and their behaviors had become sporadic because they were not walking until they heard the timer ring. To solve this problem, Ms. Jamison decided to use a variable interval schedule. She did so because she knew that the students could not predict when reinforcement was available on this schedule. In order to avoid missing a reinforcement opportunity, then, they would have to respond (walk) at a constant rate. Ms. Jamison put Donald on a VI 30 second (variable interval 30 second) schedule. During the first training session, Donald was reinforced by Ms. Jamison saying, "Good walking, Donald," after 10 seconds, 40 seconds, 25 seconds, 20 seconds, 30 seconds, 35 seconds, 50 seconds, 20 seconds, 40 seconds, 30 seconds. Thus, Donald was reinforced on a VI 30 second schedule or 10 times within a period of 5 minutes (300 seconds divided by 10 = an average of 30 seconds). Whenever the timer rang, regardless of the interval, Donald had to be walking in order to receive the reinforcers. Donald continued walking without pausing because he never knew when the reinforcement would occur. Thus, the variable interval schedule Ms. Jamison used produced a steady and constant rate of behavior (walking). Ms. Jamison also implemented a VI schedule for Jenny.

The variable interval schedule is perfect for use in the classroom because the instructor is not tied to a timer or to counted responses. In fact, it is not even necessary in some cases to calculate the average interval between reinforcers. Rather, all you must do is reinforce the student an average number of times as you observe him or her performing the desired behavior. Of course, in the beginning, you would want to make the intervals short until the behavior achieves the rate you desire. The variable interval schedule also permits you to control and reinforce the behavior of a large number of students. For example, you could keep all of your students in their seats if you did nothing more than randomly reinforce those who were seated and then stretched out the time between reinforcers.

There are two advantages of using variable interval schedules of reinforcement:

1. They produce rapid, constant behavior because, unlike fixed interval schedules, the student cannot predict when the reinforcer will be available.

2. They are easy for the teacher to use because they allow time to work with a group of students. For example, when the intervals are set for 10 or more minutes, the teacher has time to attend to more than one student and still reinforce the student(s) who is on the variable interval schedule.

Variable interval schedules are common in our own lives. For example, the frequency with which your boss delivers raises may occur on a variable interval schedule. You are never quite sure when a raise will be forthcoming, but it occurs on an average schedule. Or, how often do you attend the movies? Is it an average of once every two weeks? Variable interval schedules approximate the contingencies in the natural environment more so than any other type of schedule. This, of course, is another reason why it is such a good schedule to use because it helps program the student for normal contingencies or normalization.

Before continuing, check those situations that are examples of variable interval schedules of reinforcement and answer the questions.

_____ 1. A teacher randomly gives happy faces stickers to any student who is in his or her seat. Is this a VI schedule?

_____ 2. Susie receives an orange slice on a VI schedule if she is not rocking. The intervals after which she will be reinforced for not rocking are 1 minute, 45 seconds, 2 minutes, 30 seconds, 15 seconds, 1 minute, and 20 seconds. Susie is on a VI _____ schedule.

_____ 3. John receives a coin if he is still finger painting after 3 minutes have elapsed. Is this a VI schedule?

_____ 4. A child who is quietly playing in his room is periodically visited by his mother and praised for playing nicely. Is this a VI schedule?

_____ 5. Josie is reinforced after he picks up three toys, then five toys, and finally after he picks up four toys. Is this a VI schedule?

Answers are on page 97.

SUMMARY

Noncontingent reinforcement is used in the classroom for the first week of the new school year or when you are working with a new student. Noncontingent reinforcement is not related to the student's behavior. Contingent reinforcement is the opposite of noncontingent reinforcement because it depends upon the occurrence of a specific response. Contingent reinforcement is used to strengthen and maintain the responses of your students. The two types of contingent reinforcement are continuous reinforcement and intermittent reinforcement.

Continuous reinforcement is used when you begin to teach a new behavior. Every response is reinforced. For instance, if you use continuous reinforcement to reinforce toileting, the student will receive a reinforcer each and every time he or she uses the toilet. The main disadvantages of continuous reinforcement are:

1) when you stop reinforcing the behavior, the behavior stops, and 2) satiation can occur.

One way to avoid reinforcing every response is to deliver fewer reinforcers for the same number of responses. You can do this by using intermittent reinforcement, thereby reinforcing only some of the appropriate responses. The specification of which behaviors will be reinforced is called a schedule of reinforcement.

There are two types of intermittent schedules of reinforcement: ratio schedules, and interval schedules. A ratio schedule is based on the number of responses that are performed. Thus, we say that ratio schedules are response dependent. An interval schedule is based on the amount, or interval, of time between reinforced responses. Thus, we say that interval schedules are time dependent as well as response dependent.

There are two types of ratio schedules: fixed ratio, and variable ratio. In a fixed ratio schedule, the reinforcement follows the performance of a predetermined number of responses. In a variable ratio schedule, the reinforcer follows a different number of responses each time, such that, over time, a specific average number of responses is reinforced.

There are two types of interval schedules: fixed interval, and variable interval. In a fixed interval schedule, you reinforce the first specified response that occurs after a prespecified amount of time has elapsed. In a variable interval schedule, different amounts of time occur between reinforced behaviors.

Your goal is to use variable interval schedules in your classroom. Both fixed ratio and fixed interval schedules produce behaviors that are followed by a pause. Furthermore, the student can predict when the reinforcement will be delivered and thus will not respond at very high rates. Variable ratio schedules produce high rates of behavior, but they can be time consuming for the instructor. Variable interval schedules are the easiest to use and are the most beneficial to your students. They produce steady rates of behavior without pauses because the student cannot predict when reinforcement will be forthcoming. Also, you can use variable interval schedules to reinforce the behavior of a large group of students because you are essentially presenting a predetermined average amount of reinforcement. Thus, variable interval schedules are excellent for classroom use.

REVIEW QUESTIONS

1. The type of reinforcement that is not related to the behavior of the student who is reinforced is called _____ reinforcement.
2. When working with new students or at the beginning of the school year, you should use _____ reinforcement.
3. If students are going to perform the behaviors you attempt to teach them, they must find you to be _____.

4. Reinforcement that depends on a specific response is called _____ reinforcement.

5. Reinforcement that strengthens or that maintains a behavior is called _____ reinforcement.

6. There are two types of contingent reinforcement: 1) _____ and 2) _____.

7. When a behavior is reinforced each time it occurs, it is called _____ reinforcement.

8. The only type of reinforcement you should use when beginning to teach a new behavior is _____ reinforcement.

9. One of the disadvantages of c_____ reinforcement is that the behavior d_____ rapidly when the reinforcement ceases.

10. Another disadvantage of continuous reinforcement is s_____.

11. When only some of the appropriate responses are reinforced, you are using _____ reinforcement.

12. One way to avoid reinforcing every response is to deliver fewer r_____ for the same number of r_____.

13. After you have used c_____ r_____ to teach a new behavior, you should then use _____ reinforcement.

14. _____ schedules are based on the number of responses that are performed. Therefore, they are r_____ dependent.

15. _____ schedules are based on the amount of time between reinforced responses. Therefore, they are t_____ dependent.

16. The reinforcer is contingent on a specified number of responses occurring before one response is reinforced when you use a r_____ s_____ of reinforcement.

17. The two types of ratio schedules are_____ratio and_____ ratio.

18. A schedule where a prespecified number of responses must occur before the response is reinforced is called a _____ _____ schedule.

19. Students on fixed ratio schedules usually respond very rapidly and then p_____ after they are reinforced.

20. The reinforcer follows a different number of responses each time during a _____ _____ schedule of reinforcement.

21. The advantage of a variable ratio schedule is that it is not p_____. Thus, there is no p_____ after the reinforcer, and very steady patterns of b_____ are produced.

22. A schedule based on the amount of time between reinforced responses is called an _____ schedule.

23. A schedule where the first response that occurs after the passage of a fixed period of time is reinforced is called a _____ _____ schedule of reinforcement.

24. Students on fixed interval reinforcement schedules do not perform many behaviors because they pause after the reinforcer is delivered and do not begin responding again until _____.
25. Different amounts of time occur between reinforced behaviors in a _____ _____ schedule of reinforcement.
26. In a variable interval schedule, students cannot predict when reinforcement will be available. Therefore, they will respond at c_____ rates.
27. It is possible to reinforce the behavior of a large group of students when using a _____ _____ schedule of reinforcement.
28. Probably the best reinforcement schedule to use in the classroom is the _____ schedule.

Answers are on page 97.

SUGGESTED READINGS

Bijou, S. W., & Orlando, R. Rapid development of multi-schedule performance with retarded children. In: L. P. Ullmann & L. Krasner (eds.), *Case studies in behavior modification*, pp. 339–347. New York: Holt, Rinehart & Winston, 1965.

Ferster, C. B., & Skinner, B. F. *Schedules of reinforcement.* New York: Appleton-Century-Crofts, 1957.

Orlando, R. Shaping multiple schedule performances in retardates: Establishment of baselines by systematic and special procedures. *Journal of Experimental Child Psychology*, 1965, *2*, 135–153.

Orlando, R., & Bijou, S. W. Single and multiple schedules of reinforcement in developmentally retarded children. *Journal of the Experimental Analysis of Behavior*, 1960, *3*, 339–348.

Reese, E. P. *The analysis of the human operant behavior.* Dubuque, IA: William C. Brown Co., 1966.

Slemon, A. The effects of type of reinforcer, schedule of reinforcement, sex, and personality on response rates of mentally retarded children. *Journal of Mental Deficiency Research*, 1971, *15*, 38–43.

Spradlin, J. E., Girardeau, F. L., & Corte, E. Fixed ratio and fixed interval behavior of severely and profoundly retarded subjects. *Journal of Experimental Child Psychology*, 1965, *2*, 340–353.

ANSWERS TO CHAPTER QUESTIONS

Answers to Questions on Page 81

_____ 1. The lollipops were given contingent on being seated.
__✓__ 2. All children received a pretzel stick regardless of their behavior.
__✓__ 3. Mr. Thomas reads to Earl every night at 8:00 regardless of Earl's behavior.
_____ 4. Gwynn pushed Brian on the swing contingent on his hanging up his pajamas.
_____ 5. The lemonade was contingent on being quiet.

Answers to Questions on Page 82

_____ 1. Mr. Smith gave each child 25 cents regardless of the behaviors each exhibited. Therefore, he was using noncontingent reinforcement.

__V__ 2. Peanut butter cookies were contingent on cleaning the yard.

__V__ 3. Ten points was contingent on using the toilet.

__V__ 4. Potato chips were contingent upon swimming.

_____ 5. Popsicles were given to all students regardless of their behaviors. Therefore, the popsicles were delivered noncontingently.

Answers to Questions on Pages 83–84

_____ 1. This is not an example of continuous reinforcement because Samuel was not reinforced for putting his dishes in the sink after breakfast.

__V__ 2. This is an example of continuous reinforcement. Sally was reinforced for taking off her sweater each time the behavior occurred.

__V__ 3. This is an example of continuous reinforcement. Richie was reinforced each time he picked up his clothes.

_____ 4. Marilyn received continuous reinforcement the first week, but did not receive continuous reinforcement the second week.

__V__ 5. Jacques is receiving continuous reinforcement. Each time he sat up, he was reinforced.

Answers to Questions on Page 85

_____ 1. Joshua was reinforced for _every_ response. This is continuous reinforcement.

__V__ 2. Barbara was receiving intermittent reinforcement. Every fourth response was reinforced.

__V__ 3. Steven was receiving intermittent reinforcement. He was reinforced every 10 minutes.

_____ 4. Nicholas received continuous reinforcement. He received a kiss _every_ day.

__V__ 5. Elizabeth received intermittent reinforcement. She cleaned her room 7 days and received reinforcement on 3 of the days.

Answers to Questions on Page 87

1. Jessica will be reinforced every fourth time she hangs up her coat.
2. Alfred will receive a reinforcer after every fifth block.
3. three
4. eight
5. This example must demonstrate that the student is reinforced every second time a specific response occurs.

Answers to Questions on Pages 89

1. 4 (3 + 6 + 4 + 3 = 16 ÷ 4 = 4; VR 4)
2. 5 (8 + 3 + 7 + 2 = 20 ÷ 4 = 5; VR 5)
3. Any answer is correct if the average number of dried dishes being reinforced is five.
4. Any answer is correct if the average number of times Billy is reinforced for swallowing his saliva is nine.
5. This example must demonstrate that the student is reinforced after a predetermined average number of responses.

Answers to Questions on Page 90

√ 1. This is an example of a fixed interval schedule. The reinforcer (10 points) was contingent on a specified response (reading) occurring after a specified amount of time had elapsed (5 minutes).

√ 2. This is an example of a fixed interval schedule. The Froot Loop was contingent on speaking softly occurring at the end of each 10-second interval.

_____ 3. This is an example of a fixed ratio 6 (FR 6) schedule.

_____ 4. This is an example of a fixed ratio 5 (FR 5) schedule.

√ 5. This is an example of a fixed interval schedule. Marilyn received the reinforcer (an M&M) contingent on a specified response (playing in her back yard) occurring after a specified amount of time had elapsed (10 minutes).

Answers to Questions on Page 92

√ 1. Yes. The reinforcer (happy face stickers) is being delivered at random intervals.

_____ 2. 50 second (350 seconds ÷ 7 = 50 seconds; VI 50 second)

_____ 3. No. It is an FI 3 minute schedule.

_____ 4. Yes. The visits and reinforcer (praise) are periodic and thereby random.

√ 5. No. It is a VR 4 schedule.

Answers to Review Questions on Pages 93–95

1. noncontingent
2. noncontingent
3. reinforcing
4. contingent
5. contingent
6. continuous, intermittent
7. continuous
8. continuous
9. continuous, disappears
10. satiation
11. intermittent
12. reinforcers, responses
13. continuous reinforcement, intermittent
14. Ratio, response
15. Interval, time
16. ratio schedule
17. fixed, variable
18. fixed ratio
19. pause
20. variable ratio
21. predictable, pause, behavior
22. interval
23. fixed interval
24. the next interval has almost elapsed
25. variable interval
26. constant
27. variable interval
28. variable interval

Chapter 7

SHAPING, PROMPTING, AND FADING

After reading this chapter, you will be able to:

1. Define and give an example of shaping.
2. List the seven steps in the behavior shaping process.
3. Describe four ways of maximizing the behavior shaping process.
4. Define prompting.
5. List the three types of prompts and give an example of each.
6. Give an example of the use of prompting to teach a complex skill.
7. Define fading.
8. Describe the ways to fade the three types of prompts.
9. Give an example of how prompting and fading are used to teach a complex skill.
10. List the two cardinal rules to follow when you use prompting and fading.

Much of an instructor's time is spent teaching his or her students new, functional behaviors. This process is enhanced by the use of reinforcement. However, with retarded students, problems often arise because their various physical and intellectual deficits have limited the range of appropriate behaviors available for reinforcement. It is thus difficult to raise their level of functioning by teaching them new skills because you cannot reinforce a behavior that does not occur. The teaching task then becomes that of creating completely new behaviors in your students. The technique for doing this is called *shaping*.

In addition to this absence of behaviors, there are two other problems you will encounter in teaching retarded students. First, these students often need additional help, or cues, in order to perform the desired behaviors. *Prompting* is the technique by which we provide these extra discriminative stimuli or prompts (see Chapter 4).

The other problem arises from the use of prompting. Students often become dependent on the prompts and will not perform their newly learned behaviors on their own. Instead, they wait for the instructor to provide a prompt that they are to perform the behavior. In order to foster independence and decrease the student's reliance on prompts, we use a technique called *fading*.

In this chapter, these three techniques—shaping, prompting, and fading—for producing or increasing behaviors are discussed.

SHAPING

SHAPING, OR THE METHOD OF SUCCESSIVE AP-
PROXIMATIONS, IS USED TO PRODUCE A BEHAVIOR
THAT IS CURRENTLY NOT IN THE STUDENT'S
BEHAVIORAL REPERTOIRE.

Shaping is used to increase the number of behaviors in a student's behavioral repertoire (i.e., the pool of behaviors the student can perform). We first select the *target* or *terminal behavior,* which is the desired behavior that does not occur but which we wish to establish. Then we select a behavior or response that the student does perform and that resembles the target behavior in some way. This behavior is called the *initial behavior*.

Shaping, or the method of successive approximations, is then used. Once we have increased the frequency of the initial behavior through reinforcement, that behavior will not be reinforced again until it more closely approximates the target behavior. We continue to require these "successive approximations" of the target behavior until the target behavior fully occurs. Shaping works so well because the student must continue to change his or her behavior in the direction of the target behavior in order to be reinforced.

Shaping is a very important part of everyone's life because it is used to teach us new skills. Just about every complex skill we learned was acquired through a shaping procedure, as are skills which we are now learning or will learn in the future. For example, as young children we eventually learned to speak clearly because our parents selectively reinforced sounds that made sense like "Mommy" and ignored nonsensical sounds like "Bommy." In effect, the more clearly we spoke, the more reinforcing attention we received and the greater impact we had on our environment. As we entered school, we were taught to write through shaping. First, we practiced printing by tracing dotted lines that represented the letters of the alphabet. The lines on our writing paper were large and divided by a dotted line. As we became proficient printers, the dotted lines that represented the letters were eliminated as was the dotted line that divided the lines on our writing paper. Later, the lines on our papers were reduced in size and we were taught cursive writing. As adults, all of our complex skills were developed by shaping techniques regardless of whether we were learning to play tennis, speak a foreign language, cook, drive a car, or master the behavioral principles in this book.

The Behavior Shaping Process

Shaping is comprised of the following steps:

1. Select the target behavior.
2. Select the initial behavior that the student currently performs and that resembles the target behavior in some way.
3. Select powerful reinforcers with which to reinforce the initial behavior, the successive approximations of the target behavior, and the target behavior.
4. Reinforce the initial behavior until it occurs frequently.
5. Reinforce successive approximations of the target behavior each time they occur.
6. Reinforce the target behavior each time it occurs.
7. Reinforce the target behavior on an intermittent schedule of reinforcement.

There are important factors to consider when you follow these steps so that you can avoid potential problems.

Selecting the Target Behavior   The target behavior must be specified precisely so that you will know when the student has performed it and so that the chances of strengthening other, irrelevant behaviors through reinforcement are reduced. (Strengthening irrelevant behaviors will only serve to prolong the shaping process.) A clear-cut criterion level for success must be specified. Specifying what constitutes an acceptable level of performance of the target behavior will tell you when the behavior shaping process is complete.

Selecting the Initial Behavior   The best way to determine the initial behavior to be reinforced is to observe the student in the natural or training setting for a few days before you begin shaping. By doing so, you will observe a behavior that resembles the target behavior enough to be used as the starting point in the shaping process. Another way is to prompt the student to make responses that are the steps in your task analysis.

Selecting a Powerful Reinforcer(s)   The student's motivation to perform must be kept at a high level. Accordingly, select the most powerful reinforcers available to you (see Chapter 5). We must bear in mind that we will be requiring the student to continuously change his or her behavior as the student proceeds toward the target behavior. The use of powerful reinforcers will ensure that the student will be motivated to keep trying various approximations until he or she performs one that is reinforced.

Reinforcing the Initial Behavior Until It Occurs Frequently   By reinforcing the initial behavior frequently, you will be increasing the chances that a slight variation of it will occur that is a closer approximation to the target behavior. (It is a good idea to set a criterion level of performance for the initial behavior.)

Reinforcing Successive Approximations of the Target Behavior A good deal of skill is involved in knowing how long to reinforce one level of performance before requiring the next level. Shaping places increasing demands on the student, and only your skill will ensure its success. For example, if you reinforce one level of performance (approximation) too long, that behavior will become so rigidly established that it will be very difficult to motivate the student to move to the next performance level. On the other hand, the student's new behavior may extinguish (disappear) if you attempt to make the student progress too rapidly because he or she will not have had time to associate the new behavior with reinforcement. There is no simple way of learning how to make these decisions; they depend on the shaper's skill and the behavior of the student. The shaper must learn to attend to the feedback by observing and recording the student's responses and using these data to modify the shaping process and recognize when a behavior is occurring at a stable frequency. The data will provide a cue for the shaper to start prompting the next approximation.

Reinforcing the Target Behavior Each Time It Occurs Use continuous reinforcement to firmly establish the target behavior in the student's behavioral repertoire.

Reinforcing the Target Behavior on an Intermittent Reinforcement Schedule The use of intermittent reinforcement will ensure the maintenance of the target behavior in the student's behavioral repertoire.

Example The following example illustrates the use of these steps to shape eye contact, the most rudimentary of skills.

Target Behavior When requested to do so, Merle will maintain eye contact with the instructor for 2 consecutive seconds. Merle will have successfully achieved the criterion level for the target behavior when he gives eye contact for 2 seconds on at least 90% of all requested occasions for 100 trials (i.e., Merle must respond correctly on at least 90 of 100 trials.) Eye contact is a complex skill. It requires several different responses to discriminate stimuli such as head and eye.

Initial Behavior The initial behavior is an operant requiring several different responses. The responses will be Merle's orienting his head and eyes so that he is facing the instructor and their eyes make fleeting contact (a glance).

Reinforcers Whenever Merle responds appropriately, he will be given an edible reinforcer (peanuts, his favorite food), a tactual reinforcer (a touch on his cheek), and a social reinforcer (praise—"Good looking at me, Merle"). In order to be reinforced, all instances of eye contact must occur within 5 seconds of the instruction, "Merle, look at me."

Reinforcing the Initial Behavior Merle's orienting of his head and glancing at the instructor will be reinforced until it reaches at least 90% of all requested trials for 50 trials (i.e., Merle must respond correctly on at least 45 of 50 trials).

Successive Approximations of the Target Behavior Merle's successive approximation, 1 second of eye contact, will be reinforced until it reaches at least 90% of all requested trials for 50 trials.

Initial behavior	—Glance
Successive approximation	—Eye contact for 1 second
Target behavior	—Eye contact for 2 seconds

Reinforcing the Target Behavior Each instance of 2 seconds of eye contact will be reinforced until Merle achieves the 90% criterion level of eye contact on 100 trials. Thereafter, 2 seconds of eye contact will be reinforced intermittently until Merle responds at a 90% criterion level on an FR 5 schedule for 100 trials. When criterion is reached, the peanut near the instructor's eyes will be faded (technique described below), and a generalization program for eye contact will be implemented.

Behind a partition in the corner of the classroom, the instructor and Merle are seated at a table facing each other. A bowl of peanuts is located to the instructor's right and out of Merle's reach. In front of the instructor is a recording sheet and a pencil. The instructor begins by taking a peanut out of the bowl and placing it in Merle's mouth. She does this several times until Merle's eyes track the peanut from the bowl to his mouth. The instructor is now ready to shape eye contact because Merle is intently tracking the peanut in her hand with his eyes. The next time she reaches for a peanut, she lifts the peanut to her eyes. As Merle's eyes follow the peanut to her eyes, she says, "Merle, look at me." As soon as his eyes meet hers, she quickly places the peanut in his mouth, strokes his cheek, and says, "Good looking at me, Merle." She then scores a correct response on her recording sheet.

Each eye contact shaping session consists of 20 trials, and there are 100 trials each day. The use of the five sessions throughout the day eliminates the possibility that Merle will become bored or satiated (see Chapter 3). Once Merle has glanced at the instructor 90% of the time or better over 50 trials, the instructor is ready to require Merle to maintain eye contact for 1 second. Now, when his eyes make contact with hers, she counts to herself, "thousand and one." If Merle maintains eye contact during the second, she reinforces him in the manner described above.

Once Merle has given the instructor 1 second of eye contact on at least 90% of 50 requested trials, she is ready to begin reinforcing the target behavior of 2 seconds of eye contact. She conducts the eye contact shaping trial as she has always done with the exception that Merle must maintain eye contact with her for 2 seconds. When he does so, he is reinforced. When he fails to maintain eye contact for 2 seconds or does not respond within 5 seconds of the instruction (verbal prompts are described later in this chapter), she returns the peanut to the bowl and records an incorrect response on her recording sheet. The eye contact shaping program ends when Merle gives her 2 seconds of eye contact on at least 90 of 100 trials (90% eye contact or better). At this point, the instructor is ready to begin reinforcing Merle's eye contact intermittently. Accordingly, she reinforces eye contact on every other successful trial (FR 2), on every third trial (FR 3), and finally after every fifth trial (FR 5). Once Merle gives her 2 seconds of eye contact on at least 90 of 100 trials on the FR 5 schedule, the instructor is ready to begin her generalization and maintenance program (see Chapter 14). Also, she must fade holding the peanut by her eyes (described later in the chapter).

Maximizing Success   There are several ways of maximizing the success of the shaping process. One way is to combine a discriminative stimulus with shaping. (Recall that a discriminative stimulus is a stimulus that sets the occasion for the response because it has been associated with reinforcement.) In the above example, two discriminative stimuli were used to occasion the eye contact response. They were the peanut held near the instructor's eyes and the verbal instruction (verbal prompt), "Merle, look at me." It is hard to imagine an instance in which you would not use a discriminative stimulus to facilitate the shaping process.

A second way to maximize the shaping process is to combine physical guidance (a physical prompt) with the shaping. (As you will learn shortly, all prompts are discriminative stimuli.) In the above example, the instructor could have used physical guidance to increase the likelihood of a correct eye contact response by gently guiding Merle's chin with her left hand so that his head was oriented toward hers. She would give this physical guidance at the same time she said, "Merle, look at me."

A third way is to combine an imitative prompt with the shaping. An example of the use of an imitative prompt in shaping that is somewhat similar to shaping eye contact would be shaping speech. In that case, the instructor would hold the peanut next to her lips, say "Merle, say 'mm'," form her lips so that she could make the "mm" sound, and then make the "mm" sound. The instructor's formed lips and the "mm" sound she made would both be examples of imitative prompts. A final way to maximize success is to combine fading with shaping (discussed below).

Shaping is one of the most important and powerful techniques available for increasing positive behaviors. It requires great skill, and this skill can only be acquired by practicing as much as you can and by attending to feedback. Central to learning any new skill is feedback. Feedback on whether or not the behavior is changing controls your behavior during the shaping process. Data must be collected and used for evaluative purposes and to improve your shaping skills.

Before continuing this chapter, answer the following questions:

1. There are seven steps in the behavior shaping process:
   a. Select a _____ behavior.
   b. Select the _____ behavior that the student currently performs.

    c. Select powerful _____.

    d. _____ the initial behavior until it occurs frequently.

    e. Reinforce _____ _____ of the target behavior each time they occur.

    f. _____ the target behavior each time it occurs.

    g. Reinforce the target behavior on an _____ schedule of reinforcement.

2. Ms. Wolf would like to use shaping to teach Laura to eat independently with a spoon. Currently, Laura will raise the spoon to her mouth when told to as long as Ms. Wolf's hand is guiding Laura's hand, and she praises Laura, "Good eating, Laura." Ms. Wolf decides that the best way to use shaping would be for her to move her hand further and further up Laura's arm so that Laura will have to perform more of the feeding action herself each time she takes a bite. Ms. Wolf thinks that Laura will eventually feed herself once Ms. Wolf's hand is merely touching Laura's shoulder. At that point, Ms. Wolf plans simply to stop touching Laura and just give the instruction, "Laura, take a bite." In this example:

    a. What is the target behavior?

    b. What is the initial behavior?

    c. What are the reinforcers?

    d. How will Ms. Wolf ensure that the initial behavior occurs frequently?

    e. What are the successive approximations and how will they be reinforced?

    f. How will the target behavior be reinforced continuously?

    g. How will the target behavior be reinforced intermittently?

3. When using shaping, it is important to specify a c_____ l_____ for success for the initial behavior, the successive approximations, and the target behavior.

4. The best way to determine the initial behavior to be reinforced is to o_____ the student in the natural or training setting for a few days prior to beginning the shaping program.

5. The shaping process can be maximized by:

    a. Combining a d_____ s_____ with shaping.

    b. Combining p_____ g_____ with shaping.

    c. Combining an i_____ p_____ with shaping.

    d. Combining f_____ with shaping.

Answers are on page 116.

PROMPTING

A PROMPT IS AN ADDITIONAL DISCRIMINATIVE STIMULUS THAT IS PRESENTED IN ORDER TO CUE THE STUDENT TO PERFORM A SPECIFIED BEHAVIOR.

A discriminative stimulus is a stimulus that sets the occasion for a behavior to occur because that stimulus has been associated with reinforcement. Thus, all behaviors that are reinforced are preceded by discriminative stimuli. It makes no difference whether the reinforcer is delivered by someone (for example, an instructor giving a student a piece of candy) or by the environment (for example, the student opens a jar and takes a piece of candy). In either case, some type of discriminative stimulus sets the occasion for the reinforced response to occur. Discriminative stimuli can generate either appropriate or inappropriate behaviors in your students. For example, a plate of food can be a discriminative stimulus for the appropriate response of eating with a spoon or an inappropriate response of throwing the plate.

The use of discriminative stimuli to cue the student to perform a particular appropriate behavior is called *prompting*, and the discriminative stimuli themselves are called *prompts*. What differentiates prompts from other discriminative stimuli is that the prompt is delivered by someone (the instructor) for a specific purpose. Thus, a prompt is nothing more than a cue to the student that you want him or her to behave in a certain way and that this behavior will be followed by a reinforcer. We refer to a prompt as an additional discriminative stimulus because it is given *in addition to* whatever natural discriminative stimuli are associated with the behavior. For example, if you wanted a student to pull up his pants, you might prompt him to do so by telling him, "Pull up your pants," pointing to his pants, and guiding his hands in raising his pants. Your delivery of these prompts (discriminative stimuli) affects complex human behavior; in most cases a wide variety of discriminative stimuli set the occasion for the behavior of pulling up pants. You would use the prompts to teach the student to pull up his pants because the natural discriminative stimuli have not been sufficient to set the occasion for pants raising.

The importance of prompts, then, is that they enable us to greatly increase the likelihood that a behavior will occur. Prompting is an especially valuable technique for teaching profoundly and severely retarded students because they have so few appropriate behaviors or skills. By incorporating prompting into our training programs, we can greatly increase the students' acquisition of appropriate behaviors and complex sequences of behaviors.

Types of Prompts

There are three types of prompts: verbal, gestural, and physical. Verbal prompts are no more than a verbal instruction. The instruction, "Merle, look at me," is a verbal prompt, as is any instruction that we give (for example, a teacher telling her aide to conduct an eye contact training session with Merle: "Sally, you should take Merle with you and work with him on eye contact"). A gestural prompt might include pointing, looking in a particular direction, or raising your hand. Two common gestural prompts that are understood by everyone is a policeman extending his arm with his palm facing you to indicate that you are to stop, or someone placing his finger over his lips to indicate that you should be silent. Physical prompts involve actual physical contact with someone. For example, physically guiding a student to sit in a chair would be a physical prompt.

How to Prompt

For high functioning students and normal persons, it is only necessary to use prompting during the first few training trials. After that, the individual usually understands what to do and does it. For low functioning students, however, it is often necessary to use prompting for many trials, especially when you are attempting to teach a complex sequence of behaviors. This presents a problem because the student can become dependent on the prompter (instructor) and the prompts. For example, the student may stand in the bathroom with his pants around his knees waiting to be prompted to raise his pants. To overcome this problem, we fade the prompts (described below) as soon as possible, so that the student will have to rely on his or her own initiative, motivation, and memory.

Prompts can range from very obvious, conspicuous events to very faint, almost undetectable events. As would be expected, the more obvious the prompt, the more dependent the student is on the instructor. Conversely, the less obvious the prompt, the more the student must take responsibility to initiate the behavior.

Whenever you use prompts, you should begin with those prompts that will ensure that the desirable behavior will occur. These beginning prompts are likely to be very obvious to the student and involve your active participation. In general, it is a good idea to use all three types of prompts when you begin teaching a new skill. Over time, you will fade these prompts.

FADING

FADING IS THE GRADUAL CHANGE OF THE STIMULUS CONTROL.

Fading is used to foster independence by eliminating the control that the prompter and prompts have had over the student's behavior. Thus, fading is really the elimination of the control of a discriminative stimulus (or the gradual change of the discriminative stimulus).

Fading is accomplished by providing the student with a less obvious or active stimulus than you had given previously. For example, the first time you provide a discriminative stimulus to have a student raise his pants, you may have to guide his hands to the waistband and assist him in raising his pants. The next time you provide a discriminative stimulus, you might only guide his hands to the waistband. Thus, you have gone from actually physically guiding the student in raising his pants to just placing his hands on the waistband, and you have

Table 1. Prompts for teaching a student how to pick up a spoon

---

General Guidelines

1. Determine the minimal prompt to which the student will respond. This may be physically touching the student, gesturing toward the spoon, or giving a verbal command.
2. Use a less active prompt the next time you prompt the student.
3. Wait a few seconds after you give the prompt before you give it again.
4. A sequence of prompts is listed below, from most active prompt to least active prompt, for your guidance. The student will usually begin picking up the spoon before the least active prompt is given.

Sequence of Steps

Prompt	Example
1. Verbal prompt	"(Student's name), pick up the spoon."
+	
Gestural prompt	Point to the spoon.
+	
Physical prompt	Move the student's hand next to the spoon (place his fingers around the handle of the spoon if necessary).
2. Verbal prompt	"(Student's name), pick up the spoon."
+	
Gestural prompt	Point to the spoon.
No physical prompt	
3. Reduced verbal prompt	"(Student's name), spoon."
+	
Gestural prompt	Point to the spoon.
No physical prompt	

---

changed the stimulus control gradually. Eventually, of course, you will fade stimulus control so that the student raises his pants himself.

How to Fade Prompts

There are two ways to fade a verbal prompt. For example, let's say you want to shift control from a specific direction to the instruction "Get dressed." First, you can simply reduce the number of words in the instruction, e.g., "James, raise your pants," to "James, raise pants," to "Raise pants," and then "Get dressed." Second, you can speak more softly each time so that the student must pay more attention to what you are saying. It is possible to fade a verbal prompt in this manner until the student must practically read your lips.

Gestural prompts are faded by reducing the size of the gesture, e.g., from a sweeping motion of your arm and pointing to just simply pointing.

Table 1. (*continued*)

4.	Reduced verbal prompt + Gestural prompt No physical prompt	"Spoon." Point to the spoon.
5.	No verbal prompt Gestural prompt No physical prompt	Point to the spoon with your arm fully extended and motion toward the spoon with your head.
6.	No verbal prompt Reduced gestural prompt No physical prompt	Point to the spoon with your arm partially extended and with full head motion.
7.	No verbal prompt Reduced gestural prompt (no arm motion) No physical prompt	Point to the spoon with full head motion.
8.	No verbal prompt Reduced gestural prompt No physical prompt	Motion toward the spoon with your head.
9.	No verbal prompt Reduced gestural prompt (No head motion) No physical prompt	Move your eyes toward the spoon.

Physical prompts are the most difficult to fade because the physical prompt involves actually touching the student, who can easily tell whether or not you are touching him. Thus, the transition from touching to not touching is difficult to make. Fortunately, there are three ways to overcome this problem. The first is to progressively reduce the amount of the touch, e.g., from touching the student with your hand, to touching the student with only a part of your hand, to touching the student with just your fingers, to just touching the student with one finger. The second way is to move the location of where you touch the student away from the focal point of the behavior, e.g., progressively moving your touch further up the student's arm away from his hands when you are prompting pants raising. You would still be physically prompting pants raising, but the student would be required to use his hands without their being touched. The third and final way is to use all three types of prompts in the beginning of training and fade the physical prompts first while retaining the gestural and verbal prompts. Because gestural and verbal prompts are easier to fade, they are faded last.

Table 1 provides an example of prompting for a self-help skill that would typically be part of a training program for a severely retarded student. The first part of the table lists general guidelines to follow in shaping a student to pick

Table 2.   Prompts for teaching a student how to take off a T-shirt and put it on

General Guidelines
1. Determine the minimal prompt to which the student will respond. This may be physically touching the student, gesturing toward his T-shirt, or giving a verbal command.
2. Use a less active prompt the next time you prompt the student to take his shirt off or put it on.
3. Wait a few seconds after you give the prompt before you give it again.
4. A sequence of prompts is listed below, from most active prompt to least active prompt, for your guidance. The student will usually begin independently taking off his shirt or putting it on before the least active prompt is given.

Sequence of Steps for Taking Off a T-Shirt

	Prompt	Example
1.	Verbal prompt	"(Student's name), shirt off."
	+	
	Gestural prompt	Point to the student's T-shirt.
	+	
	Physical prompt	Grasp the bottom of the student's T-shirt and guide him in pulling it over his head and off.
2.	Reduced verbal prompt	"Shirt off."
	+	
	Gestural prompt	Point to the student's T-shirt.
	+	
	Physical prompt	Grasp the bottom of the student's T-shirt if necessary and guide him in pulling it off.
3.	Reduced verbal prompt	"Off."
	+	
	Gestural prompt	Point to the student's T-shirt.
	+	
	Reduced physical prompt	Guide the student's hands to the bottom of his T-shirt if necessary.
4.	No verbal prompt	
	Reduced gestural prompt	Looks at the student's T-shirt.
	+	
	Physical prompt, if necessary	Guide the student's hands to the bottom of his T-shirt if necessary.
5.	No verbal prompt	
	Reduced gestural prompt	Look at the student's T-shirt.
	No physical prompt	

(*continued*)

Table 2. (*continued*)

Sequence of Steps for Putting On a T-Shirt

    Note: Lay the student's T-shirt facedown on a bed or table in front of him.

Prompt	Example
1. Verbal prompt	"(Student's name), shirt on."
+	
Gestural prompt	Point to the student's shirt.
+	
Physical prompt	Place your hands over the student's hands and guide his hands to the T-shirt. Put his arms in the shirt, through the armholes, pulling it over his head, and pull it down to his waist.
2. Reduced verbal prompt	"Shirt on."
+	
Gestural prompt	Point to the student's T-shirt.
+	
Physical prompt	Grasp the student's hands holding his T-shirt and guide him in putting it on.
3. Reduced verbal prompt	"On."
+	
Gestural prompt	Point to the student's T-shirt.
+	
Reduced physical prompt	Guide the student's hands to the shirt opening if necessary.
4. No verbal prompt	
Reduced gestural prompt	Look at the student's T-shirt.
+	
Physical prompt, if necessary	Guide the student's hands to the shirt opening if necessary.
5. No verbal prompt	
Gestural prompt	Look at the student's T-shirt.
No physical prompt	

up a spoon. The second part of the table presents the prompts for picking up a spoon in the order in which they should be faded. All three types of prompts are used in the beginning: verbal ("Student's name, pick up the spoon"), gestural (point to the spoon), and physical (move the student's hand next to the spoon). As training progresses, the prompts become less obvious. The physical prompt is faded first, next the verbal prompt is reduced, and finally the gestural prompt is reduced. By the end of the sequence, only a slight gestural prompt is needed. Beyond this point, fading will occur naturally as the slight gestures of the instructor blend into the everyday movements of hands and arms associated with the activity.

Table 2 provides another example of a shaping and fading program, this one for taking off a T-shirt and putting it on. The same general guidelines brought to your attention in Table 1 apply here, as they would in most any fading program. Once again, note that the prompting steps in the second part of the table are sequenced so that the most obvious prompts occur first followed by less obvious prompts each time (that is, the prompts are faded). Usually, the student will begin taking off his T-shirt or putting it on independently before you reach the fifth step.

Earlier in this chapter, we described a procedure to shape Merle's eye contact. Prompting was used in this program whenever the instructor said, "Merle, look at me," and held the peanut to her eyes. Obviously, it is cumbersome, unrealistic, and unnatural for the instructor to keep lifting the peanut to her eyes each time she wants Merle to look at her. To solve this problem, the instructor decided to fade holding the peanut by her eyes because it, in large part, is controlling Merle's eye contact more than the verbal prompt.

To fade holding the peanut near her eyes, the instructor used the following fading procedure. After Merle would reliably give her 2 seconds of eye contact, she raised the peanut to her eyes but cupped it in her hand so that it was not visible. Over successive eye contact trials, the instructor lifted the peanut (hidden behind her fingers) to slightly below her eyes, to her cheek, to her chin, to her throat, to her chest, to her side, and ultimately to where she could say, "Merle, look at me," and take the edible from the bowl and place it in his mouth. Thus, she ended the fading program at an ideal spot. Now, whenever she requests eye contact, she can simply wait for Merle to look at her and then give him an edible from either a bowl or a pocket in her apron. At this point, she can begin generalization training of eye contact outside the training area (see Chapter 14).

CORRECTLY USING PROMPTING AND FADING

As with shaping, prompting and fading require a great deal of expertise on the part of the instructor and the only way to gain this expertise is by using the techniques as often as possible and by collecting data. You will gain this expertise as you learn to interpret the data and accordingly adjust your prompting and fading. To use prompting and fading correctly, we must prompt the student regularly during the initial training phases but not at all during the final phases. Otherwise, the student becomes dependent on the prompter (instructor) and the prompts. (This is one of the major problems of retarded students: They are highly dependent on prompts. Even when you know they know what to do, they still wait to be prompted.) Thus, it is important that you make steady progress in fading the prompts.

There are two cardinal rules to follow when you use prompting and fading:

1. *Never use a prompt that has been faded when shaping one specific behavior.* In other words, once a student has correctly responded to a less obvious prompt, there is no need to return to an earlier level of prompting (that is, a more obvious prompt) that has been faded. To do so would hamper the training because the student would become more dependent on you and the more obvious prompt.
2. *Always begin each training session or day by using the prompts to which the student successfully responded on the previous session or day.* This will start the new session or day with a successful response and will take care of any possible memory lapses the student may have had.

Before continuing through this chapter, answer the following questions.

1. Why is a prompt considered to be an additional discriminative stimulus?
2. Below is a list of common prompts. Label each one according to whether it is a physical, gestural, or verbal prompt.
   a. "Do this."
   b. Guiding a student's hand to pick up a ball.
   c. Pointing to the door.
   d. Holding up a picture of a cat.
   e. "Stand by Dennis."
   f. Looking downward at the student's pants.
   g. Touching a student's shoulder.
3. What technique is used to prevent the student from becoming dependent on a prompt?
4. What kind of prompt should you use to begin training a student?
5. What are two ways of fading a verbal prompt?
6. How is a gestural prompt faded?
7. What are three ways of dealing with the problem of fading physical prompts?
8. Ms. Essex said, "Hand me the sock," and guided Marvin's hand to the sock. Did Ms. Essex use prompts?
9. Arrange the following prompts into a sequence of steps that would permit fading to be accomplished easily.
   a. "Zack, take a bit," point to the bowl of food
   b. "Zack, bite," point to the bowl of food
   c. "Zack, take a bite," point to the bowl of food, touch Zack's hand that holds the spoon
   d. "Zack, take a bite," point to the bowl of food, guide Zack's hand to the spoon
   e. "Zack, take bite," point to the bowl of food

     f. Point to the bowl of food

     g. "Zack," point to the bowl of food

10. During speech training sessions with George, Ms. Tuttle had been holding an edible near her mouth so that George would look at her mouth as she formed the words. Now that George reliably looks at her mouth, how could Ms. Tuttle fade holding the edible by her mouth?

11. At the end of yesterday's shaping session to teach Sidney to walk, Mr. Pares had gotten Sidney to respond to the word "walk" paired with a come here motion in which Mr. Pares pointed to the spot where he wanted Sidney to walk. Mr. Pares would like to begin the day by eliminating the gestural prompt. Should he?

12. During today's session, Sidney has responded to the verbal prompt "Walk" on two occasions. Mr. Pares has just given that prompt again, but Sidney has not moved. Mr. Pares is growing anxious and thinks that maybe he should resume using the gestural prompt that had worked before. What do you think of Mr. Pares' idea?

Answers are on page 117.

SUMMARY

Three techniques that are very useful for producing and/or increasing desirable behaviors are shaping, prompting, and fading. Shaping, or the method of successive approximations, is used to produce a behavior that is not in the student's behavioral repertoire. This new behavior is called the target behavior. The behavior shaping process includes seven steps: 1) selecting a target behavior, 2) selecting an initial behavior that the student performs and that resembles the target behavior in some way, 3) selecting powerful reinforcers, 4) reinforcing the initial behavior until it occurs frequently, 5) reinforcing successive approximations of the target behavior, 6) reinforcing the target behavior each time it occurs, and 7) reinforcing the target behavior on an intermittent schedule of reinforcement. The four ways of maximizing the behavior shaping process are: 1) combine a discriminative stimulus with shaping, 2) combine physical guidance with shaping, 3) combine an imitative prompt with shaping, and 4) combine fading with shaping.

    The use of discriminative stimuli to cue a student to perform a particular behavior is called prompting, and the discriminative stimuli themselves are called prompts. The importance of prompts is that they greatly increase the likelihood that the desired behavior will occur. The three types of prompts are verbal, gestural, and physical. Of the three, physical prompts are the most difficult to fade.

    Fading fosters independence because it is the gradual removal of a prompt. By using fading, the responsibility to perform a behavior can be shifted from the prompt and prompter (instructor) to other environmental discriminative stimuli and consequences. Fading is accomplished by gradually fading the stimulus control.

To use prompting and fading correctly within a behavior shaping program, two cardinal rules must be followed: 1) once a prompt has been faded, it is never given again, and 2) each training session or day is begun using the prompts to which the student responded successfully at the end of the previous session or day.

We can now state the following concerning the instructional cycle, or three-term contingency: Fading involves a gradual change in the stimulus (e.g., prompts); shaping involves a gradual change in the response; and intermittent reinforcement schedules involve a gradual change in the consequence.

REVIEW QUESTIONS

1. The method of successive approximations is called _____.
2. The goal of shaping is to develop a new behavior that is not in the student's behavioral _____.
3. The behavior you intend to establish through shaping is called the _____ behavior.
4. You begin the shaping process by reinforcing a response or behavior that is currently in the student's repertoire. This response is called the _____ behavior.
5. An additional discriminative stimulus is a _____.
6. The three types of prompts are _____, _____, and _____.
7. Which type of prompt is the most difficult to fade?
8. The gradual change of stimulus control is called _____.
9. Fading is used to foster independence by eliminating the control that the p_____ and p_____ have had over the student's behavior.
10. Fading is accomplished by providing the student with a less _____ discriminative stimulus than you had given him previously.
11. To use prompting and fading correctly, the student should be prompted regularly during the i_____ training phases and not at all during the f_____ phases.

Answers are on page 117.

SUGGESTED READINGS

Ball, T. S. Behavior shaping of self-help skills in the severely retarded child. In: J. Fisher & R. E. Harris (eds.), Reinforcement theory in psychological treatment: A symposium. *California Mental Health Research Monograph*, 1966, *8*, 15–24.

Bensberg, G. J., Colwell, C. N., & Cassell, R. H. Teaching the profoundly retarded self-help skills activities by behavior shaping techniques. *American Journal of Mental Deficiency*, 1965, *69*, 674–679.

Foxx, R. M., & Azrin, N. H. *Toilet training the retarded: A rapid program for day and nighttime independent toileting.* Champaign, IL: Research Press, 1973.

Kerr, N., Myerson, L., & Michael, J. A procedure for shaping vocalizations in a mute child. In: L. P. Ullmann & L. Krasner (eds.), *Case studies in behavior modification.* New York: Holt, Rinehart & Winston, 1965.

Larsen, L. A., & Bricker, W. A. A manual for parents and teachers of severely and moderately retarded children. *IMRID Papers and Reports,* 1968, *5*(22).

Miron, N. B. Behavior shaping and group nursing with severely retarded patients. In: J. Fisher & R. E. Harris (eds.), Reinforcement theory in psychological treatment: A symposium. *California Mental Health Research Monograph,* 1966, *8,* 1–14.

Rincover, A. Variables affecting stimulus fading and discriminative responding in psychotic children. *Journal of Abnormal Psychology,* 1978, *87*(5), 541–553.

Sidman, M., & Stoddard, L. T. The effectiveness of fading in programming a stimultaneous form of discrimination for retarded children. *Journal of the Experimental Analysis of Behavior,* 1967, *10,* 3–15.

Walsh, B. F., & Lamberts, F. Errorless discrimination and picture fading as techniques for teaching sight words to TMR students. *American Journal of Mental Deficiency,* 1979, *83*(5), 473–479.

ANSWERS TO CHAPTER QUESTIONS

Answers to Questions on Pages 104–105

1. a. target
   b. initial
   c. reinforcers
   d. Reinforce
   e. successive approximations
   f. Reinforce
   g. intermittent
2. a. Laura's independently eating with a spoon.
   b. Laura's hand being guided to her mouth by Ms. Wolf.
   c. The food on the spoon and praise, i.e., "Good eating, Laura."
   d. Ms. Wolf will continue the guidance and praise until Laura meets some specified criterion level, e.g., successfully feeding herself with direct hand guidance on 90% or more of the feeding trials at a meal.
   e. A successive approximation occurs each time Ms. Wolf moves her hand a little further away from Laura's hand. They will be reinforced by the bite of food and praise.
   f. By a bite of food and praise.
   g. Self-feeding is unique in that the behavior is always reinforced continuously because each spoonful results in the reinforcer (a bite of food). However, Ms. Wolf can deliver her praise (the other reinforcer maintaining self-feeding) on an intermittent schedule of reinforcement, e.g., praising Laura after five successive bites.
3. criterion level
4. observe
5. a. discriminative stimulus
   b. physical guidance
   c. imitative prompt
   d. fading

Answers to Questions on Pages 113–114

1. A prompt is considered to be an additional discriminative stimulus because it is given *in addition* to the naturally occurring discriminative stimuli that are associated with the behavior to be performed.
2. a. verbal
   b. physical
   c. gestural
   d. This is not a prompt; rather, it is a natural discriminative stimulus.
   e. verbal
   f. gestural
   g. physical
3. fading
4. A prompt to which the student can respond successfully. In general, this will be a very obvious prompt(s).
5. Shorten the number of words. Progressively speak more softly.
6. By progressively reducing the size of the gesture.
7. a. Progressively reduce the amount of touch that you use.
   b. Progressively move your touch (the physical prompt) away from the part of the student's body or area that is being prompted.
   c. Use physical prompts with the other two types of prompts and fade the physical prompt first.
8. Yes. She used a verbal prompt, "Hand me the sock," and a physical prompt, guiding Marvin's hand to the sock.
9. The correct sequence is d, c, a, e, b, g, f.
10. Ms. Tuttle should hold the edible next to her mouth but hidden from view. Over successive speech trials, she would raise the edible to her chin, to her throat, to her chest, to her side, and end by taking the edible directly from the bowl and placing it in George's mouth following an appropriate utterance.
11. No. He should start by using the prompts that had been successful the previous day.
12. It is a bad idea because in any training session you should never return to a prompt that has been faded.

Answers to Review Questions on Page 115

1. shaping
2. repertoire
3. target
4. initial
5. prompt
6. physical, verbal, gestural
7. physical
8. fading
9. prompter, prompts
10. active
11. initial, final

Chapter 8

STIMULUS-RESPONSE CHAINS, BACKWARD CHAINING, AND GRADUATED GUIDANCE

After reading this chapter, you will be able to:

1. Define and give an example of a behavior chain.
2. Define a terminal reinforcer.
3. Define and give an example of a conditioned reinforcer.
4. Define and give an example of a discriminative stimulus.
5. Explain the dual role of a discriminative stimulus in a behavior chain.
6. Define forward chaining.
7. Specify when forward chaining should be used to accomplish a behavioral objective.
8. Define and give an example of backward chaining.
9. Specify when backward chaining should be used to accomplish a behavioral objective.
10. List the advantages and disadvantages of backward chaining.
11. List five factors that help facilitate backward chaining.
12. Define and give an example of graduated guidance.
13. List and define the three parts of graduated guidance.
14. List the three advantages of graduated guidance.

Much of our behavior consists of behavior chains, or sequences of responses, that result in an important reinforcer at the end of the sequence. This chapter begins with a discussion of these stimulus-response or behavior chains. Two techniques that can be used to teach a complex skill or sequence of behaviors to retarded students are then discussed: 1) backward and forward chaining, and 2) graduated guidance with forward chaining.

BEHAVIOR CHAINS (STIMULUS-RESPONSE CHAINS)

A BEHAVIOR (STIMULUS-RESPONSE) CHAIN IS A SEQUENCE OF STIMULI AND RESPONSES THAT ENDS WITH A TERMINAL REINFORCER.

Most of our behavior does not consist of a simple response being followed by a reinforcer. Rather, we engage in a series or sequence of responses (a behavior chain) that results in some important reinforcer at the end of the sequence. Because the reinforcer comes at the end of the sequence, it is called a *terminal reinforcer* (S^R+). Examples of behavior chains that we perform include shopping, bathing, going out for the evening, driving to work, and bowling.

We perform these long sequences (chains) of behavior even though the only apparent reinforcer for our actions appears at the end of the behavior chain. We do this because of conditioned reinforcement. Each response in the chain is reinforced by the next step in the chain and simultaneously serves as a discriminative stimulus for the next response. A discriminative stimulus is also a *conditioned reinforcer* (S^r) because it has been associated or paired with reinforcement. Thus, a stimulus in a behavior chain serves a dual role. It is a conditioned reinforcer (S^r) for the response (R) it follows and a discriminative stimulus (S^D) for the response it precedes. In its role as a conditioned reinforcer, the stimulus maintains and strengthens the response it follows. In its role as a discriminative stimulus, it sets the occasion for next response in the chain to occur. Let us now look at a common behavior—eating at a restaurant—as a stimulus-response (S-R) chain.

S^D ------------> (restaurant sign)	R ------------> (drive into parking lot)	S^D ------------> (door of restaurant)	
R ------------> (enter restaurant)	S^D ------------> (counter)	R ------------> (walk to counter)	S^D ------------> (menu on wall)
R ------------> (read menu)	S^D ------------> (counter employee: "May I take your order?")	R ------------> (order food)	S^D ------------> (food on tray; "That will be $2.98, please.")
R ------------> (pay counter employee)	S^D ------------> (food on tray)	R ------------> (carry food to table)	S^D ------------> (food on table)
R ------------> (eat)	S^R+ ------------> (delicious food)		

As the example shows, the promise of delicious food at the end of the chain is sufficient to produce a number of responses and these responses are reinforced by the discriminative stimuli along the way. In Chapter 2, the use of a task analysis to accomplish a behavioral objective was discussed. A task analysis is nothing more than a specification of the behavior chain that must be performed in order to reach the objective (the last response in the chain) and of the reinforcer (S^R+) the instructor delivers when the objective is accomplished is simply the terminal reinforcer (S^R+) at the end of the behavior chain.

Let's return to a behavioral objective that was used in Chapter 2 and express it as a behavior chain. The behavioral objective was to teach a student to shampoo her hair (Chapter 2, page 25).

The task analysis revealed that the following behaviors were necessary in order to accomplish the objective.
1. Wet hair.
2. Apply shampoo to hair.
3. Work shampoo into a lather.
4. Rinse hair.

Now let us look at the task analysis as a S-R chain.

S^D ------------>	R ------------>	S^D ------------>	R ------------>
(sink)	(walk to sink)	(faucet)	(turn on faucet)
S^D ------------>	R ------------>	S^D ------------>	R ------------>
(water running)	(wet hair under faucet)	(wet hair)	(pick up shampoo bottle)
S^D ------------>	R ------------>	S^D ------------>	R ------------>
(shampoo bottle in hand)	(open cap of shampoo)	(open bottle of shampoo)	(apply shampoo to hair)
S^D ------------>	R ------------>	S^D ------------>	R ------------>
(shampoo in hair)	(work shampoo into lather)	(lather in hair)	(rinse hair)
S^R+ ------------>			
(praise from instructor)			

FORWARD AND BACKWARD CHAINING

In the above example, it appears that there is an apparent discrepancy between the task analysis and the stimulus-response or behavior chain. The task analysis specified four responses (tasks) that had to be performed in order to accomplish the behavioral objective of shampooing, whereas the behavior chain specified eight responses. Furthermore, the task analysis did not specify the discriminative stimuli that preceded or followed each response but the behavior chain did. There is an explanation for this discrepancy. The task analysis of shampooing was based on the fact that the student had all of the necessary responses in her behavioral repertoire. Thus, the behavioral objective, shampooing, could be accomplished by simply chaining or sequencing the responses so that each followed the other until the objective was achieved. When the student does not have the necessary responses, a more thorough task analysis must be written. Looking at the stimulus-response chains would help you in writing the more detailed task analysis.

FORWARD CHAINING IS A TEACHING PROCEDURE IN WHICH INSTRUCTION BEGINS WITH THE FIRST STEP IN THE CHAIN AND PROCEEDS TOWARD THE LAST STEP IN THE CHAIN.

Using the task analysis or stimulus-response chain to teach a behavioral objective is called *forward chaining* because the responses are chained together beginning with the first response (wetting hair) and ending with the last response (rinsing hair), which, of course, would be followed by a reinforcer. (If one of the responses were not in the student's repertoire, it would first be shaped and then the sequence of behaviors would be chained together.)

In forward chaining, successive approximations of an operant behavior are taught. Initially, reinforcement must be given after each response, in order to shape the sequencing of steps properly. The continuous reinforcement can be faded to an intermittent schedule of reinforcement and finally only the last behavior will be taught.

The use of prompting and fading are necessary in forward chaining. Forward chaining allows the behavior to be shaped under control of the responses in the chain, which act as discriminative stimuli.

Generally, normal individuals and high functioning retarded students can be taught to accomplish a behavioral objective through forward chaining. But, what happens if the student does not have any of the necessary responses that the task analysis specifies? Here the answer to the apparent discrepancy becomes clear. When a student does not have the necessary behaviors (tasks) in his or her behavioral repertoire, we must use a *backward chaining* procedure to accomplish the behavioral objective.

BACKWARD CHAINING IS A TEACHING PROCEDURE IN WHICH INSTRUCTION BEGINS WITH THE LAST STEP IN THE CHAIN AND PROCEEDS TOWARD THE FIRST STEP IN THE CHAIN.

The success of the backward chaining procedure depends on the instructor's specification of the stimulus-response or behavior chain because backward chaining involves beginning with the last response in the chain and working backward so that the first response is taught last. We begin with the last response because it is closest to the terminal reinforcer and therefore will be reinforced soonest.

Conversely, the first response is the weakest response because it is furthest away from the terminal reinforcer. Thus, in the shampooing example, the instructor's knowledge of the behavior or stimulus-response chain would be very important in setting up a backward chaining procedure to teach shampooing to a severely or profoundly retarded student who had none of the necessary behaviors. Let us look at how the instructor would use backward chaining to accomplish that objective.

The behavior chain for shampooing one's hair was as follows:

S^D ------------> (sink)   R ------------> (walk to sink) S^D ------------> (faucet)   R ------------> (turn on faucet)

S^D ------------> (water running)   R ------------> (wet hair under faucet) S^D ------------> (wet hair)   R ------------> (pick up shampoo bottle)

S^D ------------> (shampoo bottle in hands)   R ------------> (open cap of shampoo) S^D ------------> (open bottle of shampoo)   R ------------> (apply shampoo to hair)

S^D ------------> (shampoo in hair)   R ------------> (work shampoo into lather) S^D ------------> (lather in hair)   R ------------> (rinse hair)

S^R+ ------------> (praise from instructor)

The instructor uses backward chaining as follows:

Step 1   R ------------> (rinse hair) S^R+ ------------> (praise student and perhaps give hug and an edible)

Step 2   R ------------> (work shampoo into lather) S^D ------------> (lather in hair)   R ------------> (rinse hair) S^R+

The instructor has the student work the shampoo into a lather, rinse his hair, and then reinforces him.

Step 3   R ------------> (apply shampoo to hair) S^D ------------> (shampoo in hair)   R ------------> (work shampoo into lather)

S^D ------------> (lather in hair)   R ------------> (rinse hair) S^R+ ------------>

The instructor has the student apply shampoo to his hair from an open bottle, work the shampoo into a lather and rinse his hair, and then she reinforces him.

Step 4

R ------------>	S^D ------------>	R ------------>
(open cap of shampoo bottle)	(open bottle of shampoo)	(apply shampoo to hair)
S^D ----------->	R ------------>	S^D ------------>
(shampoo in hair)	(work shampoo into lather)	(lather in hair)
R ------------>	S^R+ ------------>	
(rinse hair)		

The instructor has the student open the shampoo bottle, apply shampoo, work shampoo into a lather, and rinse his hair, and then she reinforces him.

Step 5

R ------------>	S^D ------------>	R ------------>
(pick up shampoo bottle)	(shampoo bottle in hand)	(open cap of shampoo)
S^D ----------->	R ------------>	S^D ------------>
(open bottle of shampoo)	(apply shampoo to hair)	(shampoo in hair)
R ------------>	S^D ------------>	R ------------>
(work shampoo into lather)	(lather in hair)	(rinse hair)
S^R+ ------------>		

The instructor has the student pick up the shampoo bottle, open the bottle, apply shampoo, work shampoo into a lather, and rinse his hair, and then she reinforces him.

Step 6

R ------------>	S^D ------------>	R ------------>
(wet hair under faucet)	(wet hair)	(pick up shampoo bottle)
S^D ----------->	R ------------>	S^D ------------>
(bottle in hand)	(open cap of shampoo)	(open bottle of shampoo)
R ------------>	S^D ------------>	R ------------>
(apply shampoo to hair)	(shampoo in hair)	(work shampoo into lather)
S^D ----------->	R ------------>	S^R+ ------------>
(lather in hair)	(rinse hair)	

The instructor has the student wet his hair under the faucet, pick up the shampoo bottle, open the bottle, apply shampoo, work shampoo into a lather, and rinse his hair, and then she reinforces him.

Step 7

R ------------>	S^D ------------>	R ------------>
(turn on faucet)	(water running)	(wet hair under faucet)

S^D ------------>   R ------------> S^D ------------>
(wet hair)   (pick up shampoo   (shampoo bottle in
                          bottle)   hand)

R ------------> S^D ------------>   R ------------>
(open cap of the   (open bottle of   (apply shampoo to
bottle of shampoo)   shampoo)   hair)

S^D ------------>   R ------------> S^D ------------>
(shampoo in hair)   (work shampoo   (lather in hair)
                          into lather)

R ------------> S^R+ ------------>
(rinse hair)

The instructor has the student turn on the faucet, wet his hair, pick up the shampoo bottle, open the bottle, apply shampoo, work shampoo into a lather, and rinse his hair, and then she reinforces him.

Step 8   R ------------> S^D ------------>   R ------------>
              (walk to sink)   (faucet)   (turn on faucet)

              S^D ------------>   R ------------> S^D ------------>
              (water running)   (wet hair under   (wet hair)
                                     faucet)

              R ------------> S^D ------------>   R ------------>
              (pick up shampoo   (shampoo bottle   (open cap of
              bottle)   in hand)   shampoo)

              S^D ------------>   R ------------> S^D ------------>
              (open bottle of   (apply shampoo   (shampoo in hair)
              shampoo)   to hair)

              R ------------> S^D ------------>   R ------------>
              (work shampoo   (lather in hair)   (rinse hair)
              into lather)

              S^R+ ------------>

The instructor has the student walk to the sink, turn on the faucet, wet his hair, pick up the shampoo bottle, open the bottle, apply shampoo, work shampoo into a lather, and rinse his hair, and then she reinforces him.

Let us look at another example of backward chaining. In this case, a student will be taught how to pull his pants up from his ankles.

The response chain (task analysis) is as follows. The student will:

1. Reach for pants.
2. Grasp pants.
3. Pull pants up to calves.
4. Pull pants up to knees.
5. Pull pants up to thighs.
6. Pull pants over buttocks.
7. Pull pants up to waist.

Step 1   The teacher puts the pants on the student so that they are just 1 to 2 inches below his waist. She then points to his pants, says, "Pants up," and guides his hands to the waistband of his pants. The student only needs to raise his pants 1 to 2 inches to receive the reinforcer.

Step 2   The student's pants are put on him so that they are just below his buttocks. The gestural prompt (pointing to his pants) and verbal prompt ("Pants up") are given, and the physical prompt (guiding the student's hands to the waistband) is faded. The student receives a reinforcer when his pants are raised to his waist.

Step 3   The student's pants are put on him so that they are resting on his thighs. When the student responds successfully to the verbal and gestural prompts, he is reinforced.

Step 4   The student's pants are at his knees. When he raises his pants to his waist following the gestural prompt (the verbal prompt is faded), he is reinforced.

Step 5   The student's pants are at his calves. When he raises his pants to his waist following the gestural prompt, he is reinforced.

Steps 6 and 7   The student's pants are at his ankles. When he raises his pants to his waist following the gestural prompt, he is reinforced.

Remember that prompting and fading, along with reinforcing successive approximations, is also essential to the process. If responses are to be reinforced immediately, successive approximations must be reinforced. You will need to fade reinforcement as well as prompts.

The advantage of using backward chaining to teach a complex sequence of behaviors that is not in the student's behavioral repertoire is that *the response closest to the terminal reinforcer is taught first.* This is very important because it ensures that the student will be successful. The student has only to make one simple response in order to be reinforced.

There are a few disadvantages associated with the use of backward chaining. These are discussed in the next section when we compare and contrast backward chaining and graduated guidance as techniques for teaching a complex sequence of behaviors.

The following techniques will help you use backward chaining effectively:

1. Use supplemental discriminative stimuli (S^Ds) in addition to the S^Ds that are an integral part of the behavior chain. These supplemental S^Ds are, of course, prompts such as instructions, gestures, and physical guidance.
2. Combine imitative prompts with the backward chaining.
3. Combine fading with the backward chaining.
4. Combine shaping with the backward chaining. (You will note that prompts, shaping, and fading were used by the instructor in the backward chaining example of raising pants discussed above.)

5. Reinforce the chain as often as possible in the beginning (use continuous reinforcement) and only switch to intermittent reinforcement when the student has successfully performed the behavior chain over several trials.

Before continuing this chapter, answer the following questions.

1. What roles does a discriminative stimulus play in a behavior chain?
2. Below is a behavior (stimulus-response) chain of eating with a spoon. Label the responses (Rs), discriminative stimuli (S^Ds), and terminal reinforcers (S^R+s).

```
------------>            ------------>            ------------>            ------------>
(spoon beside            (pick up                 (spoon in                (scoop food
plate of food)           spoon)                   hand)                    onto spoon)
------------>            ------------>            ------------>            ------------>
(food on                 (raise spoon             (spoon near              (place spoon
spoon)                   toward mouth)            mouth)                   in mouth
------------>
(food, praise)
```

3. In the above chain, "spoon in hand" serves as a discriminative stimulus for which response and as a conditioned reinforcer for which response?
4. Assume that the student who was taught to eat with a spoon had all of the necessary self-feeding behaviors in his behavioral repertoire. Now, write out the task analysis for accomplishing the behavioral objective of eating with a spoon. Would you use forward or backward chaining in order to accomplish the objective?
5. Suppose that the student who was taught self-feeding had all the necessary behaviors in his behavioral repertoire except for picking up the spoon. How would you add this behavior to his repertoire?
6. Suppose that the student who was taught self-feeding had none of the necessary behaviors in his behavioral repertoire. What technique would you use to teach him self-feeding? How would you go about employing that technique?
7. The advantage of backward chaining is that _____.
8. Normal individuals and high functioning retarded students typically learn a complex series of behaviors through forward chaining, whereas severely retarded students may require _____.
9. The five techniques that can be combined with backward chaining to make it more effective are: 1) p_____ (or supplemental S^Ds), 2) i_____ prompting, 3) f_____, 4) s_____, and 5) r_____ the chain as often as possible in the beginning.

Answers are on page 135.

GRADUATED GUIDANCE

GRADUATED GUIDANCE IS A TECHNIQUE IN WHICH PHYSICAL GUIDANCE AND FADING ARE COMBINED SUCH THAT THE PHYSICAL GUIDANCE IS SYSTEMATICALLY AND GRADUALLY REDUCED AND THEN FADED COMPLETELY.

Graduated guidance is a recently developed technique that is used to teach a behavior chain through forward chaining. The technique represents a radical departure from backward chaining because the entire behavior chain is completed each time the graduated guidance is used. Graduated guidance is especially useful for students whose intellectual deficits make it difficult for them to understand simple verbal and gestural prompts and for students who require a lot of physical prompting. The major difference between graduated guidance and manual guidance (as in physical prompting) is that with graduated guidance the amount of the instructor's physical guidance (hand pressure) is adjusted from moment to moment depending on the student's performance (behavior) at that moment.

There are three parts to the graduated guidance technique:

1. Full graduated guidance
2. Partial graduated guidance
3. Shadowing

During full graduated guidance, the instructor keeps her hands in full contact with the student's hands throughout the trial and praises the student continuously as long as the student is moving his hand in the desired direction. During partial graduated guidance, the instructor only guides the student's hands as necessary, while in shadowing the instructor does not physically touch the student's hands but keeps her hands within an inch of the student's hands as the student completes the trial.

Let's take a closer look at the steps involved in full graduated guidance. First, throughout the trial, the instructor should never use more force than is needed to move the student's hands in the desired direction. Verbal praise should be given throughout the trial, but only when the student is actively participating in the movement, and never when he is resisting or remaining passive. At the start of the trial, apply as little force as necessary and gradually build up your guidance until the student's hand starts to move. Then immediately but gradually begin to decrease the force you are applying as long as the student's hand continues to move in the appropriate direction. If the student begins to resist the movement, instantly apply only enough force to counteract the resistance, thereby keeping the student's hand stationary. As soon as the student ceases the resisting motion, decrease the amount of force you are applying and gradually start to apply just enough force to again begin to move the student's hand in the desired direction. Once you have started a trial, *never* stop the activity until the response is complete; do not give up or interrupt the trial. At the end of the trial, be sure to give the student a reinforcer immediately. Before actually giving the reinforcer to the student, however, completely eliminate the guidance you have been providing (i.e., you should not even be touching the student).

Following is an example of the use of graduated guidance to teach a student to pull his pants up from his ankles. All three parts of the graduated guidance technique are used.

The instructor begins with *full graduated guidance*. She puts the pants on the student so that they are at his ankles. She then says, "Pants up" and guides the student's hands to the waistband of his pants. The instructor begins guiding the student's hands in raising his pants to his waist. As the pants are being raised, she praises him whenever he makes the slightest effort to raise the pants himself. The instructor keeps her hands on the student's hands throughout the training trial, that is, from the beginning of the verbal prompt "Pants up" until the pants are raised to his waist. If the student should resist the graduated guidance, the instructor would use just enough force to counteract the student's resistance and reduce and then eliminate this force when the student ceases resisting.

Once the student allows his hands to be guided without any resistance, the instructor would begin using *partial graduated guidance*. During the partial graduated guidance, the instructor merely guides the student's hands with her thumb and forefinger. In this way, the instructor fades the amount of physical contact so that the student takes more responsibility for raising his pants. She would continue to praise all of the student's efforts to raise his pants as well as when he allowed her to use the partial graduated guidance, e.g., "That's good, you're raising your pants. Good, keep raising your pants. Keep going. Good, pants up. Good boy."

When the student reliably raises his pants in response to the instructor's use of partial graduated guidance, the instructor would begin using *shadowing*. During shadowing, the instructor keeps her hands within an inch of the student's hands throughout the pants raising trial. If the student stops raising his pants at any time during the trial, the instructor reapplies partial or full graduated guidance (depending on which was necessary to motivate the student to perform the desired action) until the student once again begins raising his pants; at that point, the instructor resumes the shadowing. As before, generous amounts of praise are given whenever the student is raising his pants. The use of shadowing permits the instructor to fade her physical contact so that it no longer serves as a physical prompt. In this way, the student is forced to attend only to the instructor's verbal prompts.

Within each training trial, you can use all three parts of the graduated guidance technique. Your choice of whether to use full graduated guidance, partial graduated guidance, or shadowing depends on what the student is doing at the moment. For example, you might begin the pants raising trial using full graduated guidance, then switch to partial graduated guidance as the student begins taking over some of the pants raising action, and then begin shadowing when the student is raising his pants himself. If the student stopped the pants raising action at any time, physical guidance would be reapplied (either full or partial, whichever was necessary) until the student resumed the action, at which time you would resume the shadowing. Praise would be given throughout as long as the student was performing some appropriate pants raising action. For any instances of resistance, you would use only the amount of hand force necessary to counterbalance the resistive action.

Over time, you will eliminate the full graduated guidance, then the partial guidance so that you will only need to shadow the student's hands during the activity. When it is only necessary to use shadowing throughout a training trial, you will begin to fade the shadowing by moving your hands further and further away from the student's hands. This fading should be done by first moving your hands 2 inches from the student's hands on one trial, then 3 inches away on the next trial, and so forth, until you are approximately 2 feet away from the student. At that point, the student will be performing the requested chain (e.g., pants raising) in response to just your verbal prompt or instruction (e.g., "Pants up"). Of course, you would reapply physical guidance (either partial or full) should the student stop somewhere along the chain. However, this is rarely necessary since the student will have had a long history of performing the chain (raising his pants) and receiving reinforcers. Once you have faded yourself to the point where you are 2 feet away from the student, you should begin reducing the amount of praise that you give during the student's performance of the chain. This will be quite easy to do since the student will be performing the chain rapidly. You should systematically reduce your praise over trials so that you ultimately only praise the student at the end of the chain.

A COMPARISON OF BACKWARD CHAINING AND GRADUATED GUIDANCE

Earlier in this chapter, the two advantages of backward chaining were stated: 1) that the response closest to the terminal reinforcer is taught first, and 2) that the task (or chain) is broken down into easily mastered steps. There is, however, a disadvantage that should be noted: *you must wait for the student to respond.* No matter what step the student is on or how small that step is, no reinforcement can be provided until the student performs the step. Thus, some instructional time may be wasted while you are waiting for the student to respond.

This disadvantage of backward chaining results from the fact that each step (response) in the chain represents a distinct trial. Thus, any backward chaining program consists of many distinct trials as each response (step) is added to the chain.

The use of graduated guidance eliminates the disadvantage of backward chaining because the entire chain is taught during each trial. The only difference in each trial is the amount of physical guidance that is needed to ensure that the entire chain is completed.

Let us now look at the disadvantage of backward chaining and see how it is eliminated when graduated guidance is used. First, in graduated guidance, you do not need to wait for the student to respond (as with backward chaining). You are guiding the student in performing the response, which ensures that the student will always be successful in performing all the responses in the chain and that there will be no down time while waiting for the student to respond.

A final advantage of graduated guidance is that it incorporates *avoidance learning* which occurs when someone responds in order to avoid or escape something that is unpleasant. In the graduated guidance procedure, the instructor's physical guidance serves as a mild irritant to the student. Over time, the student learns to avoid the physical guidance by performing the requested chain or to escape ongoing guidance by beginning to perform the chain. Even the most retarded student is able to learn to avoid or escape the physical guidance because the guidance is reduced or terminated whenever the student responds appropriately. This reduction or elimination of the physical guidance on a moment-to-moment basis thus serves as a source of constant feedback to the student.

The advantages of graduated guidance are:

1. You do not have to wait for the student to respond.
2. It incorporates avoidance learning.

Despite the obvious advantages of graduated guidance, you should begin teaching your students via backward chaining because it requires less expertise than graduated guidance. Once you have gained expertise using backward chaining, you will be ready to begin using graduated guidance. Remember that graduated guidance still requires a task analysis although there is no time lost between steps. If you do not have a task analysis, the student may not be guided through all of the steps.

Before continuing this chapter, answer the following questions:

1. Graduated guidance is especially useful for students whose intellectual deficits make it difficult for them to understand simple verbal and g_____ prompts and/or for students who require a lot of _____ prompting.
2. The major difference between manual guidance and graduated guidance is that with graduated guidance the amount of the instructor's physical guidance (hand pressure) is adjusted from _____ to _____ depending on the student's performance at that moment.
3. During full graduated guidance, the instructor keeps his or her hands in _____ hands.

4. During partial graduated guidance, the instructor merely guides the student's hands with his or her t_____ and f_____.
5. During shadowing, the instructor keeps his or her hands _____.
6. All three parts of graduated guidance are used within each training t_____.
7. When the student resists the graduated guidance, the instructor uses just enough force to counteract the student's resistance and then reduces and finally eliminates this force when _____.
8. If the student is performing some action appropriately throughout graduated guidance, you will be praising him c_____.
9. When you have faded your presence to a point where you are 2 feet away from the student, you should only praise the student at the _____.
10. The disadvantage of backward chaining is that you must wait for the student to _____.
11. The advantages of graduated guidance are: 1) you do not have to wait for the student to _____, and 2) it incorporates _____.
12. Avoidance learning occurs when the student learns to respond in order to a_____ or e_____ an unpleasant event.
13. In graduated guidance, the unpleasant event that leads to avoidance learning is the instructor's p_____ g_____.

Turn to page 135 for the answers.

SUMMARY

Most of our behavior consists of a series of discriminative stimuli and responses (behavior chain) that ends with a terminal reinforcer. Discriminative stimuli in a behavior chain perform a dual role, because they serve as a conditioned reinforcer for the response they follow and as a discriminative stimulus for the response they precede.

A task analysis is simply the specification of the responses in a behavior chain. Thus, the behavioral objective in a task analysis is the completion of the behavior chain. In a typical task analysis, the behavioral objective is accomplished via forward chaining because the responses (tasks) are taught from the beginning of the chain. Forward chaining is used when a student has the necessary responses in his behavioral repertoire so that the responses only need to be chained together.

Backward chaining is used to teach a behavior chain (accomplish a behavioral objective) when the student has few, if any, of the necessary responses in his behavioral repetoire. In backward chaining, the last response in the chain is taught first and the first response in the chain is taught last because the last response is closest to the terminal reinforcer. This is an advantage of backward chaining because it increases the likelihood that the student will be successful. A second advantage of backward chaining is that it breaks the task (chain or sequence) into small, easily mastered steps. The disadvantage of backward chaining is that you must wait for the student to respond. Five ways to maximize the use of backward chaining are: 1) use supplemental discriminative stimuli, 2) add imitative prompts, 3) combine fading with the backward chaining, 4) combine shaping with the backward chaining, and 5) reinforce the chain as often as possible when it is first being taught.

Graduated guidance is a technique in which physical guidance and fading are combined such that the physical guidance is systematically and gradually reduced and then faded completely. Graduated guidance teaches a behavior chain through forward chaining and is especially useful for students who do not understand simple verbal and gestural prompts and for students who need a great deal of physical prompting. Graduated guidance can also be used with backward chaining, except the *entire* process will not be possible in one trial. The three parts of graduated guidance are full graduated guidance, partial graduated guidance, and shadowing. The two advantages of graduated guidance are: 1) you do not need to wait for the student to respond, and 2) it incorporates avoidance learning. Avoidance learning plays an important role in graduated guidance because the student learns to respond appropriately (perform the behavior chain) in order to avoid or escape the instructor's physical guidance.

You should begin teaching your students using backward chaining. Once you have acquired sufficient expertise in the use of backward chaining, you can begin trying the graduated guidance procedure as a means of teaching the students complex skills.

REVIEW QUESTIONS

1. The sequence of stimuli and responses that ends with a terminal reinforcer is called a _____ _____.
2. A behavior chain is also known as a _____-_____ chain.
3. The reinforcer that comes at the end of a behavior chain is called the t_____ reinforcer.
4. A stimulus that is associated with reinforcement is called a c_____ reinforcer.
5. A stimulus associated with reinforcement is the d_____ stimulus.
6. A discriminative stimulus in a behavior chain has a dual role. It serves as a discriminative stimulus for the response it precedes and as a conditioned reinforcer _____.
7. The abbreviation for discriminative stimulus is _____.
8. The abbreviation for reinforcer is _____.
9. The abbreviation for terminal reinforcer is _____.
10. A task analysis is nothing more than a specification of the b_____ c_____ that must be performed in order to reach the behavior objective.

11. To accomplish a behavioral objective when the student has all the necessary behaviors in the behavior chain in his or her _____ repertoire, you use _____ _____.

12. Forward chaining is when you teach the first response in the chain first and teach the _____.

13. When the student does not have the necessary behaviors in his or her behavioral repertoire, he or she should be taught a behavior chain using _____ _____.

14. In backward chaining, the last response in the chain is taught first and the _____.

15. Backward chaining breaks a task down into the smallest possible s_____.

16. A technique in which physical guidance and fading are combined to teach a behavior chain through forward chaining is called _____ _____.

17. The three parts of graduated guidance are: 1) full graduated guidance, 2) _____, and 3) _____.

18. Graduated guidance incorporates avoidance learning which occurs when a student learns to respond in order to _____.

Answers are on page 136.

SUGGESTED READINGS

Ball, T. S., Seric, K., & Payne, L. E. Long-term retention of self-help skill training in the profoundly retarded. *American Journal of Mental Deficiency,* 1971, *76,* 378–382.

Foxx, R. M., & Azrin, N. H. *Toilet training the retarded: A rapid program for day and nighttime independent toileting.* Champaign, IL: Research Press, 1973.

Foxx, R. M. Attention training: The use of overcorrection and positive reinforcement to increase the eye contact of autistic and retarded children. *Journal of Applied Behavior Analysis,* 1977, *10,* 489–499.

Foxx, R. M. An overview of the use of overcorrection with the handicapped. *Journal of Pediatric Psychology,* 1978, *3,* 97–101.

Gold, M. W. Stimulus factors in skill training of the retarded on a complex assembly task: Acquisition, transfer, and retention. *American Journal of Mental Deficiency,* 1972, *76,* 517–526.

Horner, R. D. Establishing use of crutches by a mentally retarded *spina bifida* child. *Journal of Applied Behavior Analysis,* 1971, *4,* 183–189.

Horner, R. D., & Keilitz, I. Training mentally retarded adolescents to brush their teeth. *Journal of Applied Behavior Analysis,* 1975, *8,* 301–319.

Mahoney, K., Van Wagenen, R. K., & Meyerson, L. Toilet training of normal and retarded children. *Journal of Applied Behavior Analysis,* 1971, *4,* 173–181.

Song, A. Y., & Gandhi, R. An analysis of behavior during the acquisition and maintenance phases of self-spoon-feeding skills of profound retardates. *Mental Retardation,* 1974, *12*(1), 25–28.

Striefel, S., & Wetherby, B. Instruction-following behavior of a retarded child and its controlling stimuli. *Journal of Applied Behavior Analysis,* 1973, *6,* 663–670.

Talkington, L. W. Response-chain learning of mentally retarded adolescents under four conditions of reinforcement. *American Journal of Mental Deficiency,* 1971, *76,* 337–340.

Weisberg, P. Operant procedures with the retardate. In: N. R. Ellis (ed.), *International review of research in mental retardation* (Vol. 5). New York: Academic Press, 1971.

ANSWERS TO CHAPTER QUESTIONS

Answers to Questions on Page 127

1. It serves as a discriminative stimulus for the response it precedes and as a conditioned reinforcer for the response it follows.
2. Responses: pick up spoon, scoop food onto spoon, raise spoon toward mouth, place spoon in mouth
   Discriminative stimuli: spoon beside plate of food, spoon in hand, food on spoon, spoon near mouth
   Terminal reinforcers: food, praise
3. S^D for scooping food onto spoon; S^r for picking up the spoon.
4. Task analysis:
   a. Pick up spoon.
   b. Scoop food onto spoon.
   c. Raise spoon toward mouth.
   d. Place spoon in mouth.
   You would use forward chaining since all the necessary self-feeding behaviors are in the student's behavioral repertoire.
5. You would use shaping.
6. You would use backward chaining. You would begin by teaching the last response in the self-feeding chain first. Accordingly, you would guide the student's hand so that the spoonful of food was very near the student's mouth. He would then eat the food. Next, you would guide the student's hand so that the spoonful of food was a little further away from his mouth. You would continue to move backward in the response chain until the last response you taught would be picking up the spoon (the first response in the chain).
7. the response closest to the terminal reinforcer is taught first.
8. backward chaining
9. prompting, imitative, fading, shaping, reinforcing

Answers to Questions on Pages 131–132

1. gestural, physical
2. moment, moment
3. full contact with the student's
4. thumb, forefinger
5. within an inch of the student's hands
6. trial
7. the student stops resisting
8. continuously
9. end of the trial
10. respond

11. respond, avoidance learning
12. avoid, escape
13. physical guidance

Answers to Review Questions on Pages 133–134

1. behavior chain
2. stimulus-response
3. terminal
4. conditioned
5. discriminative
6. for the response it follows
7. S^D
8. S^r
9. S^R+
10. behavior chain
11. behavioral, forward chaining
12. last response in the chain last
13. backward chaining
14. first response in the chain is taught last
15. steps
16. graduated guidance
17. partial graduated guidance, shadowing
18. avoid or escape something unpleasant

Chapter 9

OBSERVING AND RECORDING BEHAVIORS

After reading this chapter, you will be able to:

1. Determine how and when to use frequency recording.

2. Determine how and when to use duration recording.

3. Determine how to use continuous recording.

4. Determine how to use interval recording.

5. Determine how to use time sampling.

Chapter 3 briefly discussed the critical role of observing behaviors. You found that to determine the student's operant level, it was necessary to engage in an observation of behavior called a baseline. As you now know, the baseline 1) allows the observer to objectively measure the occurrence of a behavior, and 2) helps the instructor determine the effectiveness of a program after intervention begins by providing information on how often the behavior occurred prior to instruction. To increase or decrease a behavior effectively you must first determine the student's baseline behavior.

This chapter covers frequency recording and duration recording. These recording methods will enable you to record the student observations necessary to measure behavior objectively. A sample data sheet is provided in Appendix C to help you collect data that will pinpoint variables that may be cuing inappropriate behaviors for your students.

These recording methods will allow you to objectively determine when one procedure is not working and thus identify when another procedure should be initiated. Observing and recording the behaviors that occur in your classroom provide accountability in increasing or decreasing behaviors.

FREQUENCY RECORDING

Frequency recording was introduced in Chapter 3 as the procedure that tells you the number of times a behavior occurs within a set period of time.

FREQUENCY RECORDING MEASURES THE NUMBER OF TIMES A STUDENT ENGAGES IN A SPECIFIC BEHAVIOR WITHIN A SET PERIOD OF TIME.

Frequency data are recorded when you want to know how many times a response occurs. If you are beginning to teach a child to feed himself with a spoon you will collect baseline data before your program begins. During this baseline period you will engage in frequency recording to count the number of times the student independently takes the spoon from the plate and inserts the spoon in his mouth. Data will also be collected during intervention to provide you with an objective record of the progress of the self-feeding program. If the data indicate an increase in your student's self-feeding behaviors, you have evidence that the program is a successful one. If the data indicate that the self-feeding behaviors are not increasing, you can then rewrite the feeding program, using a more detailed task analysis or using additional prompts, etc.

Frequency recording is also necessary when you are attempting to eliminate an undesirable behavior. For example, Ms. Dubois has been working with Ann, a student in her class who hits other children. Before beginning an intervention to decrease these behaviors, Ms. Dubois has selected the frequency recording method because she is interested in knowing the number of times Ann hits other students. Ms. Dubois must have this information before and after intervention so that she can objectively determine the success of her program. Ms. Dubois has constructed the following chart to tally the number of times Ann hits other students.

Recorder: Ms. Dubois
Student: Ann
Behaviors: Number of times Ann hits other children

Date	Time	Frequency of behavior
3/4/80	9 a.m.–3 p.m.	//// //
3/5/80	9 a.m.–3 p.m.	////
3/6/80	9 a.m.–3 p.m.	//// /
3/7/80	9 a.m.–3 p.m.	//// ///
3/8/80	9 a.m.–3 p.m.	////

After 5 days of data collection, Ms. Dubois was surprised that the frequency of Ann's hitting behavior was not higher. Ms. Dubois began an intervention procedure and after 1 week Ann was hitting one and sometimes two times per day. After comparing the data from before and after intervention, Ms. Dubois was pleased that the intervention procedure was indeed successful. She continued the procedure for 2 more weeks and eliminated Ann's inappropriate behavior.

Another example of frequency recording is recording several behaviors for one student. Last year when Shelly first entered Ms. Dubois' room, Shelly displayed several inappropriate behaviors. She would pull her classmates' hair, run out of the classroom, and hit Ms. Dubois when she walked past her desk.

To determine how often these behaviors occurred, Ms. Dubois constructed the following chart.

Recorder: Ms. Dubois	Date: 10-4-80
Student: Shelly	Location: Classroom
	Time: 9:00 a.m.–2:00 p.m.

Behavior	Number of times behavior occurs
1. Pulled hair	//
2. Runs out of classroom	### /
3. Hits Ms. Dubois	///

During the first day of observation, Ms. Dubois recorded that Shelly pulled hair twice, ran out of the classroom six times, and hit Ms. Dubois three times. Before beginning an intervention procedure, Ms. Dubois must collect baseline data for 4 more days. The data must also be collected at the same time each day and in the same general area.

Once you have decided to collect frequency data, following four steps will guide you through the frequency recording procedure.

Step 1: *Define the response that you wish to measure.* It must be an observable behavior that two people can agree upon.

Step 2: *Determine when and how often you will be able to observe and record the response.* It is imperative that the data be recorded during the same periods each day.

Step 3: *Devise a data sheet appropriate to your measure.* Several different data sheets are presented throughout this chapter. Select an appropriate one or create one designed to accommodate your specific needs.

Step 4: *Record the behavior consistently according to your definition and procedure.* If you decide to count the number of times a student hits other students, do not count the times he hits students one day and the number of times he attempts to hit students the next day. Once you have decided what behaviors you are going to count, you must be consistent.

Before continuing with this chapter, answer the following questions.

1. Mr. Sperrich would like to know how much time Billy spends rocking. Will he use frequency recording?
2. Ms. Strunk has a student in her room who pulls hair. She would like to know how many times this student pulls hair each morning. Will she use frequency recording?
3. Justin will begin a toilet training program next month. Before the toilet training program begins, his teacher, Ms. Evans, would like to know how many times he urinates in his pants each day. Should Ms. Evens use frequency recording to collect this information?
4. Wanda is collecting frequency data on her student, Nicole. Nicole hits her head against the wall. Before Wanda intervenes in this behavior, she wants to know how often it occurs. Follow the four steps outlined in this chapter and a) define the response Wanda would like to measure, b) determine how often she will be able to observe and record the response, c) devise a data sheet, and d) explain how she would consistently record the behaviors.

Turn to page 148 to check your answers.

DURATION RECORDING

The second method of recording behavior is duration recording. Duration recording is used to measure the amount of time a student engages in a specific behavior. When the duration procedure is used, the instructor records the time the prespecified behavior begins and ends.

DURATION RECORDING MEASURES THE TOTAL AMOUNT OF TIME A STUDENT SPENDS ENGAGING IN A PRESPECIFIED BEHAVIOR.

In duration recording you are measuring the amount of time during which the student's behavior occurs. The most effective and precise way to measure duration is with a stopwatch. If you do not have access to a stopwatch, a clock or wristwatch with a sweep-second hand may be used.

Individual response duration can be measured by clicking the watch on at the beginning of the behavior and clicking it off at the end of the behavior. You would then immediately record the minutes and seconds and reset the watch in preparation for the next behavior to occur. This method would be useful in recording the amount of time required for a student to feed or dress himself.

Total duration of responses is measured in the same way, but without resetting the watch after each response. This method could be used if you wanted to measure the total amount of time that a child engaged in autistic-like behavior. To further understand individual response duration and total duration of responses, following are some examples of how it is used.

Duration Chart

Student: Mary   Date: August 19, 1980
Recorder: Mr. Bagley   Location: Classroom
Behavior: Screaming

Total length of session	Time behavior started	Time behavior ended	Total duration	Percentage of time
9:00–9:30	9:15	9:22	7 minutes	23%
10:00–10:30	10:10	10:30	20 minutes	66%
11:00–11:30	11:00	11:14	14 minutes	46%
1:00–1:30	1:12	1:22	10 minutes	33%

Figure 1. Sample chart for use in duration recording.

Mr. Bagley uses individual response duration recording to determine the duration of Mary's screams. Mary is a student who creates a disturbance by screaming throughout the day. Mr. Bagley wants to determine the duration of each scream before beginning to eliminate this inappropriate behavior. He used the chart shown in Figure 1 to record the time the behavior began and the time it stopped, and then computed the total time Mary spent screaming.

With another student, Mr. Bagley wants to decrease the amount of time Horace spends rocking. Before Mr. Bagley can plan an intervention strategy for this procedure, he must determine the amount of time Horace spends rocking.

To establish a baseline for Horace's rocking behavior, Mr. Bagley measured the total duration of Horace's rocking behavior. He recorded the time the rocking started and stopped throughout the day. At the end of the day, he wanted to compute the percentage of time spent rocking for the 9:30–3:30 day. Look at the chart in Figure 2. Mr. Bagley neglected to compute the total percentage of time for Horace's rocking behavior. Compute the total percent and turn to page 149 to check your answer.

Remember, a percentage indicates what portion of time out of the total time was spent engaged in a specific behavior; that is,

Duration Chart

Student: Horace   Date: September 29, 1980
Recorder: Mr. Bagley   Location: Classroom
Behavior: Rocking

Total length of session	Time behavior started	Time behavior ended	Total duration	Percentage of time
	9:30	9:45	15 minutes	
9:30–3:30	9:48	9:50	2 minutes	
	10:11	10:25	14 minutes	
	10:40	10:50	10 minutes	
	11:20	11:29	9 minutes	
	11:45	12:00	15 minutes	
	12:15	12:30	15 minutes	
	1:46	1:50	4 minutes	
	2:15	2:38	23 minutes	
	2:40	3:20	40 minutes	
	3:29	3:30	1 minute	
Total length:			Total duration:	Total percentage:
360 min.			148	____

Figure 2. Sample chart for use in duration recording.

$$\frac{\text{Total time engaged in behavior}}{\text{Total possible time}} \times 100 = \underline{\hspace{1cm}} \%$$

Duration recording should be used when you want to know *how long* a response occurs. Whenever you want to know the total amount of time an individual spends engaged in a specified response, you record the duration of each response. Duration, like frequency, is usually measured in conjunction with a time interval—seconds, minutes, or hours. In both of the previous examples, Mr. Bagley recorded the duration of a behavior within a prespecified time limit.

Duration recording can be used to record behaviors that you want to increase or decrease. An example of a behavior you want to increase might be a child who eats very slowly. You would use duration recording to determine just how slowly he eats before you attempt to speed him up. Then you would observe and record the behaviors of both slow and fast eaters for a period of 5 days. These data would be used to determine a reasonable length of time for eating, perhaps 30 minutes. Next you would design an intervention to decrease the length of time required by the child to eat.

Before continuing with this chapter, answer the following questions.

1. Mr. Solomon would like to know how long it takes Sylvie to put on her blouse. Would he use duration recording?
2. Ms. McMurray would like to know how many times Kelly spits. Would she use duration recording?
3. Ms. Herty wants to decrease the amount of time Craig spends fighting. Will she use duration recording?

Turn to page 149 for the correct answers.

METHODS OF COLLECTION

Discussed below are three methods that you can use when collecting frequency and duration data. These methods are: 1) continuous recording, 2) interval recording, and 3) time sampling recording.

Continuous Recording

> CONTINUOUS RECORDING IS BASED ON RECORDING THE BEHAVIOR EACH AND EVERY TIME IT OCCURS FOR A GIVEN TIME PERIOD.

Continuous recording can be used when you want to know the frequency or the duration of a response. Mr. Lox wanted to know how many times a day Kenny hit his head with his fists. All day long, Mr. Lox kept a running account of the behaviors on the data sheet shown in Figure 3. At the end of each day, Mr. Lox added the number of tally marks to determine how many times Kenny hit his head during the day.

To measure the total duration of a behavior, record the times the behavior starts and stops throughout the day. Ms. Carlton wanted to measure the length of time Jason spent rocking. She recorded the data on her data sheet as shown in Figure 4.

| Student: Kenny | | | | Date: October 14, 1980 | | | | |
| Recorder: Mr. Lox | | | | Behavior: Hitting head with fists | | | | |

/////	-##-	///	//////////////	//////	-###-	-###-		
-###-	-###-	-###-	-###-	-###-	-###-	-###-	-###-	-###-
-###-	-###-	-###-	-###-	-###-	////	////	////////	
/////	/////	//	-###-	/////////	////	////////////		

Figure 3. Sample data sheet for continuous recording.

Sometimes, however, you may not have enough time to collect data continuously. If that is the case, you may want to use interval recording or time sampling recording.

Interval Recording
The second method of observing and recording behaviors is interval recording. During interval recording, you divide the observation period into continuous intervals and record the number of times a specific behavior occurs within each interval. You will use the interval recording method when you want a running record of the occurrence or non-occurrence of a behavior. Interval recording can be used for measuring both the frequency and the duration of a behavior.

INTERVAL RECORDING IS BASED ON COUNTING
THE NUMBER OF TIMES A PRESPECIFIED BEHAVIOR
OCCURS WITHIN A SERIES OF TIMED INTERVALS.

| Student: Jason | Date: August 15, 1980 |
| Recorder: Ms. Carlton | Behavior: Rocking |

8:30– 8:35 a.m.	5 minutes
8:40– 8:42 a.m.	2 minutes
10:15–10:50 a.m.	35 minutes
11:20–11:22 a.m.	2 minutes
11:30–12:00 noon	30 minutes
1:00– 1:19 p.m.	19 minutes
1:33– 1:49 p.m.	16 minutes
2:16– 2:38 p.m.	22 minutes
2:40– 2:44 p.m.	4 minutes
3:00– 4:30 p.m.	90 minutes
4:35– 6:00 p.m.	85 minutes
7:00– 7:15 p.m.	15 minutes
7:22– 7:25 p.m.	3 minutes
7:45– 7:50 p.m.	15 minutes
Total duration	343 minutes

Figure 4. Sample data sheet for continuous recording.

Student: Brian   Date: July 21, 1980
Recorder: Mr. Baxter   Location: Mr. Baxter's classroom
Behavior: Pulls his lip   Time: 11:00 a.m.–11:10 a.m.

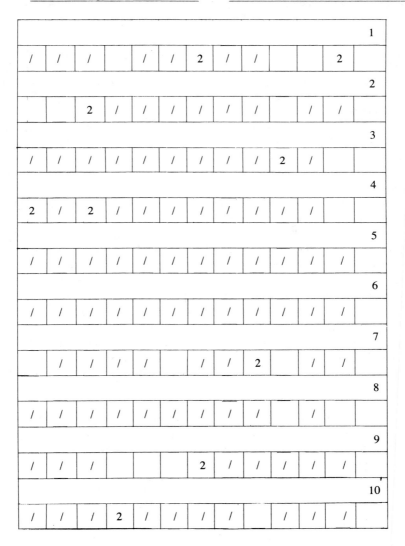

Figure 5. Sample data sheet for interval recording.

For example, Brian pulls at his lower lip all day long. He doesn't injure himself, but he does pull the lip often enough to permit a steady flow of saliva to accumulate on his chin. The saliva irritates the skin and the skin is red and chapped. Brian's teacher, Mr. Baxter, would like to eliminate this inappropriate behavior. Since he must first know how often it occurs, he uses an interval recording method to count the number of times Brian pulls his lip. Mr. Baxter used the data sheet shown in Figure 5 to record at 5-second intervals within the 10 minute sample.

Each block on the data sheet indicates a 5-second interval and each row contains 12 blocks, corresponding to 1 minute of observation time. Mr. Baxter has recorded the number of times Brian pulls his lip for 10 minutes.

Mr. Baxter used a stopwatch to keep track of the intervals on his data sheet. If Brian pulled his lip before an interval started and was still pulling it when the interval started, Mr. Baxter recorded it during the new interval. Whenever a behavior occurs during an interval, even if the behavior began before the interval started, a mark is recorded in the square for the corresponding interval. If a 5-second interval passes without Brian's pulling his lip, Mr. Baxter would have left the square for that interval blank.

Some behaviors you observe will occur more frequently than Brian's lip pulling and other behaviors will occur less frequently. Before you begin interval recording, you must determine how often the behavior occurs. Once you know how often the behavior occurs, you can then determine the size of the intervals. The interval of time should be long enough to allow you to record and short enough to show separate occurrences of the behavior. If a behavior stops and starts several times during each interval, the interval is too long.

Interval recording should be used: 1) when you are interested in the number of times the behavior occurs, 2) when you want to know how often it occurs, and 3) when the number of behaviors is not low enough to use the tally method.

Time Sampling Recording

The third method of observing and recording behavior is time sampling recording. As you know, it will not always be possible for you to observe a student(s) for long periods of time. When observational time is limited, time sampling is very useful.

> TIME SAMPLING IS BASED ON COUNTING THE NUMBER OF TIMES A PRESPECIFIED BEHAVIOR OCCURS AT THE END OF A SPECIFIED INTERVAL OF TIME.

In time sampling, you simply observe the student at fixed intervals, for a specified period of time. You may observe the student for 30 seconds every 5 minutes or you may observe for 1 minute at the end of a 1-hour interval. You then record whether or not the behavior occurred. The behavior can be expressed as a percentage, i.e., the number of instances in which the behavior was observed divided by the number of observations, times 100. Thus, rather than counting each instance of the behavior, you simply determine the percentage of time the behavior occurs. Time sampling is especially useful when the operant level of the behavior is very high (as in self-stimulatory behavior, for example (see Chapter 3)).

However, percentage should be avoided whenever possible. Frequency and rate are much better indicators of behavior. Any time you change data into a percentage, you lose some essential data characteristics. To say that a student banged his head 50% of the time and had 5 head bangs is remarkably different from the student who banged her head 50% of the time and had a count of 500 head bangs.

Before continuing with this chapter, determine which recording technique—continuous, interval, or time sampling recording—was used in the situations below.

1. Mr. Jamison counted the number of times Shelly bit her arm throughout the day.
2. Data were collected on William for 15 minutes each hour.
3. Susan screamed throughout the day. At the end of each half hour, her mother recorded the duration of the scream within a 2-minute interval.
4. Mr. Smith wanted to know how long it took his student Simon to eat his three meals. At breakfast, lunch, and dinner Mr. Smith recorded duration data. He recorded the time it took Simon to eat the three individual meals.
5. Kathleen recorded the number of times Sarah wet her pants during Sarah's waking hours.

Answers are on page 149.

SUMMARY

It is important to collect data because the information gathered: 1) allows you to objectively measure the occurrence of a behavior, and 2) helps you determine the effectiveness of a program after intervention begins by providing information on how often the behavior occurs prior to and after instruction.

There are basically two types of recording: frequency recording, and duration recording. Frequency recording is based on counting the number of times a student engages in a specific behavior within a set period of time. Duration recording is based on measuring the total amount of time the student spends engaging in a prespecified behavior.

Three methods are employed to collect frequency and duration data. The methods are: 1) continuous recording, 2) interval recording, and 3) time sampling recording. Continuous recording is based on recording the behavior each and every time it occurs throughout a given time period. Interval recording is based on counting the number of times a prespecified behavior occurs within a series of timed intervals. And time sampling is based on counting the number of times a prespecified behavior occurs at the end of a specified interval of time.

REVIEW QUESTIONS

1. Data collection allows you to measure _____.
2. Two types of recording data are f_____ recording and d_____ recording.
3. Three methods of collecting these data are c_____ recording, i_____ recording, and t_____ _____ recording.
4. When you record the behavior each and every time it occurs, you are using _____ _____.
5. When you count the number of times a prespecified behavior occurs within a series of timed intervals, you are using _____ _____.
6. When you count the number of times a prespecified behavior occurs at the end of a specified interval of time, you are using _____ _____ _____.

Answers are on page 149.

SUGGESTED READINGS

Arrington, R. E. Time-sampling in studies of social behavior: A critical review of techniques and results with research suggestions. *Psychological Bulletin,* 1943, *40,* 81–124.

Bachrach, A. J. (ed.). *Experimental foundations of clinical psychology.* New York: Basic Books, 1962.

Bijou, S. W., & Baer, D. M. The laboratory experimental study of child behavior. In P. H. Mussen (ed.), *Handbook of research methods in child development.* New York: John Wiley & Sons, 1960.

Cozley, P. C. *Methods in behavioral research.* Palo Alto, CA: Mayfield, 1977.

Sanders, R. M., Hopkins, B. L., & Walker, M. B. An inexpensive method for making data records of complex behaviors. *Journal of Applied Behavior Analysis,* 1969, 221.

Underwood, B. J. *Psychological research.* New York: Appleton-Century-Crofts, 1957.

Wright, H. F. Observational child study. In: P. H. Mussen (ed.), *Handbook of research methods in child development.* New York: John Wiley & Sons, 1960.

ANSWERS TO CHAPTER QUESTIONS

Answers to Questions on Page 140

1. No. Frequency recording is used to determine the number of times, not the amount of time, a behavior occurs.
2. Yes. Frequency recording is used to determine the number of times a response (pulling hair) occurs, and it is measured in conjunction with a time interval (each morning).
3. Yes. Frequency recording is used to determine the number of times a response (wetting pants) occurs, and it is measured in conjunction with a time interval (each day).

4. a. head banging
   b. Any response similar to chapter examples is correct.
   c. Any response similar to chapter examples is correct.
   d. Every time Nicole hits her head against the wall, Wanda will place a hash mark on the data sheet.

Answer to Question on Page 142
41%

Answers to Questions on Page 143
1. Yes. Duration recording is used to measure the length of time a student spends engaging in a prespecified behavior (putting on blouse).
2. No. Duration recording is used to measure the length of time, not the number of times, a student spends engaging in a prespecified behavior.
3. Yes. Duration recording is used to measure the length of time a student spends engaging in a prespecified behavior (fighting).

Answers to Questions on Page 147
1. continuous recording
2. interval recording
3. time sampling recording
4. continuous recording
5. continuous recording

Answers to Review Questions on Page 148
1. the occurrence of a behavior
2. frequency, duration
3. continuous, interval, time sampling
4. continuous recording
5. interval recording
6. time sampling recording

Part II

Using the Least Restrictive Environment to Eliminate Inappropriate Behaviors

Chapter 10

DECREASING INAPPROPRIATE BEHAVIORS
Reinforcement Procedures

After reading this chapter, you will be able to:

1. Define the Least Restrictive Model of Treatment.

2. List five steps to follow when using the Least Restrictive Model of Treatment.

3. Define and give an example of DRO (differential reinforcement of other behavior).

4. List the advantages and disadvantages of DRO.

5. Define and give an example of DRA (differential reinforcement of appropriate behavior).

6. List the advantage and disadvantages of DRA.

7. Define and give an example of DRI (differential reinforcement of incompatible behavior).

8. List the advantage and disadvantage of DRI.

9. List three rules to follow when designing a program to reduce a misbehavior.

10. Name the cardinal rule for using a reinforcement procedure to decrease behavior.

11. Describe the most important rule to follow in using DRO.

12. Describe the most important rule to follow in using DRA.

13. Describe the most important rule to follow in using DRI.

In the next four chapters, you will learn about a variety of behaviorally based procedures for decreasing inappropriate behaviors. The procedures are presented according to the Least Restrictive Model of Treatment, which was designed to protect retarded persons' civil liberties. It is important that this model be understood before the procedures are actually used in the classroom.

THE LEAST RESTRICTIVE MODEL OF TREATMENT

The Least Restrictive Model of Treatment is more than just a list of behaviorally based treatment procedures for decreasing the inappropriate behavior of retarded persons. The Least Restrictive Model also includes treatment procedures for increasing appropriate behaviors. It includes not only treatment procedures, but also environmental conditions. Using only aversive consequences raises serious legal questions; therefore, before you attempt to eliminate undesirable behavior with an aversive procedure, you should first use those techniques in which reinforcing consequences are applied. In the Least Restrictive Model, the procedures are ranked according to their aversiveness, severity, and intrusiveness, beginning with the procedures that are the least aversive and ending with those that are the most aversive. The purpose of the model and this ranking is to ensure that individuals who work with retarded persons use only those procedures that are necessary and sufficient to eliminate a misbehavior. The model dictates that we cannot use a more aversive procedure until we have demonstrated that a less aversive procedure was ineffective. Thus, the model guarantees that the least restrictive treatment, i.e., least restrictive of the retarded person's rights, will always be tried first whenever an attempt is made to decrease the person's misbehavior.

The model was developed just a few years ago as one of the by-products of litigation against institutions for retarded persons. During the course of these lawsuits, it was determined that a number of abuses of retarded persons' civil liberties had occurred. To correct these abuses, some of the following major judicial rulings emerged: 1) retarded persons are entitled, as is everyone, to live in the least restrictive environment, 2) humane and ethically defensible treatment or educational programs must be developed and implemented for retarded persons, and 3) a least restrictive treatment model must be followed when attempts are made to decrease a retarded person's inappropriate misbehavior. As an educator of retarded persons, you are primarily concerned with the last two points. You may recognize that point 2 was the forerunner of Public Law 94-142 (Education for All Handicapped Children Act) which mandates that all persons of school age are entitled to an education regardless of their handicap.

Point 3 is no less important to you. It is imperative that you understand and follow the Least Restrictive Treatment Model in your classroom. Failure to do so could make you subject to a lawsuit if, for example, a parent were to sue you. However, if you correctly follow the Least Restrictive Model of Treatment, and have administrative approval of those procedures utilizing aversive consequences, you will be following the mandate of Public Law 94-142.

1. Take baseline data on the student's misbehavior (see Chapter 3).
2. Choose the least restrictive behavioral treatment procedure and use it for the misbehavior.
3. Collect accurate, reliable data to determine whether the procedure is effective (see Chapter 9).
4. Only select a more restrictive procedure if your treatment data indicate that the previous procedure was ineffective (the minimum duration for trying a procedure should be about 7 to 10 days).
5. When punishment procedures are being considered, always obtain written permission from the student's parents and the school administrator before you implement such procedures. The message is: *Document what you are doing*.

To summarize, when attempting to decrease inappropriate behavior, use the least restrictive treatment procedure first, and if it is ineffective, move to the next procedure and so forth up through the list of procedures.

Before proceeding, answer the following questions.

1. The ranking of procedures according to their aversiveness is the _____ _____.
2. The Least Restrictive Model of Treatment is a by-product of litigation against institutions for _____.
3. The five steps to follow in using the Least Restrictive Model of Treatment are:
   a. Take _____ on the student's behavior.
   b. Choose the _____ and use it for the misbehavior.
   c. Collect accurate, r_____ _____.
   d. Only select a more restrictive procedure if the treatment data indicates that the _____.
   e. When considering the use of a punishment procedure, always obtain written permission from the student's p_____ and the s_____ a_____ before you implement such a procedure.

Answers are on page 166.

REINFORCEMENT PROCEDURES FOR DECREASING BEHAVIOR

The least restrictive of all procedures for decreasing behavior involves the use of reinforcement of positive consequences. These procedures are often called reductive procedures because they are designed to decrease or reduce behavior. It is highly unlikely that you would ever encounter any legal problems as a result of using reinforcement procedures.

There are three reinforcement procedures that can be used to decrease behavior. They are:

1. DRO (differential reinforcement of other behavior)
2. DRA (differential reinforcement of appropriate behavior)
3. DRI (differential reinforcement of incompatible behavior)

A fourth reinforcement procedure, DRL (differential reinforcement of low rates), requires great expertise and will not be discussed.

DRO (Differential Reinforcement of Other Behavior)

DRO (DIFFERENTIAL REINFORCEMENT OF OTHER BEHAVIOR) IS A PROCEDURE IN WHICH A REINFORCER IS GIVEN AT THE END OF A SPECIFIED PERIOD OF TIME PROVIDED THAT A PRESPECIFIED MISBEHAVIOR HAS NOT OCCURRED DURING THE SPECIFIED INTERVAL.

DRO requires data collection procedures not only on the prespecified behavior to decrease, but on the other behaviors that are reinforced. In this way you can determine whether or not you are shaping up inappropriate behaviors or rate of behaviors.

DRO is perhaps the simplest of all reductive procedures. In a DRO procedure, you are *reinforcing the absence of the misbehavior*. The procedure is so simple because all you must determine is whether or not the misbehavior occurred. The following example illustrates the correct use of a DRO procedure.

Bobby is a 10-year-old severely retarded boy who engages in self-abusive behavior. He self-abuses by repeatedly striking the sides of his head with his fists throughout the school day. His teacher, Ms. Santos, decides to use a DRO procedure to reduce Bobby's self-abuse. Ms. Santos's first task is to determine how often Bobby hits himself. After conducting a brief, 3-day baseline, Ms. Santos finds that Bobby hits himself on the average of about once every 30 seconds. Based on this information, Ms. Santos makes five important decisions: 1) she will set the DRO interval at 15 seconds, 2) she will only use the DRO procedure with Bobby during a 1-hour period each day, 3) the session will be one-to-one and will be conducted behind a partition in the classroom, 4) a variety of objects will be made available to Bobby during the session, and 5) she will select Bobby's most preferred reinforcer, carrot sticks, as the reinforcer for non-hitting.

During the sessions, Ms. Santos is seated at a table across from Bobby. Every time 15 seconds elapses without Bobby having hit himself, Ms. Santos says, "Good, Bobby, you did not hit yourself," and places a piece of carrot in Bobby's mouth. Once Bobby has not hit himself for several days under the 15-second DRO procedure, Ms. Santos increases the DRO interval to 30 seconds. When several days have passed without any hits, Ms. Santos increases the

DRO interval to 1 minute. She continues to increase the DRO interval until Bobby can go 15 minutes without hitting himself. At that point, she begins using the 15-minute DRO procedure throughout the 6-hour school day.

Ms. Santos's use of the DRO procedure was perfect, no doubt, because she carefully planned how she would use the procedure. The five decisions she made were extremely important in making the program a success. Let's examine why.

Ms. Santos's first decision followed the cardinal rule in using a DRO procedure: *Always select a DRO interval that is shorter than the interval between occurrences of the prespecified behavior.* Ms. Santos selected 15 seconds as the DRO interval because Bobby normally hit himself every 30 seconds. She thus ensured that the DRO interval was shorter than the interval between hits.

Her next three decisions followed the general rules necessary to obtain programmatic consistency. These general rules are:

1. *Select a time period each day that can be completely devoted to the student's program.* Ms. Santos limited the DRO program to 1 hour per day, ensuring that the program would be consistent since she could afford to devote that much time to Bobby's program.
2. *Have one person take responsibility for the program.* Ms. Santos used a one-to-one session approach, with herself as the only reinforcing agent. By doing this, she eliminated the possibility that there would be any inconsistencies across reinforcing agents.
3. *Create activities that are as incompatible as possible with the inappropriate behavior.* Bobby was provided with a variety of objects during the session. The distraction function of these objects provided a greater likelihood that Bobby could go for 15 seconds without hitting himself.

Ms. Santos's fifth and final decision followed one of the cardinal rules in using a reinforcement procedure: *Always select the most preferred (powerful) reinforcer available.* She selected carrot sticks as the reinforcer because they are Bobby's favorite food and would therefore ensure that Bobby's motivation to not hit himself would be as great as possible. You will see the application of this reinforcement rule and the rules for programmatic consistency throughout the remaining chapters of this book.

The advantages of using a DRO procedure include:

1. It is an easy procedure to use. All you must do is determine whether or not the misbehavior occurred.
2. You are reinforcing other appropriate behaviors. Therefore you are not working directly on the inappropriate behavior.

However, there are two disadvantages associated with using a DRO procedure:

1. The procedure is not designed to deliberately teach or increase any appropriate behaviors.
2. In using DRO, you are committed to reinforcing the student at the end of the DRO interval provided that the misbehavior has not occurred. In doing so, you run the risk of reinforcing another type of inappropriate behavior. For example, consider the following. Bobby had gone 15 seconds without hitting himself. Just as Ms. Santos places the carrot in Bobby's mouth, Bobby throws an object. What has Ms. Santos reinforced? She just reinforced object throwing which is clearly an inappropriate behavior. Regardless of whether or not object throwing is less inappropriate than self-abuse, it is undesirable. Thus, we see one of the inherent limitations of the DRO procedure. To overcome this limitation, it is best *to specify any other behaviors that will not be followed by a reinforcer*. In other words, it is better to let a DRO interval pass without delivering a reinforcer than to reinforce an inappropriate behavior.

Before continuing this chapter, answer the following questions.

1. After taking a baseline, Ms. Washington found that Shari bites her hand every 20 seconds. Ms. Washington should set the DRO interval at _____.
2. Mr. Rogers is using a DRO procedure of 15 minutes to treat David's saliva smearing. At the end of the 15-minute interval, David rips his shirt just as Mr. Rogers is about to give him an edible reinforcer and praise him for not smearing during the interval. Should Mr. Rogers reinforce David? Why?
3. Ms. Carson, the mother of one of your students, asks you to help design a home program for her daughter. What three general rules would you tell her to follow to ensure programmatic consistency?
4. You would like Ms. Carson to try a DRO procedure at home. Accordingly, you will tell her about the advantages and disadvantages of the procedure. What two advantages will you list? What two disadvantages will you caution her about?
5. Don, a screamer, likes physical contact with an instructor more than any kind of edible reinforcer or praise. If you decided to use a DRO procedure to reduce Don's screaming, what would you use as a reinforcer? Why?

Answers are on page 166.

DRA (Differential Reinforcement of Appropriate Behavior)

> DRA (DIFFERENTIAL REINFORCEMENT OF APPROPRIATE BEHAVIOR) IS A PROCEDURE IN WHICH A REINFORCER IS GIVEN FOLLOWING THE PERFORMANCE OF A PRESPECIFIED APPROPRIATE BEHAVIOR.

The DRA (differential reinforcement of appropriate behavior) procedure offers the instructor more control than a DRO procedure because it specifies an appropriate behavior to be increased by reinforcement. As a result, the first disadvantage of DRO—that appropriate behaviors are not deliberately being increased—is eliminated. Furthermore, DRA minimizes the second disadvantage of DRO since there is almost no chance that an inappropriate behavior will be increased.

The rationale for using a DRA procedure to decrease behavior is that increasing an appropriate behavior may produce a simultaneous decrease in the targeted inappropriate behavior. In essence, the instructor is hoping to increase the student's performance of the appropriate behavior to a point where the student has little, if any, time to perform the inappropriate behavior. The following example illustrates the correct use of a DRA procedure.

Ms. Santos has decided to use a DRA procedure to reduce Bobby's self-abuse. After taking a baseline of Bobby's hitting, Ms. Santos decides that a good behavior to increase would be Bobby's eye contact. She decides to use eye contact because Bobby would occasionally look at someone when instructed to do so. Ms. Santos arranges to give Bobby four 15-minute eye contact training sessions per day. The training will be one-to-one and will be conducted at a table behind a partition. Ms. Santos will use bite-size bits of carrot as the reinforcer for eye contact. She will not bring any objects into the training area because they might distract Bobby during the training sessions (see Chapter 3).

During the sessions, Ms. Santos sits directly across the table from Bobby. She takes a piece of carrot out of a bowl located to her right (and out of Bobby's reach) and moves the carrot toward her eye. As Bobby begins tracking the carrot with his eyes, Ms. Santos says, just as the carrot reaches her eye, "Bobby, look at me." When Bobby's eyes make brief contact with her eyes, Ms. Santos says, "Good, Bobby, you looked at me," and places the carrot in Bobby's mouth. Ms. Santos then lightly strokes the side of Bobby's face and says once again, "Good, Bobby, you looked at me." She then records Bobby's correct response after which she begins another trial. Over time, she finds that Bobby's rate of looking at her has increased and that Bobby's frequency of hitting his head has decreased. Eventually, Ms. Santos plans to require Bobby to look at her for a full 2 seconds when instructed to do so and to fade the use of the carrot near her eyes (see Chapter 7). Later, she will add other educational activities to the sessions as well as using these activities during the entire school day.

Ms. Santos used the DRA procedure quite effectively and it accomplished its intended purpose: Bobby's eye contact increased and his self-hitting decreased. Ms. Santos followed the three rules necessary to ensure the success of any program designed to decrease an inappropriate behavior, one of the rules for using a reinforcement procedure (i.e., select a powerful reinforcer), and finally the cardinal rule when using a DRA procedure: *Always select a behavior to increase that the student already performs at a low rate* (data must be taken). This, of course, is why Ms. Santos chose eye contact as the behavior to increase.

DRA is the procedure we use whenever we wish to increase a behavior regardless of whether or not any misbehaviors are occurring. DRA is simply the use of reinforcers to increase a behavior. During its use, most other behaviors, either appropriate or inappropriate, will usually decrease in frequency because of the increase in frequency of the reinforced behavior.

The advantage of using a DRA procedure to decrease a misbehavior is that an appropriate behavior is increased. This is a major advantage because it allows the instructor to incorporate a part of the student's educational program into a program to decrease a misbehavior. However, this may not always be the case as we shall see in our discussion of the disadvantages of DRA.

There are two disadvantages associated with the use of DRA.

1. We are not working directly on the misbehavior.
2. The misbehavior can still occur during the DRA program. For example, Bobby could still hit himself during the eye contact training sessions. In fact, he could hit himself and look at Ms. Santos simultaneously. (If this happened, Ms. Santos should not reinforce the eye contact, but rather ignore the hit, wait for the hitting to stop, and then resume the eye contact training. Otherwise, she would run the risk of having reinforced hitting.)

What can the instructor do to remedy these inherent disadvantages of DRA? The answer can be found in the discussion of our third and final reinforcement procedure for reducing a misbehavior.

Before continuing this chapter, answer the following questions.

1. Ms. Goldstein would like to use a DRA procedure with Terri, who rocks almost constantly. Terri does respond to simple commands such as ''Look at me'' and ''Hand me the (object).'' Ms. Goldstein also has been considering teaching Terri to point to objects. She is undecided as to which appropriate behavior she should choose to reinforce. Which behavior should she pick?
2. You would like Ms. Carson to try a DRA procedure at home with her daughter. What will you tell her is the advantage of the procedure? What two disadvantages will you describe?
3. Mr. Hendry has been reinforcing John every 10 minutes for not belching. Although this program has been successful, Mr. Hendry is concerned that John is not displaying enough appropriate behaviors. What could Mr. Hendry do to answer this concern? What type of procedure was he using initially?

Answers are on page 166.

DRI (Differential Reinforcement of Incompatible Behavior)

DRI (DIFFERENTIAL REINFORCEMENT OF INCOM-
PATIBLE BEHAVIOR) IS A PROCEDURE IN WHICH A
REINFORCER IS GIVEN FOLLOWING THE PERFOR-

MANCE OF A PRESPECIFIED BEHAVIOR THAT IS
PHYSICALLY AND FUNCTIONALLY INCOMPATIBLE
WITH THE TARGETED INAPPROPRIATE BEHAVIOR.

The DRI procedure (differential reinforcement of incompatible behavior) offers the instructor the greatest reinforcement control over the inappropriate behavior. This control comes from the fact that the appropriate and inappropriate behaviors cannot occur simultaneously because they are physically and functionally incompatible.

The rationale for using a DRI procedure is that increasing the targeted incompatible appropriate behavior guarantees that the inappropriate behavior will decrease in frequency. Under ideal conditions, there should be no opportunity for the student to perform the inappropriate behavior if the appropriate behavior occurs often enough. The following example illustrates the correct use of a DRI procedure.

Ms. Santos has decided to use a DRI procedure to reduce Bobby's self-abuse. After taking a baseline of Bobby's hitting, she decides that the best incompatible behavior to reinforce would be one that kept Bobby's hands on the table and away from his head. She selects the behavior of having Bobby scribble on a piece of paper because Bobby has performed this behavior in the past. Ms. Santos plans to have Bobby hold the paper on the table with the palm of his left hand and scribble on the paper with a crayon in his right hand. To obtain a reinforcer, both of Bobby's hands must be in contact with the paper. Ms. Santos arranges to give Bobby four 15-minute coloring sessions behind a partition with just the two of them present. No other materials will be present in the area where the sessions are to be conducted. Bits of carrot will be used to reinforce the scribbling.

During the sessions, Ms. Santos sits beside Bobby. She begins by guiding Bobby's left hand to the paper and his right hand in a scribbling or coloring motion. Within a second or two, Ms. Santos pops a carrot into Bobby's mouth, simultaneously says, "Good coloring, Bobby," and then caresses Bobby's cheek as she repeats the phrase. Over time, Ms. Santos increases the duration between reinforcers from 3 seconds to 5 seconds to 10 seconds, etc., until Bobby colors for 5 minutes between reinforcers. Since Ms. Santos paced Bobby very carefully, only a few head hits occurred.

When Bobby is coloring for 5 minutes in order to receive a reinforcer, Ms. Santos begins introducing new activities into the session that require Bobby to use both his hands. She begins reinforcing Bobby every few seconds for performing these activities and then gradually increases the interval between reinforcers as she had done for the scribbling. After Bobby performs a variety of incompatible activities for a reinforcer every 5 minutes, Ms. Santos returns Bobby to the classroom proper where the activities will be scheduled to occur all day. After a few days in which no hitting occurs in the classroom, Ms. Santos plans to schedule some activities for Bobby that do not have to be incompatible with his hitting.

Ms. Santos did an excellent job of conducting the DRI procedure. Bobby's hitting disappeared quickly because he had learned that, when he did hit, he relinquished the opportunity to be reinforced because his hands had left the table. Ms. Santos followed all the rules for ensuring that a reinforcement procedure successfully increased an appropriate behavior and decreased an inappropriate behavior as a result. And, she followed the rule in using the DRI procedure: *Always select a behavior to increase that is physically and functionally incompatible with the misbehavior and that the student already performs.*

The major advantage of DRI is that the inappropriate behavior cannot occur when the incompatible behavior is occurring. This aspect of DRI provides the instructor with the highest possible reinforcement control over the misbehavior since, if the reinforcer is powerful enough and the response requirement for achieving it is reasonable, there is little motivation for the student to perform the misbehavior.

The major disadvantage of using a DRI procedure is that it is sometimes difficult to find an appropriate, incompatible behavior. Finding a behavior that is incompatible with the inappropriate behavior is difficult enough, but finding one that is also appropriate can require a good deal of thought and creativity. For example, consider the kinds of incompatible behaviors that could have been selected for Bobby. Several possibilities include having Bobby sit on his hands. keeping his hands in his pockets, keeping his hands flat on the table, keeping his hands in his lap, interlocking his fingers and keeping his hands on the table, or holding onto an object with both hands. All of these behaviors are incompatible with hitting his head with his hands, yet none would be appropriate for Bobby to perform for very long. If he performed them for long periods, he would not be learning anything that would raise his level of functioning. However, the incompatible behavior that was selected, scribbling, offers the advantage of increasing Bobby's motor coordination while it is developmentally appropriate. *Remember, when using DRI, it is important to select a behavior not only for its incompatibility with the misbehavior but also for its social and educational appropriateness.* Sometimes this is difficult to do, but it is certainly a worthy goal.

Before continuing this chapter, answer the following questions.

1. Below is a list of incompatible behaviors that could be reinforced in a DRI procedure. Match the incompatible behaviors on the right to the inappropriate behaviors on the left.

1. ____hand in mouth	a. placing pegs in pegboard
2. ____shouting	b. urinating in the toilet
3. ____running around the room	c. hand on table
4. ____urinating on the floor	d. keeping clothing on

5. ____removing clothing   e. whispering
6. ____throwing pegs   f. sitting in a chair

2. You believe that a DRI procedure is appropriate for Ms. Carson to use at home with her daughter. What will you tell her is the advantage of a DRI procedure? What disadvantage will you describe?
3. Which of the three reinforcement procedures would be most appropriate to use in treating self-abusive behavior?

Answers are on page 166.

Below are some examples of the use of reinforcement procedures to decrease a behavior. Please identify which reinforcement procedure is being used.

____1. A child is allowed to watch TV as long as his thumb stays out of his mouth.
____2. Jenny is frequently out of her seat. Her teacher begins a program in which she reinforces Jenny for remaining in her seat.
____3. Paul picks at his face with his fingernails. His teacher begins reinforcing Paul for correctly identifying pictures of common objects.
____4. Josie, a screamer, is reinforced every 10 seconds for being quiet.
____5. Dorothy receives a sip of cola every 2 minutes if she has not removed her clothes.
____6. Linda, a drooler, is reinforced every 15 seconds for working on a puzzle.

Answers are found on page 167.

SUMMARY

The Least Restrictive Model of Treatment evolved out of litigation to correct the abuses by institutions of retarded persons' civil rights. The guidelines for following the model are: 1) take baseline data on the student's misbehavior, 2) choose the least restrictive treatment procedure, 3) collect accurate data to determine whether the procedure is effective, 4) only select a more restrictive procedure if your data indicate that the previous procedure was ineffective, and 5) when punishment procedures are being considered, always obtain written permission from the student's parents and the school administrator before implementing such procedures.

There are three reinforcement procedures that can be used for decreasing an inappropriate behavior: DRO (differential reinforcement of other behavior), DRA (differential reinforcement of appropriate behavior), and DRI (differential reinforcement of incompatible behavior). All three involve little, if any, restriction of the retarded student's rights.

DRO is a procedure in which the absence of misbehavior is reinforced following a specified interval of time. The DRO interval must always be a shorter interval than the average interval of the misbehavior. DRO is the simplest reinforcement procedure, and it works directly on the misbehavior; however, it does not increase an appropriate behavior, and an inappropriate behavior may be inadvertently reinforced.

DRA is a procedure in which a specific appropriate behavior, which the student already performs, is reinforced. DRA permits the instructor to increase an appropriate behavior; however, it does not work directly on the misbehavior and does not prevent the misbehavior from occurring.

DRI is a procedure in which a behavior is reinforced that is physically and functionally incompatible with the inappropriate behavior. When using DRI, it is very important to select an incompatible behavior that is socially and educationally appropriate and that the student already performs. DRI offers the tightest reinforcement control of the three reinforcement procedures because the misbehavior and appropriate behavior cannot occur simultaneously. When using reinforcement procedures, the most powerful reinforcer possible must be used.

The three general rules to follow in designing any program to decrease behavior are: 1) select a time period that can be devoted exclusively to the program, 2) have one person take programmatic responsibility, and 3) in general, create activities that are incompatible with the inappropriate behavior.

REVIEW QUESTIONS

1. A procedure in which you reinforce the absence of the misbehavior is _____.

2. The cardinal rule in using DRO is that the DRO interval must always be shorter than the interval between occurrences of _____.

3. One advantage of a DRO procedure is that it is so _____.

4. A second advantage of DRO is that you are reinforcing other behaviors; therefore, you are not _____.

5. The two disadvantages of a DRO procedure are: 1) it does not teach any appropriate behaviors, and 2) _____.

6. To overcome the second disadvantage of DRO, it is best to specify any behavior that will not be followed by _____.

7. The procedure used when a reinforcer is given following the performance of a prespecified appropriate behavior is _____.

8. By increasing an appropriate behavior with a DRA procedure, the instructor hopes that the student will have less time to perform the _____ behavior.

9. The advantage of a DRA procedure is that a specific _____ behavior is increased. This allows us to incorporate a part of the student's educational program into a program to decrease inappropriate behavior.

10. One disadvantage of DRA is that the inappropriate behavior can still occur. A second disadvantage is that the procedure does not work _____.

11. A procedure where a reinforcer is given following the performance of a

prespecified behavior that is physically and functionally incompatible with the inappropriate behavior is _____.

12. The advantage of a DRI procedure is that the inappropriate behavior cannot occur when the _____.

13. The disadvantage of DRI is that it is often difficult to find an _____ appropriate behavior that is socially and educationally relevant.

14. The three general rules to follow in designing a program to reduce behavior are: 1) select a _____ period that can be devoted exclusively to the program, 2) have one _____ take responsibility for the program, and 3) in general, create activities that are _____ with the inappropriate behavior.

15. The rule for using any reinforcement procedure to decrease behavior is to always select the most powerful _____.

16. The rule in using DRA is to always select a behavior to increase that the student already _____.

17. The rule in using DRI is to always select an _____ behavior to increase that the student already _____.

Answers to questions are on page 167.

SUGGESTED READINGS

Allen, K. E., Hart, B. M., Buell, J. S., Harris, P. R., & Wolf, M. M. Effects of social reinforcement on isolate behavior of a nursery school child. In: M. P. Ullmann & L. Krasner (eds.), *Case studies in behavior modification,* pp. 307–312. New York: Holt, Rinehart & Winston, 1965.

Flavell, J. E. Reduction of stereotypes by reinforcement of toy play. *Mental Retardation,* 1973, *11*(2), 21–23.

Foxx, R. M. Weight reduction in an obese retarded adolescent through social reinforcement. *Mental Retardation,* 1972, *10,* 21–23.

Frankel, F., Moss, B., Schofield, S., & Simmons, J. Q. Case study: Use of differential reinforcement to suppress self-injurious and aggressive behavior. *Psychological Reports,* 1976, (Dsc. Vol.) *39*(3 Pt. 1), 843–849.

Martinez, S. S. Comparison of extinction, DRO 0-sec. and DRO 6-sec. in the elimination of imitative responding under discrete trial paradigms. *Journal of Applied Behavior Analysis,* 1977, *10*(2), 315.

Mulhern, T., & Baumeister, A. A. An experimental attempt to reduce stereotypy by reinforcement procedures. *American Journal of Mental Deficiency,* 1969, *74,* 69–74.

Myers, D. V. Extinction, DRO, and response-cost procedures for eliminating self-injurious behavior: A case study. *Behavior Research and Therapy,* 1975, *13,* 189–192.

Ragain, R. D., & Anson, J. E. The control of self-mutilating behavior with positive reinforcement. *Mental Retardation,* 1976, *14,* 22–25.

Repp, A. C., Deitz, S. M., & Speir, N. C. Reducing stereotypic responding of retarded persons by the differential reinforcement of other behavior. *American Journal of Mental Deficiency,* 1974, *79,* 279–284.

Risley, T. R., & Wolf, M. M. Establishing functional speech in echolalic children. *Behaviour Research and Therapy,* 1967, *5,* 73–88.

Spradlin, J. E., Fixsen, D. L., & Girardeau, F. L. Reinstatement of an operant response by the delivery of reinforcement during extinction. *Journal of Experimental Child Psychology*, 1969, 7, 96–100.

ANSWERS TO CHAPTER QUESTIONS

Answers to Questions on Page 155

1. Least Restrictive Model of Treatment
2. retarded persons
3. a. baseline data
   b. least restrictive behavioral treatment procedure
   c. reliable data
   d. least restrictive procedure was ineffective
   e. parents, school administrator

Answers to Questions on Page 158

1. less than 20 seconds. A DRO interval of 10 seconds would be a good place to start.
2. No. Mr. Rogers would be reinforcing David's shirt ripping as well as his not smearing. It would be best to wait for the next interval of non-smearing to elapse.
3. a. Select a time period each day that can be completely devoted to the program.
   b. One person in the family should take responsibility for the program.
   c. Create activities that are as incompatible as possible with the inappropriate behavior.
4. Advantages:
   a. It is a simple procedure.
   b. It works directly on the misbehavior.
   Disadvantages:
   a. It does not teach an appropriate behavior.
   b. There is a risk of reinforcing some other type of misbehavior.
5. Physical contact. Physical contact is Don's most preferred reinforcer and would therefore be the most powerful reinforcer.

Answers to Questions on Page 160

1. Ms. Goldstein should pick a behavior that Terri already performs. Thus, she would pick either having Terri look at her when instructed or having Terri hand her objects. She would not pick pointing at objects because Terri does not, at this time, perform that behavior.
2. Advantage:
   DRA increases an appropriate behavior.
   Disadvantages:
   a. DRA does not work directly on the misbehavior.
   b. The misbehavior can still occur during the program.
3. Mr. Hendry could institute a DRA program. He was initially using DRO.

Answers to Questions on Pages 162–163

1. 1-c
   2-e
   3-f
   4-b

5-d

6-a

2. Advantage:

The inappropriate behavior cannot occur when the incompatible behavior is occurring.
Disadvantage:

Ms. Carson may have trouble finding a socially appropriate incompatible behavior.

3. DRI. The severity of the misbehavior dictates that we reduce the self-abuse as soon as possible. DRI would be the best procedure because it guarantees that the misbehavior cannot occur when the reinforced behavior is occurring. In other words, DRI offers the tightest form of reinforcement control over the self-abuse.

Answers to Questions on Page 163

1. DRO
2. DRI
3. DRA
4. DRI
5. DRO
6. DRA

Answers to Review Questions on Pages 164–165

1. DRO
2. the inappropriate behavior
3. simple
4. working directly with the inappropriate behavior
5. there is a possibility that an inappropriate behavior may be reinforced at the end of the DRO interval
6. a reinforcer
7. DRA
8. inappropriate
9. appropriate
10. directly on the inappropriate behavior
11. DRI
12. incompatible appropriate behavior is occurring
13. incompatible
14. time, person, incompatible
15. reinforcer
16. performs at a low rate
17. incompatible, performs at a low rate

Chapter 11

DECREASING INAPPROPRIATE BEHAVIORS
Satiation, Negative Practice, and Extinction

After reading this chapter, you will be able to:

1. Define and give an example of satiation.
2. List the advantage and disadvantages of satiation.
3. Define and give an example of negative practice.
4. List the advantages and disadvantages of negative practice.
5. Distinguish between satiation and negative practice.
6. Define and give an example of extinction.
7. List the advantages and disadvantages of extinction and the phenomena associated with its use.

In the preceding chapter, you learned about the Least Restrictive Model of Treatment and reinforcement procedures that are used to decrease inappropriate behaviors. In this chapter, you will be introduced to three more reductive procedures and how they fit within the Least Restrictive Model. These three procedures are satiation, negative practice, and extinction.

SATIATION

SATIATION IS A PROCEDURE IN WHICH UNLIMITED AMOUNTS OF A REINFORCER THAT HAS BEEN MAINTAINING A MISBEHAVIOR ARE PRESENTED NONCONTINGENTLY IN ORDER TO REDUCE THAT BEHAVIOR.

A satiation procedure can be used to decrease a misbehavior; however, it is appropriate for only a few types of misbehavior. To understand how and why a satiation procedure works, recall that satiation occurs when a reinforcer has been presented so much that it is no longer effective in producing or maintaining a behavior. Since students misbehave because some type of reinforcer follows their misbehavior, you can use satiation to reduce a misbehavior by simply determining what reinforcer maintains the misbehavior and then providing unlimited access to that reinforcer whether or not the misbehavior occurs. In effect, the student does not have to respond (misbehave) in order to obtain the reinforcer because he or she has received either large amounts of it or prolonged exposure to it. The misbehavior is reduced because the student is not motivated (there is no deprivation, see Chapter 5) to perform it. The following example illustrates how satiation works in this fashion.

Eddie steals food from the other students during lunch. He waits until a student is not looking, and then grabs the student's sandwich, fruit, or dessert. Eddie's misbehavior is stealing food and the reinforcer for this behavior is probably the food (the reinforcer also could be attention from the instructors or other students). What would happen if Eddie was given as much food to eat at lunch as he desired? Would Eddie still steal food? The answer depends on what reinforcer is maintaining food stealing. If food was the reinforcer, the stealing should stop, because Eddie would be full (satiated on food) and therefore would have no motivation to steal. Of course, if he continued to steal food but did not eat it, we could state with confidence that attention was probably reinforcing and maintaining food stealing. Either way, however, we would have identified the reinforcer for food stealing.

The most important points to remember in using a satiation procedure to reduce a misbehavior are:

1. Always provide large quantities of the reinforcer before the student has had a chance to misbehave. Otherwise, you run the risk of reinforcing the misbehavior. *Remember, in a satiation procedure, the reinforcer is always presented noncontingently or prior to the misbehavior.*
2. Always make sure that you have identified the particular reinforcer that is maintaining the misbehavior.

As mentioned earlier, there are very few misbehaviors for which a satiation procedure is appropriate. Most people are hesitant to use a procedure that involves providing the reinforcer that has been maintaining the misbehavior. As a result, satiation has been used mostly for misbehaviors related to food or those that are annoying but not a serious threat to the student or others. For example, satiation has been used to treat food stealing (as in the above example), rumination, and clothes tearing or ripping.

An especially interesting use of satiation is in the treatment of rumination. Rumination is a maladaptive behavior in which the student regurgitates (vomits) and then either chews and re-swallows the vomitus or expels it from his mouth. In either case, the student usually ruminates repeatedly for 45 minutes or more after each meal. If the student expels the vomitus, a serious health hazard may arise because vital nutrients are being lost. In fact, the situation can become life-threatening since the student is retaining little, if any, food in his stomach. Such students sometimes have an emaciated look and are hospitalized. Fortunately, life-threatening rumination is somewhat rare and there is little chance you will encounter it in your classroom. Non-life-threatening rumination (i.e., when the vomitus is re-swallowed) is, unfortunately, not uncommon in classrooms for severely and profoundly retarded students. Although it does not present a major health hazard, there are problems associated with the behavior. The ruminator is unsightly; the student usually has some vomitus on his clothing and around his mouth, smells bad, and may have irritated skin around his lips and face due to the moist vomitus. Furthermore, rumination is a form of self-stimulation since it is repetitive, nonfunctional, and interferes with the student's education. This, of course, is the major reason why rumination cannot be tolerated in the classroom.

Treating non-life-threatening rumination with a satiation procedure is simply a matter of providing the ruminator with double or triple portions of his meal; in other words, allowing the ruminator to eat until he is full (satiated). If this is done, the student's rumination following the meal generally decreases by anywhere from 50% to 90%. The rumination is decreased because the reinforcer for rumination is the sensation produced by food in the stomach. In essence, the ruminator is still hungry following the meal and engages in behaviors such as chewing and swallowing vomitus because they lead to the sensations of food in the stomach. However, the student is not motivated to ruminate (misbehave) when large amounts of food (the reinforcer) are delivered noncontingently (independent of and prior to the misbehavior). You have probably anticipated the major concerns associated with using satiation to treat rumination. They are: Always keep accurate records of the student's weight and how much food is consumed at each meal and collect data on the frequency of the target behavior.

The major advantage of satiation is that it is a nonaversive procedure. As such, it permits the instructor to partially control the student's misbehavior without resorting to a more intrusive procedure. Thus, we consider satiation to be a level 1 procedure in the Least Restrictive Model of Treatment. However, research has shown that, in general, misbehaviors treated by satiation are not eliminated until a more aversive procedure such as punishment is coupled with the satiation procedure.

There are several disadvantages associated with the use of satiation.

1. The procedure is rarely, if ever completely effective in eliminating the undesirable behavior.
2. It is only temporarily effective because the effects of satiation will wane and deprivation will begin to occur.

3. There is always the danger that the reinforcer will be delivered following the misbehavior, rather than independent of the misbehavior, thereby reinforcing and strengthening it.
4. There are many undesirable behaviors for which a satiation procedure is not appropriate because of the potential dangers associated with using the procedure. For example, you would hardly consider using satiation to treat self-abuse, aggressive behavior toward other persons, or many other forms of highly disruptive behavior.

In summary, great care should be exercised when you consider the use of satiation. To prevent any problems, always remember to: 1) ensure that you have determined the reinforcer that is maintaining the undesirable behavior, and 2) make sure that the reinforcers are given independent of, i.e., prior to, the misbehavior.

Before continuing this chapter, answer the following questions.

1. For which of the following misbehaviors would it be possible to try a satiation procedure?

Climbing window ledges	Hoarding toys
Masturbation	Screaming
Food stealing	Banging tables with a toy
Air swallowing	Rumination (non-life-threatening)
Picking at scabs	

2. Mr. Edwards would like to try satiation to treat his daughter's hoarding of her dirty clothes in her closet. What would you suggest that he do in order to use satiation correctly?
3. Travis engages in non-life-threatening rumination in the classroom following lunch. If you choose to treat his rumination with a food satiation procedure, what will you do? What safeguard(s) will you follow? What is your rationale for choosing to treat Travis's rumination by satiation?

Turn to page 183 for the answers.

NEGATIVE PRACTICE

> NEGATIVE PRACTICE IS A PROCEDURE IN WHICH THE MISBEHAVING PERSON IS REQUIRED TO RE-PEATEDLY PRACTICE THE INAPPROPRIATE BE-HAVIOR.

Negative practice has been used most often in treating normal individuals who wish to reduce annoying habits such as nail biting, facial and body tics (e.g., eye blinking, facial grimacing, and body jerking), and stuttering. The procedure basically consists of simply instructing the person to practice the habit repeatedly during a specified period of time. If these instructions are followed religiously, there is often a subsequent decrease in the frequency of the habit.

Negative practice has been used by instructors to decrease the misbehaviors of retarded persons, but only in a few instances. There are several reasons why.

1. Retarded students typically will not practice their misbehaviors when instructed to do so because they are not as motivated to eliminate inappropriate behaviors from their behavioral repertoires. This lack of motivation results from their behavioral and intellectual deficits. With so few appropriate behaviors that could receive reinforcement, their inappropriate behaviors become their source of reinforcement. When they behave inappropriately, they often receive some type of powerful reinforcer such as attention. Normal individuals, of course, do not have this problem since they have an elaborate behavioral repertoire that leads to many varied sources of attention. Because the retarded student is usually unwilling to engage in negative practice, he must be physically guided so that he will perform the misbehavior. As you can guess, such a physical encounter between student and instructor can lead to some serious problems (discussed later).
2. Instructors often feel uncomfortable, and rightly so, with the idea of requiring the student to perform the inappropriate behavior. The general feeling is that it is difficult enough to reduce or eliminate an inappropriate behavior without attempting to do so by giving the student opportunities to practice and possibly refine his inappropriate behavior.
3. There are only a few misbehaviors for which negative practice is applicable. For example, one certainly would not endeavor to use negative practice to treat aggressive behaviors, self-abuse, or disruptive behaviors, and the potentially hazardous consequences of doing so can be easily imagined.

Although there are disadvantages associated with the use of negative practice, there are times when negative practice can be an extremely effective treatment procedure. The rationale for using negative practice is that the physical effort involved in repeatedly performing the misbehavior will become so aversive that the student will stop misbehaving in order to avoid the negative practice consequence. The following example illustrates the correct use of a negative practice procedure.

Brenda is a 16-year-old severely retarded student who frequently rips her clothing both at school and at home as well as the sheets on her bed. Her instructors are greatly concerned about Brenda's behavior because the ripping is costly, it interferes with their educational efforts, and it makes it chancy, at best, to take Brenda on field trips. They feel that Brenda's ripping is maintained by the attention she receives following an episode of tearing. In order to eliminate clothes ripping at school, Brenda's instructors decide to use a negative practice procedure. Their program plan is as follows. Whenever Brenda attempts to rip her clothing, she will be told "No" and taken to a corner of the classroom where she will be given a sack full of old clothing and rags to rip. Brenda will be told to rip all of the sack's contents and that she cannot return to her desk until she has done so.

To increase the likelihood that Brenda will want to return to her desk, a DRO program will be instituted throughout the school day in which Brenda will be reinforced frequently with attention when she has not ripped her clothing for specified intervals of time. Furthermore, no attention will be paid to Brenda while she is engaging in the negative practice.

Brenda's behavior during the negative practice sessions suggests that she finds the sessions aversive. She tries to run away from the instructor who is attempting to take her to the corner and she cries during the sessions. Within a week, Brenda's rate of clothes ripping decreases from a baseline average of 20 incidents per day to 2. Her teachers plan to continue using the negative practice until the ripping is eliminated at school, at which point they intend to suggest to Brenda's mother that she institute the negative practice procedure at home following any episodes or attempts by Brenda to rip her clothes or sheets.

Brenda's instructors were successful because they carefully designed and followed their negative practice program. In designing the program, they 1) ensured that the negative practice required a sufficient amount of physical effort to make it aversive by having Brenda rip a sack of old clothing and rags, and 2) ensured that attention, the suspected reinforcer for clothes ripping, was only delivered following the absence of clothes ripping and that no attention was given during the negative practice. This use of attention ensured that Brenda would be motivated to stop clothes ripping during class time and that the negative practice period would be aversive because of the opportunities for attention that Brenda missed during that period.

Negative practice is often confused with satiation because the inappropriate response or behavior seems to also be the reinforcer. For example, clothes ripping is a response, yet perhaps the act itself is reinforcing. The same can be said about appropriate behaviors. For example, dancing is a behavior, yet dancing is also reinforcing. The same analysis applies to jogging, sexual behavior, singing, and many other activities. Thus, in many situations, we are never quite sure whether we are dealing with the misbehavior or the reinforcer for that misbehavior or both. However, there are ways to distinguish between satiation and negative practice.

Negative practice is given following the misbehavior and as such it is a behavioral consequence. Satiation is given prior to, or independent of, the misbehavior; thus, satiation cannot be used as a consequence. Also, negative practice deals with the misbehavior or response whereas satiation deals with the reinforcer. Thus, if you wished to treat clothes ripping with satiation, you would provide the student with the opportunity to rip a bag of rags *before* she rips her clothing. If, on the other hand, you wished to use negative practice, you would require the student to rip a bag of rags *after* she has ripped her own clothing.

The advantages of negative practice are:

1. As an aversive consequence, it can be effective in eliminating an undesirable behavior.
2. Its suppressive effects may be long lasting (the misbehavior may be completely eliminated) if the negative practice sessions are sufficiently aversive.
3. It provides the instructor with control over the student's behavior during the consequence; i.e., if the instructor is guiding the student in performing the negative practice tasks, she can physically prevent him from engaging in undesirable behaviors.

There are several disadvantages associated with negative practice.

1. There is a good chance that the student may become combative when the instructor attempts to guide the student through the negative practice. If so, either the student, the instructor, or both of them could be injured. You must carefully consider this potential risk and take steps to minimize the possibility that someone will be injured.
2. We must ask ourselves whether or not it is even a good idea to allow a student to practice his misbehavior. It may well be that all we are doing is simply allowing him to learn how to misbehave better. To avoid this problem, keep very complete records of the misbehavior during the first few days of the negative practice condition. If the misbehavior is not greatly reduced during this period as compared to its frequency during baseline, terminate the negative practice procedure and institute another type of reductive or inhibitory procedure or structure the negative practice procedure differently.
3. There are many undesirable behaviors for which a negative practice procedure is inappropriate because of the potential dangers associated with using the procedure. For example, you would hardly consider using negative practice to treat self-abusive behavior.
4. Negative practice is often confused with satiation. Besides the differences between the two that have been mentioned, there remains one final and most important difference: Satiation is a nonaversive procedure whereas negative practice is an aversive procedure. As a result, we consider negative practice to be a level 2 procedure in the Least Restrictive Model of Treatment. We define level 2 procedures as those that contain some aversive properties.

Great care should be exercised when you consider the use of negative practice. You can avoid the potential problems described above by following, to the letter, the Least Restrictive Treatment Model guidelines that were discussed in Chapter 10. Negative practice can be a useful way of reducing or eliminating certain behaviors; but, as we shall see in the next chapter, there are some other inhibitory procedures that are applicable to a greater number of misbehaviors and that are more effective.

Before continuing this chapter, answer the following questions:

1. For which of the following misbehaviors would it be reasonable to try a negative practice procedure?

   Masturbation   Screaming
   Self-stimulatory behaviors Hitting other students
   Rumination   Paper tearing
   Spitting   Running away
   Eye poking

2. Ms. Parsons would like to try negative practice to treat her students' plant and grass pulling on the school grounds. What would you suggest that she do in order to use negative practice correctly?

3. Negative practice differs from satiation in at least three ways. Can you name them?

Answers are on page 183.

EXTINCTION

EXTINCTION IS A PROCEDURE IN WHICH THE REIN-
FORCER THAT HAS BEEN SUSTAINING OR INCREAS-
ING AN UNDESIRABLE BEHAVIOR IS WITHHELD.

In Chapter 4, you learned that a behavior or response is increased and then maintained when it is followed by a reinforcer, that is, a positive or pleasurable event. However, if the positive reinforcer is withheld permanently, that behavior will cease. When this occurs, we say that the behavior was extinguished; the procedure itself is called extinction.

Undoubtedly, extinction is the most widely used procedure for decreasing the behavior of retarded students. There are three reasons why. To begin with, the procedure is so simple: First you must discover what the reinforcer is. A teacher does not always deliver the reinforcers. Second, you must figure out how to withhold the reinforcer. (Withholding the reinforcer can sometimes be a difficult task.) Third, everyone has had a great deal of practice ignoring the undesirable behavior of others. All of us at one time or another have ignored the behavior of our children, spouses, bosses, parents, and in-laws, as well as that of salespersons, beggars, and teachers. Thus, the use of extinction comes naturally to most people.

Unfortunately, however, the use of extinction in the classroom is not as easy as it seems. It can be fraught with potential pitfalls, which are discussed later in this chapter when the disadvantages of extinction are described. Right now, however, let's look at an example of the proper way to conduct an extinction program.

Bruce is a profoundly retarded student who constantly demands attention from his instructors. In fact, he will do just about anything to gain their attention whether it be exposing himself, blowing his nose and smearing the mucus on himself, or pushing his face very close to another person and then hugging him. His instructors have chosen to work on his self-exposure since they are convinced that their attention has been maintaining his behavior. For example, they have always told Bruce to pull up his pants whether or not they discovered that he had lowered them.

During a 7-day baseline period, the instructors continue to treat Bruce's exposing himself as they have always done, i.e., telling him to raise his pants. They find after 7 days that, on the average, Bruce exposes himself about 14 times per day. Having ensured that the behavior was stable during baseline, the instructors institute an extinction program the following day. They all agree that none of them will look at or speak to Bruce when he pulls his pants down or is discovered with them down. Furthermore, they decide to give him generous amounts of attention when he is not misbehaving. During the first extinction day, Bruce's rate of exposing himself increases to 30. It remains higher than baseline the second day, and, in addition, Bruce begins throwing tantrums and attempting to attack the instructors and other students. On day three, Bruce exposes himself 40 times and begins attempting to smear mucus from his nose on the instructors.

The instructors have not reacted to all of Bruce's inappropriate behaviors; rather, they have maintained impassive faces and a stony silence. Their only interactions with Bruce when he has exposed himself come when he attempts to attack people or wipe mucus on them. In these instances, they calmly guide him away without speaking or looking at him. Over the next few days, there is a dramatic reduction in the number of times Bruce exposes himself and an equally dramatic increase in his appropriate behavior. After 2 weeks of the extinction program, Bruce ceases exposing himself.

The instructors' use of extinction with Bruce was excellent and they were rewarded for their efforts by the elimination of Bruce's self-exposure. Let's look at why their extinction program worked. First and foremost, the instructors were consistent and persistent. All of them ignored Bruce's self-exposure as well as the other undesirable behaviors he displayed. Second, they did not become dismayed when Bruce's exposing himself dramatically increased in frequency during the first few days of the program. Third, they provided Bruce with attention for appropriate behaviors while withholding attention whenever he exposed himself. By doing so, they helped Bruce begin to realize that attention would be forthcoming for appropriate behaviors but withheld for inappropriate behavior.

To use extinction correctly and successfully, you must be prepared for the following phenomena that usually occur when a student's behavior has been placed on extinction.

1. *The undesirable behavior gets worse before it gets better.* In most cases, the rate and severity or intensity of the undesirable behavior increases during the first few days to a week that the extinction program is in effect. The student is attempting to force you to abandon the program, no doubt because such efforts have been successful in the past. The student has usually had a history of successfully forcing his instructors and parents to attend to him by becoming extremely persistent in the misbehavior. This is one of the major reasons it may initially seem difficult to extinguish the misbehavior.

2. *There is a gradual reduction in the misbehavior.* Usually, extinction does not have an immediate effect on the misbehavior. The misbehavior will continue for some indeterminate amount of time before it stops. The length of time required for extinction to take effects depends on: 1) how many times the student received reinforcement for the misbehavior in the past, 2) whether or not every misbehavior was reinforced with attention (if the misbehavior was reinforced continuously, then the misbehavior tends to extinguish fairly rapidly whereas it will persist if it has been reinforced intermittently—see Chapter 6), 3) the student's deprivation level, i.e., how badly he wants the attention, how long he has been without it, and whether or not he has alternative sources of obtaining attention (this is why a combination of extinction with either a DRO or DRA procedure will reduce a misbehavior more rapidly than the use of either procedure alone), and 4) how much effort is required to perform the response (in general, the more effort that is required, the sooner extinction will be successful).

3. *Extinction-induced aggression may occur.* Especially during the first few days of extinction, the student may act aggressively toward his teachers or classmates, objects, or himself. This same phenomenon occurs when you hit or kick a vending machine that has taken your money but has not delivered the item you chose.

4. *Spontaneous recovery may occur.* Occasionally, the misbehavior will reappear after it has been extinguished for a time. This phenomenon is called spontaneous recovery. You need not worry about it: Simply ignore the misbehavior as you did before and it will quickly disappear. *Under no circumstances should you regard the extinction program as unsuccessful and thus abandon it.*

5. *It only takes one person attending to the misbehavior on one occasion to wreck an extinction procedure.* We cannot overemphasize the need for everyone in the student's environment to be committed to the extinction program. There are some ways of preventing uninformed individuals from inadvertently paying attention to the misbehavior. One way is to post a sign on the outside of the classroom door, alerting anyone entering the room that no attention is to be given to the student unless permission to do so is given by one of the classroom instructors. Or you could intercept any visitors to your classroom and explain the extinction program to them. Another way is simply

to not allow visitors to enter the classroom. All of the instructors in the classroom must be kept up to date about the extinction procedure. When instructors return from sick leave or a vacation, for example, be sure to call and inform them about the extinction procedure before they return to work. Failure to prevent inadvertent attention will result in all your efforts at extinguishing the misbehavior going for naught. When your classroom contains severely and profoundly retarded students, it is usually unnecessary to ensure that a student's classmates do not attend to his misbehavior. However, if the classroom contains moderately retarded students, you must gain the cooperation of the student's classmates so that they do not reinforce his undesirable behavior with their attention. This cooperation can be gained by reinforcing them for not attending to the student's misbehavior and/or instituting a negative consequence for them if they do.

An excellent example of what happens during extinction can be found in those rare, bad arguments that occur between a married couple. During the argument, the arguing behavior of both parties is reinforced by the other's verbal behavior. But what happens when one spouse chooses to quit arguing and merely clams up? The other spouse, who wishes to pursue the argument, has been placed on extinction because the arguments go unanswered. What does this person typically do first? The intensity of the response is increased, i.e., the talk grows louder. But still there is no reinforcement. So what does the person do next? Unrelated issues are brought into the argument. But still there is no response from the spouse who is tired of arguing. Then what happens? The spouse on extinction begins to loudly attack and question the other's general worth as a person. Still no response. At this point, the spouse seeking a reaction has only one alternative left. The one taboo subject that the quiet spouse has confessed in a moment of weakness or for which the spouse had been forgiven and told would never again be brought up is in fact brought up. And what usually happens? The quiet spouse responds angrily and thereby reinforces the behavior of the verbal attacker. However, if the silent spouse remains silent, there is nothing left for the arguer to say. The arguer may throw a few dishes or call a lawyer but the verbal behavior has been successfully extinguished. The point is, if you want to end the argument, do not respond under any circumstances even if the verbalizations you hear are cutting you very deeply.

The advantages of extinction are:

1. It is simple, provided that all of the instructors are consistent and persistent.
2. It will effectively eliminate a misbehavior.
3. It will produce a long-lasting effect.
4. It is a relatively nonaversive procedure. However, because it may produce aggression and emotional behavior by the student, we classify it as a level 2 procedure in the Least Restrictive Treatment Model.

The disadvantages of extinction are:

1. The misbehavior is initially likely to increase in frequency and intensity.
2. The procedure requires incredible consistency and persistence on the part of the instructor.
3. It is not rapid—the elimination of the misbehavior takes time.
4. The student may become aggressive during the initial stages of the procedure.
5. Sometimes it is difficult to determine the reinforcer that is maintaining the undesirable behavior.
6. The schedule of reinforcement is unknown so you are never sure how long extinction will be necessary. For example, if an inappropriate behavior is reinforced on a VR 30 (every thirtieth response on the average is reinforced) or a VI 2 hour (reinforcement occurs on the average of every 2 hours), it will take a considerable amount of time to extinguish the behavior.
7. Some misbehaviors simply cannot be ignored. For example, you would not use extinction to treat self-abuse, aggression toward others or objects, or many types of highly disruptive behavior such as screaming or stripping.

In summary, the success of an extinction procedure depends on your being *consistent, patient, and persistent.*

Before continuing, answer the following questions.

1. For which of the following misbehaviors would it be reasonable to try an extinction procedure?

Masturbation	Hitting others
Self-stimulatory behaviors	Out-of-seat behavior
Whining	Running away
Screaming	Throwing objects
Pestering	Cursing

2. Dick steps in front of the teacher whenever she is talking or working with another student. How could his teacher use extinction to eliminate Dick's attention seeking?
3. Ms. Kelly has been using an extinction procedure for 2 days in an attempt to eliminate Conrad's whining. She is concerned because Conrad has been whining very loudly and acting aggressively toward other students since she started the program. What would you tell her regarding her concerns?
4. You are describing the advantages of extinction to a group of teachers at a workshop. What would you tell them?
5. What disadvantages of extinction would you describe to them?

Turn to page 183 for the answers.

THE LEAST RESTRICTIVE TREATMENT MODEL

Thus far, we have discussed seven procedures that will decrease an undesirable behavior and we have grouped them into two levels within the Least Restrictive

Treatment Model. Level 1 procedures contain no aversive properties, while level 2 procedures do contain some aversive properties. However, the level 2 procedures are not very restrictive of the student's rights. Still, you should obtain written approval from the school administration before using a level 2 procedure.

Level 1 procedures	Level 2 procedures
DRO (differential reinforcement of other behavior)	Negative practice
DRA (differential reinforcement of appropriate behavior)	Extinction
DRI (differential reinforcement of incompatible behavior)	
Satiation	

SUMMARY

Three procedures for decreasing a misbehavior are satiation, negative practice, and extinction.

Satiation is a procedure in which unlimited amounts of a reinforcer that has been maintaining a misbehavior are presented noncontingently in order to reduce that misbehavior. The advantage of satiation is that it is nonaversive. Its disadvantages are: 1) it does not eliminate the misbehavior, 2) it is only temporarily effective, 3) there is a danger of reinforcing the misbehavior, and 4) there are few misbehaviors for which it is an appropriate consequence.

Negative practice is a procedure in which the misbehaving person is required to repeatedly practice his or her misbehavior. Satiation and negative practice are sometimes confused. They can be differentiated as follows. Satiation is used noncontingently, whereas negative practice is used as a consequence (it follows the misbehavior). The advantages of negative practice are: 1) it will eliminate the misbehavior, 2) it is long lasting, and 3) it provides the instructor with control over the student's physical movements during the consequence. The disadvantages of negative practice include: 1) the student may become combative when required to go through negative practice, 2) it is sometimes questionable whether a student should be allowed to practice a misbehavior, and 3) it is not an appropriate procedure for many undesirable behaviors.

Extinction is the withholding of the reinforcer that has been maintaining the undesirable behavior. Some common phenomena associated with the use of extinction are: 1) the behavior gets worse before it gets better, 2) the behavior is reduced gradually, 3) extinction-induced aggression may result, 4) spontaneous recovery may occur, and 5) the procedure is easily rendered ineffective if one person in the student's environment does not follow the extinction program. The advantages of extinction are: 1) it is simple, 2) it eliminates the misbehavior, 3) it produces a long-lasting effect, and 4) it is relatively nonaversive. The disadvantages include: 1) an initial increase in the intensity and frequency of the behavior, 2) the need for consistency, 3) the procedure takes time, 4) the student may become aggressive, 5) it may be difficult to determine what reinforcer is maintaining the undesirable behavior, 6) the schedule of reinforcement is unknown, and 7) some behaviors cannot be ignored.

Satiation and stimulus change are nonaversive procedures and thereby are considered to be level 1 procedures in the Least Restrictive Model of Treatment. Negative practice and extinction are considered to be level 2 procedures in the model because they contain some aversive properties.

REVIEW QUESTIONS

1. The noncontingent presentation of large amounts of a reinforcer is called _____.

2. Satiation is always presented n_____.
3. Satiation does not suppress behavior; rather, it merely _____.
4. The effects of satiation are t_____.
5. Satiation is effective for only a f_____ _____.
6. Requiring a student to repeatedly practice his misbehavior is called _____ _____.

7. Negative practice follows the misbehavior whereas satiation is presented _____.

8. The effects of negative practice are long lasting and the misbehavior may well be e_____.
9. Sometimes during negative practice it is necessary to guide the student physically in performing _____.
10. Students may become combative when required to undergo _____ _____.
11. The withholding of a reinforcer is called _____.
12. Some characteristics of extinction include: 1) the behavior gets worse before it gets better, 2) the misbehavior is reduced gradually, 3) extinction induced aggression may occur, and 4) _____.
13. Extinction will eliminate a misbehavior and produce a l_____ _____.
14. There are several disadvantages associated with extinction. They are: 1) an initial _____ in intensity and frequency, 2) the procedure works g_____, 3) the student may become a _____, 4) it is sometimes difficult to identify the r_____ that is maintaining the misbehavior, and 5) the _____ of reinforcement is unknown.

Answers are on page 184.

SUGGESTED READINGS

Ayllon, T. Intensive treatment of psychotic behavior by stimulus satiation and food reinforcement. *Behavior Research and Therapy*, 1963, *1*, 53–61.

Barton, E. J., & Ascione, T. R. Social reinforcer satiation outcome of frequency, not ambiguity—sometimes. *Developmental Psychology*, 1978, *14*, 363–370.

Gewirtz, J. L., & Baer, D. M. Deprivation and satiation of social reinforcers as drive conditions. *Journal of Abnormal and Social Psychology*, 1958, *57*, 165–172.

Knepler, K. N., & Sewall, S. Negative practice paired with smelling salts in the treatment of a tic. *Journal of Behavior Therapy and Experimental Psychiatry*, 1974, *5*, 189–192.

Lowenstein, L. F. The treatment of moderate school phobia by negative practice and desensitization procedures. *Association of Educational Psychologists' Journal and Newsletter*, 1973, *3*, 46–49.

Martin, P. L., & Foxx, R. M. Victim control of the aggression of an institutionalized retardate. *Journal of Behavior Therapy and Experimental Psychiatry*, 1973, *4*, 161–165.

Myers, D. V. Extinction, DRO, and response-costs procedures for eliminating self-injurious behavior: A case study. *Behaviour Research and Therapy*, 1975, *13*, 189–192.

Williams, C. D. The elimination of tantrum behavior by extinction procedures. *Journal of Abnormal and Social Psychology*, 1959, *59*, 269.

ANSWERS TO CHAPTER QUESTIONS

Answers to Questions on Page 172

1. Satiation could reasonably be tried for food stealing, hoarding toys, and rumination. All of the other misbehaviors are too serious in nature to consider treating them by satiation.
2. Since his daughter apparently is reinforced by collecting and hoarding her dirty clothes, Mr. Edwards should place all of his family's dirty laundry in her closet. When her closet becomes filled with dirty clothes, she may just stop hoarding her dirty clothes.
3. Let Travis eat as much as he wants to at lunch. You will want to keep accurate records of his weight and how much food he consumes at lunch. If Travis is full (satiated), he will not be motivated to engage in rumination.

Answers to Questions on Page 176

1. Negative practice should reasonably be tried for self-stimulatory behaviors, paper tearing, and running away. The other misbehaviors listed are too serious in nature to consider treating them with negative practice.
2. Ms. Parsons should require her students to repeatedly practice pulling grass and plants whenever she discovers them exhibiting this behavior. To avoid damaging the grounds, Ms. Parsons should select a place full of weeds as the site for the negative practice sessions.
3. Negative practice:
   a. Follows the misbehavior (it is a consequence)
   b. Deals with the response
   c. Is an aversive procedure

   Satiation:
   a. Is given independent of the misbehavior
   b. Deals with the reinforcer
   c. Is a nonaversive procedure

Answers to Questions on Page 180

1. Extinction could be tried for masturbation, whining, pestering, out-of-seat behavior, or cursing. The other behaviors listed are too serious in nature to consider treating them with extinction.

2. The teacher should ignore Dick when he seeks attention by stepping between her and another student.
3. You would tell Ms. Kelly not to worry because Conrad's behaviors are very characteristic of what happens when a student is placed on extinction. Simply tell her that if she persists with the program, Conrad will stop whining and acting aggressively.
4. The advantages of extinction are that it is simple, effective in eliminating the undesirable behavior, long-lasting, and relatively nonaversive.
5. The disadvantages of extinction are: 1) the behavior may initially increase in frequency and intensity, 2) it requires a consistent approach, 3) it takes time to work, 4) the student may become aggressive, 5) it is sometimes difficult to identify the reinforcer, 6) the schedule of reinforcement for the undesirable behavior is unknown, and 7) it cannot be used for dangerous or highly disruptive behaviors.

Answers to Review Questions on Page 182

1. satiation
2. noncontingently
3. reduces it
4. temporary
5. few misbehaviors
6. negative practice
7. noncontingently
8. eliminated
9. the repeated acts
10. negative practice
11. extinction
12. spontaneous recovery may occur
13. long-lasting effect
14. increase, gradually, aggressive, reinforcer, schedule

Chapter 12

DECREASING INAPPROPRIATE BEHAVIORS
Physical Restraint and Punishment by Timeout

After reading this chapter, you will be able to:

1. Define behavioral physical restraint.

2. Define custodial physical restraint.

3. List three ways in which behavioral physical restraint and custodial physical restraint differ.

4. Give an example of the two methods of instituting behavioral physical restraint.

5. List the advantages and disadvantages of behavioral physical restraint.

6. Define punishment.

7. Define and give an example of the two types of punishment.

8. List four variables that influence the effectiveness of a punishment procedure.

9. List the advantages and disadvantages of punishment.

10. Define and give an example of a conditioned aversive stimulus.

11. Define timeout.

12. Define exclusionary timeout and give examples of three different types.

13. List the advantages and disadvantages of the three types of exclusionary timeout.

14. Define nonexclusionary timeout and give examples of three different types.

15. List the advantages and disadvantages of the three types of nonexclusionary timeout.

This chapter deals with two methods of reducing behavior: physical restraint and timeout. Because both methods are aversive, we need to add a third level to the Least Restrictive Model of Treatment, discussed in the last two chapters. Physical restraint, discussed first in this chapter, is an aversive procedure; it is not a punishment procedure per se. The discussion of punishment that follows focuses on the variables that make it a humane, effective procedure. In the last section, a punishment procedure called timeout, which is commonly used in classrooms, is discussed. Two types of timeout are covered: nonexclusionary and exclusionary timeout.

PHYSICAL RESTRAINT

> BEHAVIORAL PHYSICAL RESTRAINT IS A PROCE-
> DURE IN WHICH THE STUDENT IS PREVENTED
> FROM MOVING HIS OR HER LIMBS AND/OR BODY
> FOR A PRESPECIFIED PERIOD FOLLOWING THE PER-
> FORMANCE OF A MISBEHAVIOR.

Physical restraint is an aversive procedure that is seldom used in the classroom. It is used almost exclusively to treat severe cases of self-abusive behavior, and is occasionally used to treat dangerous or highly disruptive behavior, e.g., severe cases of aggression toward others or constantly pestering one's classmates. There are two types of physical restraint—behavioral physical restraint and custodial physical restraint—and it is important from the outset that a clear distinction be made between them.

Behavioral physical restraint is used as a negative consequence to follow an undesirable behavior. The duration of behavioral physical restraint is pre-specified, i.e., the exact amount of time the student is to be restrained is determined before the procedure is implemented. Behavioral physical restraint is brief and it should never last more than 30 minutes. Because behavioral physical restraint is used as a consequence, the procedure requires that data be collected.

> CUSTODIAL PHYSICAL RESTRAINT IS A PROCEDURE
> IN WHICH THE STUDENT IS NONCONTINGENTLY
> PREVENTED FROM MOVING HIS OR HER LIMBS
> AND/OR BODY FOR AN INDEFINITE PERIOD.

Custodial restraint, on the other hand, is not used as a consequence. Rather, it is often applied noncontingently and arbitrarily. The duration of custodial physical restraint is rarely specified and it can often last indefinitely. There are two types of custodial physical restraint. One type is used in institutions to subdue agitated residents. It is ordered by a physician and usually consists of tying or strapping the agitated person to the bed in a spread-eagle fashion. An intramuscular injection of a tranquilizer often accompanies the restraint. The restraint remains in force until canceled by the physician which means the individual can remain in restraint long after his or her agitation has subsided.

The other type of custodial restraint involves the use of restraint to prevent self-abuse, either in the institution or in the classroom. This restraint may take many forms depending on the type of self-abuse. For example, a head banger may wear a football helmet that is locked so that it cannot be removed. Or an individual who smashes his face with his fists could be outfitted with arm splints that prevent him from bending his arms to hit his face. The self-abusive individual often wears his restraints day and night. Although these forms of custodial restraint prevent self-abuse from occurring, they do present several problems. First, the restraint may prevent the individual from participating in a variety of educational activities; for example, the number of activities available to someone in arm splints is severely limited. Second, the restraint may cause muscle deterioration or atrophy if it has been worn for long periods of time. Third, when the person struggles against the restraints, he is in effect performing a series of isometric exercises that will only serve to make him stronger and more difficult to manage. Fourth, for some self-abusive retarded persons, the restraints themselves may become reinforcing over time. If this happens, you are faced with the difficult problem of eliminating the person's reliance on the restraints. What follows is the classic catch-22 situation. If you remove the restraints, the person hits himself; if you do nothing, he will not hit himself. Yet he will continue to suffer physical problems and restriction from educational activities previously described. For these reasons, it is highly recommended that custodial physical restraint not be used. If restraint must be used, it should be behavioral physical restraint. Otherwise, restraint is not a true treatment technique; it merely serves the interests of staff and not the best interests of the student. If custodial restraint is to be used at all, it should only be used until a treatment program is written and implemented.

Now let us summarize the important distinctions between custodial physical restraint and behavioral physical restraint. Custodial restraint is often applied noncontingently and arbitrarily and it serves a purely custodial function. Behavioral restraint is contingent on behavior and is prespecified; it is a programmatic intervention that includes collection of treatment data.

There are two ways of implementing behavioral physical restraint. You can restrain the student with your hands and body or use some type of mechanical restraint for a prespecified period of time. Mechanical restraints include straps, auto seat belts, football helmets, and equipment especially designed for particular body parts. The following example illustrates the use of behavioral physical restraint when the instructor uses her hands to restrain a student.

Ms. Santos has decided to use a physical restraint procedure to decrease Bobby's self-abuse. Following a brief period of baseline recording, she is ready to implement the procedure. Whenever Bobby hits himself, or attempts to hit himself, Ms. Santos says, "No, don't hit yourself," and immediately restrains his hands with her hands. She stands behind Bobby while he is seated at his desk so that she can hold his arms to his sides. She does not look at him or say anything. Although Bobby struggles somewhat, Ms. Santos continues to hold his hands with sufficient force to prevent him from being self-abusive. The program plan calls for her to restrain Bobby for 5 minutes. She releases him at the end of that time because he is not struggling. (Had he been struggling at the end of the 5-minute interval, she would have continued to restrain him until he had ceased struggling. In this way, Bobby would learn that release from restraint was contingent on his being relaxed.) As she releases his arms, she says, "Don't hit yourself." She then attempts to involve him in working a puzzle and reinforces him with a piece of carrot stick when he touches a puzzle part. Bobby's struggling during the physical restraint suggested that it was aversive to him. Over time, the combination of 5 minutes of physical restraint for self-abuse plus reinforcement for appropriate behavior decreases Bobby's self-abuse to the point where he can sit in class all day without hitting himself.

This next example illustrates the use of behavioral physical restraint when the instructor uses a mechanical device.

Ms. Santos has decided to treat Bobby's self-abuse by employing a physical restraint procedure that involves the contingent application of mechanical restraints. Whenever Bobby hits himself, she says, "No, don't hit yourself," and immediately slips a splint-like device over each of his arms. Bobby is required to wear the restraints for 5 minutes after which they are removed. While he is wearing them, Ms. Santos does not look at him or say anything. When he is not restrained, Ms. Santos or her aide provides him with reinforcers for engaging in appropriate behaviors. Ms. Santos is confident that the arm splints will reduce Bobby's self-abuse because he often cries and becomes agitated when he is required to wear them. Her observations were ultimately confirmed because within 2 weeks Bobby's self-abuse had been eliminated in the classroom.

The success of these two behavioral physical restraint procedures was a direct result of Ms. Santos's consistent use of the procedures in combination with a DRA procedure. Furthermore, Ms. Santos made every effort to minimize the attention associated with the use of physical restraint.

There are several advantages associated with the use of behavioral physical restraint:

1. The major advantage is that the misbehavior cannot occur during the procedure. Thus, physical restraint procedures produce immediate and complete suppression of the misbehavior as long as the procedures are in force.
2. There may be complete elimination of the misbehavior; that is, it may be reduced to zero *when the restraints are removed.*
3. The misbehavior may remain at zero; that is, the procedure may have long-lasting effects.

All of these advantages are the result of the aversive nature of behavioral physical restraint procedures.

There are several disadvantages associated with the use of behavioral physical restraint:

1. The procedure is aversive so great care and judgment must be exercised when it is used.
2. The restraint can become reinforcing if a lot of attention is associated with the implementation of the procedure. Many profoundly retarded persons find being touched a very powerful reinforcer, especially if the majority of their physical interactions with people are limited to being touched during a restraint procedure. To minimize this possibility, you should use physical contact (e.g., a hug, touch, or caress) as a reinforcer for appropriate behavior. Some students even find mechanical restraints to be reinforcing if their use represents the major source of attention that they receive. Such an iatrogenic effect (where the cure is worse than the problem) usually results from the long term use of mechanical restraint in a custodial, rather than behavioral, fashion. In such situations, your use of behavioral physical restraint may be counterproductive to the successful elimination of the student's misbehavior. You can usually identify such students because they will self-restrain in their own clothing if denied access to the mechanical restraints. For these students, it is best to use an alternative reductive procedure.
3. The student's struggling during the restraint can constitute a period of isometric exercise. When this occurs, we are presented with another iatrogenic effect; namely, the use of the restraint procedure creates a stronger student who is thereby able to better resist the restraint procedure.
4. There is the danger that the procedure could be used in an arbitrary and punitive fashion. For example, a bothersome student could be placed in mechanical restraints simply as a method of "getting him out of the instructor's way." This is usually not a problem if the instructor uses his or her hands to apply the physical restraint, since the instructor would be required to interact with the student.
5. The procedure requires the full participation of a staff person when the physical restraint is not mechanical. This can be a problem when there are not enough instructional staff members available to provide one-to-one attention to a misbehaving student.
6. There is a distinct possibility that someone may be injured because of the procedure's physically intrusive nature. The student may become combative when you attempt to implement the restraint which can greatly increase the likelihood that one of you will be injured. Thus, it should come as no surprise that we do not advocate the use of physical restraint with large, aggressive students. For any student, it is best to try other treatment procedures first (*less restrictive*) unless there is an immediate danger to someone. For any student

in a behavioral restraint program, other procedures such as differential reinforcement of other behaviors (DRO) or differential reinforcement of incompatible behaviors (DRI), etc., should be used to ensure success.

In summary, you should never consider using a physical restraint procedure
until you have tried all of the less restrictive procedures. And the misbehavior
should be serious enough to warrant accepting the potential dangers associated
with the use of restraint. Above all, *document what you are doing and obtain
written permission from all relevant parties,* i.e., parents and school administrators, before you undertake a physical restraint procedure.

Before continuing this chapter, answer the following questions.

1. For which of the following misbehaviors would it be reasonable to try a
   physical restraint procedure:

Masturbation	Face scratching
Rectal digging	Clothes ripping
Running away	Screaming
Throwing objects	Out-of-seat behavior
Hitting others	Pestering

2. What are three ways in which custodial physical restraint and behavioral
   physical restraint differ?
3. Larry hits his ears with his fists. How could his teacher use her hands to
   implement a behavioral physical restraint procedure to treat Larry's self-
   abuse?
4. How could Larry's teacher use a mechanical device to treat his self-abuse by
   behavioral physical restraint?
5. Why is it so important to reinforce an appropriate behavior with physical
   contact when using a physical restraint procedure to treat a misbehavior?

Answers are on page 208.

PUNISHMENT

PUNISHMENT IS AN EVENT THAT DECREASES THE
FREQUENCY OF THE BEHAVIOR IT FOLLOWS.

In Chapter 4, you learned there are two basic types of consequences: reinforcing
consequences and punishing consequences. Thus far, you have learned much
about reinforcing consequences. It is now time to turn our attention to the use of
punishing consequences.

ONE TYPE OF PUNISHMENT INVOLVES THE APPLI-
CATION OF AN AVERSIVE EVENT FOLLOWING THE
MISBEHAVIOR.

There are two types of punishment. The first is the application of some aversive event following the misbehavior. Examples of this type include spanking, punching, and shouting at someone. This type of punishment is typically used in situations and environments where the punisher has nearly complete control over the person being punished. Thus, it is not surprising that this type of punishment is most commonly used by parents, on military bases, and in prisons.

A SECOND TYPE OF PUNISHMENT INVOLVES THE WITHDRAWAL OF A POSITIVE REINFORCER FOLLOWING THE MISBEHAVIOR.

The second type of punishment will be of more interest to you because it is the type you will probably use *if it is necessary* to use punishment. The second type involves the withdrawal of positive reinforcement. Examples of this type include social disapproval (withdrawing your attention from the student), fines, and penalities. The most pervasive form of this second type that is used in classrooms for severely and profoundly retarded students is timeout from positive reinforcement, which is discussed later in this chapter.

There are several variables that influence whether or not a punishment procedure will be effective. One of these is whether or not the punishment is implemented *immediately*. The sooner the punishment follows the misbehavior, the more likely it is that the punishment will effectively reduce the misbehavior. The importance of immediacy cannot be overstressed, especially when you are dealing with profoundly and severely retarded students who do not mediate time spans well. As a result, the most humane way of using punishment with these students is to use the punishment immediately following the misbehavior so that the students will remember and associate the misbehavior with the punishment.

A second variable is the *intensity* of the punisher. As a rule, the more intense a punisher, the more effective it will be in suppressing the unwanted behavior.

A third variable is the schedule of punishment, i.e., whether or not the punishment is delivered each time the misbehavior occurs. To maximize the effectiveness of a punishment procedure, it should follow each occurrence of the undesirable behavior.

The final and most important variable is whether or not an alternative behavior will be reinforced. The cardinal rule in using punishment is to *always provide reinforcement for an alternative appropriate behavior*. For example, if attention is suspected to be the reinforcer that is maintaining the misbehavior, provide attention for an appropriate behavior and punishment for the misbehavior. In addition to making your punishment procedure work effectively, the reinforcement of an alternative behavior offers another benefit; namely, it will not be necessary to use an intense punisher. Scientific research has shown that mild forms of punishment are highly effective when the student has some means of obtaining reinforcement other than via the misbehavior that is being punished.

To summarize, by carefully considering these four variables when you design a punishment procedure, you will be treating the misbehaving student in a humane fashion. When you maximize the effectiveness of a punishment procedure, it will work more quickly, thus reducing the number of times punishment will be necessary.

We have all encountered students or individuals who do not seem to be affected by what we would consider to be punishing consequences. For example, there is general agreement that being scolded is a punishing or aversive experience, yet some children are unaffected when their parents scold them. By unaffected, we mean that the scolding does not produce a subsequent decline in their behavior. Scolding was obviously not a punishing consequence and in fact might even be maintaining (reinforcing) the misbehavior. An even more extreme example is masochism. Someone who is excited by a certain type of pain hardly finds that pain to be a punishing experience. The point is, it is very unwise to make sweeping generalizations about what is punishing for someone (or, for that matter, what is reinforcing). This is why you should always *specify or define a consequence by its effect on the behavior*. If it increases the behavior, it is a reinforcing consequence; if it decreases the behavior, it is a punishing consequence. Thus, we attend to how a consequence effects the behavior rather than to the nature of the consequence itself. The following example illustrates this point.

A kiss, hug, or extra piece of pie can under certain conditions function as punishers. For example, you are sitting next to a person who is writing on a note pad. If you were to kiss him every time his pen touches the writing pad, one of two things would probably happen. If he found your kisses reinforcing, his note writing frequency, or rate, would increase as long as kissing was contingent on note writing and the behavior did not become satiated. If he found your kisses offensive, his rate of writing notes in your presence would decrease markedly. In this latter instance, your kisses by definition would be a punisher. Similarly, a hug from you, if it were offensive to him, would decrease his note taking. Or if he had just finished a large lunch and was satiated, your force feeding him bits of his favorite food, say apple pie, each time he wrote on the pad would decrease his note taking. Thus, we see that under certain circumstances events we ordinarily regard as powerful reinforcers can serve as punishers, and vice versa. This example clarifies that when we speak of punishing a response, we are discussing the use of an ethically defensible behavioral event that will decrease that response. We are certainly not referring to some barbaric technique or procedure that is designed to cause physical or psychological harm.

There are several advantages of using punishment to decrease a behavior:

1. Punishment immediately suppresses the behavior. When applied correctly, punishment will immediately stop the student's misbehavior.
2. Punishment produces an enduring effect when generalization has occurred. The future probability of the misbehavior's occurrence is greatly reduced

when punishment is used effectively. In other words, the procedure is long-lasting.

3. Punishment may produce complete suppression of the misbehavior; that is, the misbehavior may be reduced to a zero level (eliminated) by punishment.

4. Punishment may be instructive to the misbehaving student's classmates. The use of punishment to treat a student's misbehavior reduces the chance that the student's classmates will imitate the misbehavior. Having observed the punishing consequence being applied, other students are less likely to misbehave since they do not wish to receive the punishment.

5. Punishment may produce an irreversible effect. When punishment is maximally used, the behavior may be eliminated forever in those situations in which it was punished. This advantage distinguishes punishment from any other reductive procedures because no procedure, other than punishment, can produce an irreversible effect. However, if a misbehavior is taken totally out of the student's behavioral repertoire, it can be shaped up again if the contingencies are arranged in a manner to do so.

Lest we regard punishment as a panacea, we must carefully consider its disadvantages or side effects. The disadvantages of punishment are:

1. Punishment may produce emotional behavior. The student may become nervous and upset when punished or about to be punished. There is also the chance that others will engage in aversive behaviors which are cued by the punishment procedure.

2. The punished student may become aggressive when punished. This aggression can either be elicited or operant. In elicited aggression, the student attacks a classmate or an inanimate object. The aggression is said to be elicited because it was not directed toward the source of the punishment. In operant aggression, the punished student attacks the source of the punishment, i.e., the instructor. The purpose of this attack, of course, is an attempt to end the punishment.

3. Negative modeling may occur. When you punish a student, you run the risk of teaching the student how to punish others. Negative modeling occurs when you, the punisher, serve as a model for the student to imitate. In this case, you are modeling how to punish others. Negative modeling explains why children who were abused by their parents grow up to become child abusers.

4. The student may attempt to escape or avoid the punishing situation or person. This is a very serious disadvantage because your opportunities to have positive interactions with the student would be severely limited if he or she avoided interacting with you or attempted to escape an interaction.

Fortunately, there is a very simple way of avoiding or reducing the possibility that these disadvantages or side effects will occur. Follow the cardinal rule when using punishment: *Always reinforce an alternative appropriate response.* By doing so, you will reduce the student's anxiety, the possibility that he or she will attack you or someone else, and the student's desire to avoid or escape interacting with you. You will also be helping the student to form the discrimination that appropriate behavior is reinforced while inappropriate behavior is punished. And you will be serving as a positive model.

CONDITIONED AVERSIVE STIMULI

A CONDITIONED AVERSIVE STIMULUS IS A NEUTRAL STIMULUS THAT HAS ACQUIRED AVERSIVE PROPERTIES BECAUSE IT HAS BEEN REPEATEDLY PAIRED WITH A PRIMARY AVERSIVE STIMULUS.

When using a punishment procedure, your ultimate goal is to reduce and eventually eliminate its use. To do this, you should always pair a conditioned aversive stimulus with the punishment.

The word "No," frowns, and negative gestures, such as shaking your fist at someone, are conditioned aversive stimuli. We regard these events as aversive because they have been paired in the past with punishing events, such as spankings, scoldings, and even physical attacks. The word "No" itself had no meaning for us until it was paired with these punishing events. Eventually, however, "No" came to mean that we were to stop what we were doing or that we were being instructed not to do something. It is very important for you to always pair the word "No" with the delivery of punishment. By doing so, the word "No" will eventually suppress the student's misbehavior. The use of "No" to function as a conditioned aversive stimulus is crucial to you because it offers you a simple way of controlling the student's misbehavior without having to resort to the punishment procedure each time.

Before continuing this chapter, answer the following questions.

1. After Marilyn bit her little sister, Marilyn's mother spanked her. Marilyn's mother used what type of punishment?
2. After Alice broke her mother's vase, her mother sent Alice to her room for 30 minutes. What type of punishment did Alice's mother use?
3. Ms. Jefferson, Jonathan's teacher, has instituted a punishment program to reduce his screaming in class. As part of her program, she intends to liberally reinforce Jonathan for on-task behavior. Ms. Jefferson is following the cardinal rule for using punishment. What is it?
4. You are describing the four variables that influence the effectiveness of a punishment procedure to some of your fellow instructors. What would you tell them?
5. Ms. Ryland has been requiring Robert to sit in the corner for 5 minutes whenever he hits one of his classmates. She sends him to the corner because

she thinks it is punishing. There has been no decrease in Robert's hitting in the 2 weeks that she has been using the procedure. What has Ms. Ryland learned about this supposed punishing consequence?

6. Name the five advantages of punishment.
7. Name the five disadvantages of punishment.
8. On one occasion Elliot tried to hit his teacher when she sent him to the corner. On another occasion he kicked the trash can on his way to the corner. Elliot's attack toward his teacher represented what kind of aggression? His kicking the trash can represented what kind of aggression?
9. Ms. Klein said, "No, Rose don't pick your nose!" Ms. Klein was using the word "No" as what?

Answers are on page 208.

TIMEOUT

> TIMEOUT IS A PUNISHMENT PROCEDURE IN WHICH POSITIVE REINFORCEMENT IS WITHDRAWN FOR A PRESPECIFIED PERIOD OF TIME FOLLOWING THE PERFORMANCE OF THE MISBEHAVIOR.

Timeout punishment is widely used in classrooms for severely and profoundly retarded students. There are two basic types of timeout: exclusionary and nonexclusionary. Both types are used in a variety of ways. An exclusionary timeout procedure consists of removing the misbehaving student from the reinforcing environment for a specified period of time. The student's removal is accomplished by placing him in a timeout room, requiring him to remain behind a partition located in a corner of the classroom, or requiring him to stand in the hallway. A nonexclusionary timeout procedure consists of allowing the student to remain in the reinforcing environment but not allowing him to engage in reinforcing activities for a specified period of time. Nonexclusionary timeout is accomplished by removing or withdrawing a specific reinforcer, requiring the student to sit in a chair in the corner and observe his classmates receiving reinforcers, or by a timeout ribbon procedure (described below). Basically, the difference between these two types of timeout is that exclusionary timeout requires that the student be removed from the reinforcers while nonexclusionary timeout requires that the reinforcers be removed from the student.

Before these procedures are discussed in detail, we must first discuss the common characteristics of any sound timeout program. The first and perhaps most important characteristic is that there must be a *high density of reinforcement* in the classroom. This high density of reinforcement ensures that timeout will be aversive and thereby effective because the student will be missing reinforcement opportunities while in timeout. The most common reason why timeout programs fail is that the density of reinforcement in the "reinforcing environment" is too low. As a result, there is not enough contrast between the reinforcing environment and timeout. In these instances, the student is essentially in timeout in both situations. The establishment of a high density of reinforcement in the classroom also minimizes the possibility that the student may misbehave in order to escape or avoid a stressful learning situation. Some students will actually misbehave in order to receive timeout, because they prefer the timeout over the required educational activity. This usually occurs when there are high response requirements associated with the activity (e.g., the student must actively respond) and little reinforcement available for performing the activity (a low density of reinforcement). However, if the density of reinforcement during the activity is high, the student will be less motivated to misbehave in order to escape or avoid the activity.

A second characteristic of a sound timeout program is that there is little, if any, reinforcement available to the student during the period he is in timeout. This, of course, maximizes the aversiveness of the timeout period.

A third characteristic is that the duration of the timeout has been pre-specified and is brief. Under normal circumstances, the maximum period for any single timeout should be 30 minutes. At the end of that time, the student is returned to the reinforcing environment provided he is not misbehaving when the timeout interval ends. (What to do if the student is still misbehaving is discussed below.) Failure to specify the duration and keep it brief can result in abuses and misuses of timeout. For example, you may have read newspaper articles about so-called "behavior modification programs" in centers for juvenile delinquents. The article probably noted the use of solitary confinement for several weeks and called that confinement "timeout." Clearly, that procedure was not timeout; it was an abuse of authority.

A fourth characteristic is that the student is not released from timeout if he is misbehaving when the timeout period ends. Releasing a misbehaving student from timeout is a major error because it pairs the student's misbehavior with release from timeout and such release would be reinforcing for the student. The student could then be expected to misbehave each time he was placed in timeout. To avoid this problem, the student is released from timeout at the end of the timeout period only if he is not misbehaving. Thus, we are pairing release from timeout with appropriate behavior. If the student is misbehaving when the timeout period ends, recycle the timeout interval in 1-minute blocks of time and require that the student behave appropriately during the last 15 seconds of that interval. In other words, the student must not misbehave during the final 15 seconds of timeout in order to leave the timeout. *Under no circumstances should you recycle the entire timeout period if the student is misbehaving at the end of the timeout period.* Otherwise, the student might not ever get out of timeout.

Remember that when returning to the activities from which the student was excluded, the student may be reinforced or punished immediately, depending on the stimuli present at that time, e.g., the responses of the other students. Reinforcement for returning must be given. If the return is punished, students may try to escape the return.

A fifth characteristic is that the timeout is applied immediately following the misbehavior as is the case with any punishment procedure.

Sixth, verbal interactions with the student are brief, to the point, and are paired with the word "No" (a conditioned aversive stimulus). When the student misbehaves, simply say, "No, you (*name the misbehavior*), and you must go into timeout." There is nothing else you need to say, except possibly, "You cannot leave timeout if you are misbehaving (*name the specific misbehavior*)" and "You must stay here _____ minutes (*specify the duration of timeout*)." These limited verbal interactions while you institute the timeout will reduce the possibility that your attention will reinforce the student for misbehaving. While the student is in timeout, do *not* talk to him. If, at the beginning of the timeout period, you did not tell him that he could not leave timeout while misbehaving, simply let him figure that out.

Seventh, efforts are taken to prevent "bootleg" reinforcement which occurs when a student's classmates give him attention (social reinforcement) while he is in timeout. Although this is more of a problem with moderately retarded and normal students, it can occur in classrooms for severely and profoundly retarded students. If it does, the timeout program will lose much of its effectiveness because of the reinforcement the student is receiving while in timeout.

The eighth and final characteristic is that detailed records must be kept. These records list the name of the student receiving timeout, the misbehavior that resulted in timeout, the time the student began timeout, the time the student was released from timeout, and the name of the instructor who instituted and terminated the timeout. (These records are especially important when a timeout room is being used.) Maintaining detailed timeout records will, in part, allow you to determine the effectiveness of the procedure and whether or not it is being used in an arbitrary and punitive fashion. Furthermore, these records will offer you some legal protection if something by chance goes awry.

Although exclusionary timeout is generally considered to be more aversive than nonexclusionary timeout in the Least Restrictive Model of Treatment, it is discussed here first so that the added advantages of nonexclusionary timeout can be compared to some of the disadvantages of exclusionary timeout.

Before continuing this chapter, answer the following questions.

1. What is the basic difference between exclusionary and nonexclusionary timeout?
2. According to the Least Restrictive Model of Treatment, is exclusionary timeout or nonexclusionary timeout considered to be more aversive?
3. To ensure that a timeout program will be aversive and thereby effective, a high density of reinforcement must be provided _____.

4. If possible, there should be no reinforcement available to the student when he or she is in _____.
5. To use timeout properly, the duration of timeout should be prespecified and it should be b_____.
6. A student should never be released from timeout if he or she is m_____ _____.
7. To be effective, timeout should be applied immediately following the _____ _____.
8. In a timeout program, all verbal interactions with the student should be b_____ to the p_____ and paired with the word "_____."
9. When a misbehaving student's classmates give the student attention while he or she is in timeout, it is called _____ _____.
10. In any sound timeout program, you must collect _____.

Turn to page 209 for the answers.

Exclusionary Timeout

There are three ways to use exclusionary timeout: 1) remove the student to a timeout room, 2) place the student behind a partition that is located in a corner of the classroom, and 3) require the student to stand in the hallway.

Timeout Room   A timeout room is a small room devoid of any reinforcing stimuli; that is, the room is bare. The ideal timeout room is located adjacent to, or near, the classroom, has good lighting and ventilation, and a window (made of Plexiglas) or one-way-vision mirror on the door to permit unobtrusive observations of the student. A record sheet (described earlier) should hang on the outside of the timeout room door or on a nearby wall. The following example illustrates the use of a timeout room.

Bobby occasionally hits other children. To reduce this behavior, Ms. Santos has decided to use a timeout room. The next time Bobby hit a classmate, Ms. Santos said, "No, you hit Charlie, you must go to the timeout room." Ms. Santos quickly took Bobby's hand and rapidly escorted him to a nearby, small, vacant room. She opened the door, placed Bobby in the room, said, "You must stay here 10 minutes," and closed the door. She then recorded the time, Bobby's name, her name, and the misbehavior on the record sheet that was hanging on the door. Ten minutes later, Ms. Santos returned to the timeout room, opened the door, and said, "You can come out now and go back to class." She recorded the time she let Bobby out of timeout on the record sheet and then escorted him back to class. Within 2 weeks, the use of the timeout room had eliminated Bobby's hitting others.

The advantages associated with using a timeout room are:

1. The disruptive student is removed from the reinforcing environment, thus increasing the possibility that the timeout will be aversive.

2. The timeout room is devoid of any reinforcing stimuli so there are few reinforcers for the student while in timeout.
3. There is no possibility of bootleg reinforcement.
4. Entrance in and out of the room provides the student with a clear signal as to when timeout is in effect.
5. Highly agitated students can be removed from the classroom, thereby eliminating the possibility that they might injure someone, destroy property, or disrupt the educational activities of the other students.

The disadvantages of a timeout room procedure are:

1. It is difficult, if not impossible, to institute the timeout immediately because the student must be taken to the timeout room.
2. A special room must be set up to function as the timeout room, which can present difficulties when room space is at a premium.
3. There is the distinct possibility that the student may receive some attention for his or her misbehavior during the process of being taken to the timeout room. For example, if the student becomes combative while you are attempting to go to the timeout room, you will be providing the student with attention in your efforts to overcome his or her resistance. The student could also, at this time, be receiving attention from classmates while you are struggling.
4. The continuity of the classroom educational tasks is interrupted. Whenever a student is to be placed in a timeout room, one of the classroom instructors must escort the student there. That person must immediately terminate whatever he or she is doing with the students so that the timeout program can be instituted. Thus, when the timeout room is used frequently, the daily classroom schedule can be disrupted by the frequent absences of the instructors.
5. The procedure can only be used in those situations in which a timeout room is available. When you rely on a timeout room procedure, you are limited to where you can use the procedure. As a result, it is difficult to program for generalization of the procedure. For example, what do you do on a field trip when the student misbehaves?
6. The procedure is less likely to be effective for the self-isolate (i.e., the student who enjoys being alone), for students who engage in high rates of self-stimulatory behavior, or for students who masturbate frequently. To overcome this problem, you must ensure that the classroom contains a high density of reinforcement.
7. The student may engage in behaviors while in timeout that require you to enter the timeout room and intervene. For example, if the student becomes self-abusive, rips off clothing, or smears feces on the walls, you must intervene to interrupt these behaviors. (This would be especially true in the case of self-abuse where the student's well-being was threatened.) By doing so, you are providing the student with attention (social reinforcement) and hence have

nullified the timeout program. It is entirely possible that the student may display such bizarre behaviors because there is little else to do in the timeout room. Thus, the student has more control in the timeout room than might at first be expected. Fortunately, only a small number of students engage in such bizarre behaviors while they are in timeout. Nevertheless, it is a potential problem that you may encounter.

Timeout Behind a Partition in the Classroom   A timeout area can be created by partitioning off a corner of the classroom. Ideally, the partitions should be stable enough so that the student cannot move them or knock them over. The record sheet can be hung on the partition.

The timeout area procedure essentially offers the same advantages as the timeout room with one notable exception. The student may receive bootleg reinforcement because he or she may be able to generate sufficient noise to disturb classmates and thereby gain their attention. In fact, if the student is loud enough, the entire classroom routine may be disturbed. The timeout area does, however, offer an advantage over the timeout room. It allows the procedure to be implemented more quickly. Also, it does not require the use of a special room or disrupt the continuity of the educational activities as much as a timeout room procedure does. The timeout area does suffer from the other disadvantages listed above for the timeout room.

Timeout in the Hallway   This is a seldom used form of exclusionary timeout, for a very good reason. In addition to having the disadvantages listed above for the timeout room, the misbehaving student may run away or go into other classrooms and cause a disturbance. As a result, a student should not be placed in timeout in the hallway unless: 1) he is quite docile and under good instructional control, i.e., he will follow your instructions to remain in the hallway, and 2) the duration of timeout is quite brief, i.e., 5 minutes or less.

Before continuing this chapter, answer the following questions.

1. Name three ways of using exclusionary timeout.
2. List five advantages associated with using a timeout room.
3. List seven disadvantages associated with using a timeout room.
4. List one disadvantage that timeout behind a partition does not share with a timeout room. List three advantages the procedure does not share with a timeout room procedure.
5. List the two criteria for using a hallway timeout procedure. What is the major disadvantage of this procedure?

Answers are on page 209.

Nonexclusionary Timeout

There are three ways to use nonexclusionary timeout: 1) withdrawing a specific reinforcer, 2) requiring the student to sit in a corner of the classroom, and 3) employing the timeout ribbon procedure.

Timeout by Withdrawing a Specific Reinforcer   This type of nonexclusionary timeout is useful when the student misbehaves during a specific activity in which a very powerful reinforcer is available to him. For example, if a student attempts to eat with his fingers during mealtime, you can place him in timeout simply by removing his plate of food for a minute or two. Because the food is a powerful reinforcer and an integral part of the educational activity (i.e., teaching appropriate table manners), the inappropriate eating behavior will be suppressed quickly. Another example would be a student who is misbehaving while playing with his favorite toy. Removing the toy for a brief period contingent on the misbehavior should produce a rapid decrease in that misbehavior.

The advantages of this nonexclusionary timeout procedure are:

1. Timeout can be implemented immediately.
2. The student sees what he or she is missing which should help to make the procedure aversive (punishing).
3. The presence or absence of the reinforcer provides a clear signal as to when timeout is in effect.
4. No special room or area is required.
5. There is little chance that bootleg reinforcement will be a problem since the reinforcer from which the student is being timed out should be more powerful for the student than attention from classmates. Also, there is less chance that your attention will reinforce any misbehavior because you are not required to escort the student anywhere.
6. There is less interruption of the classroom routine since the timeout is implemented in the classroom environment.
7. The procedure can be used in a variety of locations and situations. For example, timing a student out from a plate of food can be accomplished in any situation in which the food is available.
8. There is less chance the student will misbehave during the timeout period. The student quickly learns that by misbehaving during timeout, he or she is only delaying access to the powerful reinforcer.
9. The procedure will be effective with self-isolates, self-stimulators, and masturbators because those reinforcing behaviors are competing with a powerful reinforcer (the timed out reinforcer) for which the student is highly deprived.

The disadvantages of the procedure are:

1. The student may become agitated and/or combative when the reinforcer is removed. If the agitation is serious enough, some type of backup procedure such as a timeout room will be required.
2. The student may disturb classmates because he or she is remaining in the educational environment.
3. The success of the procedure is dependent on a powerful reinforcer and a sufficient level of deprivation for that reinforcer.

4. Another disadvantage of this procedure is that if a reinforcer is withheld, an appropriate behavior is not being reinforced.

Timeout by Requiring the Student to Sit in a Corner of the Classroom This is a general type of nonexclusionary timeout that can be used for a variety of misbehaviors that occur in the classroom. The procedure can be implemented in either of two ways. One way is to require the student to sit in a chair located in the corner of the classroom during timeout. This is sometimes called a timeout chair procedure. The other way (sometimes called contingent observation) is simply to require the student to sit at the perimeter of the classroom during timeout. The only real difference between the two procedures is that one specifies that the student must be seated in a chair during the timeout period. The rationale underlying both procedures is that the student will be learning appropriate forms of behavior by observing classmates during his or her timeout.

Ms. Santos has decided to try a timeout chair procedure to punish Bobby when he hits his classmates. When Bobby hits someone, Ms. Santos says "No, you hit Charlie, you must go sit in the timeout chair." She then quickly takes Bobby's hand and rapidly escorts him to a chair located in the corner of the classroom. She seats Bobby and tells him, "You must sit here for 5 minutes." Ms. Santos returns to her desk, fills out her timeout record sheet, and then begins working with the other students. Five minutes later, she returns to Bobby and tells him he may return to his desk, provided he is not misbehaving at the time.

These two procedures—the timeout chair procedure and contingent observation—offer the same advantages and disadvantages as timeout by withdrawing a specific reinforcer with the following exceptions. The additional advantages of these procedures are:

1. They can be used to punish a variety of misbehaviors.
2. Positive modeling may take place. If the timed out student observes classmates behaving appropriately and receiving reinforcers for such behaviors, the student may imitate these positive behaviors when returned to the reinforcing environment.
3. The student will not miss the ongoing educational activities because they can still be observed.

The additional disadvantages are:

1. The student may not stay in the chair or seated at the perimeter of the classroom.
2. Because there is no single powerful reinforcer involved, there is a greater chance that bootleg reinforcement may nullify the procedure, or that self-isolates, self-stimulators, or masturbators will find the timeout period reinforcing.

The Timeout Ribbon Procedure The timeout ribbon procedure offers some distinct advantages over the other nonexclusionary timeout procedures.

The timeout ribbon procedure can be used with one student, a few students, or your entire class. When it is used with all of your students, the program is set up as follows. All the students in the classroom are given a ribbon to wear around their necks or on their wrists. Each ribbon is a different color so that the ribbons are individualized. Whenever a student is reinforced, the instructor describes the appropriate behavior and mentions the fact that the student is wearing his ribbon, e.g., "Good, Dave, you are working the puzzle and wearing your ribbon." Pairing the requirement that the ribbon be worn with the delivery of reinforcers establishes the ribbon (a neutral stimulus) as a discriminative stimulus for reinforcement and hence a continued reinforcer (see Chapter 8). Over time, the students learn that they must be wearing their ribbons in order to receive any reinforcement.

Once the ribbons have been established as a prerequisite for reinforcement (ribbons have acquired reinforcing properties when the students cease trying to remove them), the timeout procedure is implemented. Whenever a student misbehaves, the instructor removes the student's ribbon and says, for example, "No, Dave, you are screaming, you cannot have your ribbon." The ribbon is removed for a specified period (the timeout interval) and all forms of instructor-dispensed reinforcement and the student's participation in classroom activities are discontinued. At the end of the timeout period, the ribbon is returned provided that the student is not misbehaving.

The timeout ribbon procedure offers all of the advantages of the other two nonexclusionary timeout procedures as well as several additional benefits:

1. Group treatment is possible. The timeout procedure can be implemented at any time with any and all students who have misbehaved. Thus, there is no problem of running out of timeout rooms, partitions, or chairs.
2. Bootleg reinforcement can be quickly terminated because all the instructor needs to do is remove the ribbon(s) of the student(s) who is providing attention to the misbehaving classmate.
3. Any bizarre misbehaviors that the student performs during timeout, such as self-abuse, can be interrupted by the teacher in the early parts of the response chain. The instructor would simply stop the misbehavior by commenting or looking at the student. There is less danger that the teacher will be reinforcing the misbehavior because the instructor is already in the timeout situation with the student.
4. The presence or absence of the ribbon provides a clear signal to classroom visitors when it is appropriate to interact with a student. One of the major problems that can occur during the use of a reductive procedure such as extinction or timeout is that a visitor often inadvertently reinforces the student with attention. The timeout ribbon procedure, however, eliminates this prob-

lem. By placing a large sign outside the classroom door that explains the purpose of the timeout ribbon procedure, you will not have to intercept each classroom visitor to explain which of your students are allowed a social interaction.

5. The highly visible ribbons serve as a reminder to the instructor of who to reinforce. Similarly, the absence of the ribbon helps the instructor to remember who is in timeout and to let the student out of timeout.
6. The procedure can be used across settings (e.g., across classes, at home and school, at school and in a residential setting) because the student can *always* wear the ribbon. This benefit makes it an excellent procedure to teach to parents and thereby helps ensure a consistent programming effort throughout the student's waking hours.
7. There is no concern about keeping the timed out student in one location as is the case with the other nonexclusionary timeout procedures.

Aside from sharing the disadvantages already noted for nonexclusionary timeout procedures, the timeout ribbon has one additional disadvantage. Because the timed out student is free to move about the classroom, he or she could easily disturb other students or possibly destroy classroom property (e.g., ripping pictures off the wall). One way to minimize this problem is to keep all teaching materials in locked cabinets unless they are being used in the current activity and to ensure that any objects on the walls are either firmly attached, indestructible, or expendable.

The key to the success of a timeout ribbon procedure is that the ribbon be established as a requirement for reinforcement. Other objects can also be used in the same fashion as the ribbon. A happy face button or some type of tag can serve as the timeout object. We prefer the use of ribbon wrist bands with Velcro tape on each end rather than a ribbon necklace because the wrist band is less obtrusive and therefore fits in better with the spirit of normalization. To ensure that the object acquires reinforcing properties, you must provide liberal amounts of reinforcement when you are beginning the program. Along this line, the frequency of reinforcement must be shorter than the timeout interval. If the timeout period is 3 minutes, reinforcement should be delivered to the other students about every 2 minutes. By doing this, you will be ensuring that the timed out student misses at least one reinforcement opportunity.

Before continuing this chapter, answer the following questions.

1. List three ways of using nonexclusionary timeout.
2. List the nine advantages of placing a student in timeout by withdrawing a specific reinforcer.
3. List the four disadvantages of placing a student in timeout by withdrawing a specific reinforcer.
4. List three advantages of placing a student in timeout in the corner of the

classroom that are not shared with the timeout procedure of withdrawing a specific reinforcer.
5. List two disadvantages of placing a student in timeout in the corner of the classroom that are not shared with the timeout procedure of withdrawing a specific reinforcer.
6. List seven advantages of the timeout ribbon procedure that are not shared with the other nonexclusionary timeout methods.
7. List the one disadvantage of the timeout ribbon procedure that is not shared with the other nonexclusionary timeout methods.

Answers are on page 210.

THE LEAST RESTRICTIVE TREATMENT MODEL

We have now discussed nine procedures that will decrease an undesirable behavior and have grouped them into three levels. Level 1 procedures contain no aversive properties, while level 2 procedures do contain some aversive properties. Procedures in level 3 are completely aversive which is why written approval must be obtained before you use them.

Level 1 procedures	Level 2 procedures	Level 3 procedures
DRO (differential reinforcement of other behavior)	Negative practice Extinction	Nonexclusionary timeout Exclusionary timeout Physical restraint
DRA (differential reinforcement of appropriate behavior)		
DRI (differential reinforcement of incompatible behavior)		
Satiation		

SUMMARY

Three aversive procedures for decreasing a misbehavior are physical restraint and the two punishment procedures of exclusionary and nonexclusionary timeout.

Behavioral physical restraint is a procedure in which the student is prevented from moving limbs and/or body for a prespecified period following performance of a misbehavior. Custodial physical restraint is a nonbehavioral procedure that is used to prevent and control agitated or self-abusive persons. The procedures differ in that behavioral physical restraint is a brief negative consequence whose duration is prespecified whereas custodial physical restraint is applied noncontingently for indeterminate periods of time. The two ways of implementing behavioral physical restraint are with your hands or with mechanical devices.

Punishment is an event that decreases the frequency of the behavior it follows. There are two types of punishment. One type involves the application of an aversive event following the misbehavior. The other type involves the withdrawal of a positive reinforcer following the misbehavior. We cannot state whether a consequence is a punisher or reinforcer until we specify the consequence by its effect on the behavior it follows. If the behavior increases, the consequence is reinforcing. If the behavior decreases, the consequence is punishing. A conditioned aversive stimulus is a neutral stimulus that has acquired its aversive properties because it has been repeatedly paired with a primary aversive stimulus. A classic example of a conditioned aversive stimulus is the word "No."

Timeout is a punishment procedure in which positive reinforcement is withdrawn for a prespecified period of time following the performance of the misbehavior. There are two types of timeout: exclusionary and nonexclusionary. In exclusionary timeout, the student is removed from the reinforcers. In nonexclusionary timeout, the reinforcers are removed from the student.

There are three ways to use exclusionary timeout: 1) remove the student to a timeout room, 2) place the student behind a partition located in the corner of the classroom, and 3) require the student to stand in the hallway. There are also three ways to use nonexclusionary timeout: 1) withdraw a specific reinforcer such as food, 2) require the student to sit in a corner of the classroom, and 3) use the timeout ribbon procedure.

The two timeout procedures as well as physical restraint are highly aversive and are therefore considered to be level 3 procedures in the Least Restrictive Model of Treatment. Written permission must be obtained from parents and school administrators before you can use these procedures.

REVIEW QUESTIONS

1. A procedure in which the student is prevented from moving limbs and/or body is called _____ _____.
2. Physical restraint is used almost exclusively to treat severe cases of s_____-a_____ behavior.
3. Behavioral physical restraint is a behavioral consequence whereas custodial physical restraint is not because _____.
4. The advantages of physical restraint are: a) the misbehavior cannot occur, b) the misbehavior may be eliminated, and c) _____.
5. The disadvantages of physical restraint are: a) it is a_____, b) the restraint can become r_____, c) the student's struggling during restraint can be a form of i_____ e_____, d) it may be used in an a_____ or p_____ fashion, e) the full participation of a s_____ p_____ is required when the

restraint is not mechanical, and f) it is p_____ i_____, thereby increasing the chance that someone may be injured.

6. An event that decreases the frequency of the behavior it follows is called _____.

7. One type of punishment involves the application of an aversive event following the _____.

8. A second type of punishment involves the withdrawal of a p_____ r_____ following the _____.

9. The cardinal rule in using punishment is to *always provide reinforcement* for an _____ _____ behavior.

10. You should always specify or define a consequence by its e_____ on the _____.

11. Punishment immediately suppresses a behavior, produces an _____ effect, may produce c_____ suppression, and may produce an i_____ effect.

12. The negative side effects of punishment are e_____ behavior, a_____, and n_____ m_____, as well as the student's attempting to e_____ or a_____ the punishing situation or person.

13. A neutral stimulus that has acquired aversive properties because it has been repeatedly paired with a primary aversive stimulus is a c_____ a_____ s_____.

14. A punishment procedure in which positive reinforcement is withdrawn for a prespecified period of time following the performance of the misbehavior is called _____.

15. A procedure that consists of removing the misbehaving student from the reinforcing environment is _____ _____.

16. A procedure that consists of allowing the misbehaving student to remain in the reinforcing environment but not allowing the student to engage in reinforcing activities is _____ _____.

17. A student should never be released from timeout while misbehaving. Rather, the student should be released _____.

18. The entire timeout period should never be recycled when the student is misbehaving at the end of the timeout period. Rather, the timeout interval should be recycled in 1-_____ blocks of time.

19. The three ways of using exclusionary timeout are: a) remove the student to a _____ room, b) place the student behind a p_____ located in a corner of the classroom, and c) require the student to stand in the h_____.

20. The ideal timeout room is located near the c_____, has good l_____ and v_____, and has a w_____ or one-way-vision _____ to permit unobtrusive observation of the student.

21. The three ways of using nonexclusionary timeout are: a) withdrawing a _____ reinforcer, b) requiring the student to sit in a c_____ of the c_____, and c) using the t_____ r_____ procedure.

22. The student is required to sit in a chair located in the corner of the classroom in the _____ _____ procedure.
23. The student is required to sit at the perimeter of the classroom during timeout in the c_____ o_____ procedure.
24. In the timeout ribbon procedure, the frequency of reinforcement must be shorter than the t_____ _____.
25. Because they are aversive, p_____ r_____, e_____ t_____, and n_____ t_____ are level ____ procedures in the Least Restrictive Model of Treatment.
26. Before a level 3 procedure is used you must obtain written permission from _____ and _____.

Answers are on page 210.

ANSWERS TO CHAPTER QUESTIONS

Answers to Questions on Page 190

1. Assuming that less restrictive methods have failed, physical restraint could be used for rectal digging, hitting others, face scratching, and clothes ripping. The other behaviors listed are treatable by less restrictive methods.
2. a. Behavioral physical restraint is a negative consequence whereas custodial physical restraint is often applied independent of any misbehavior.
   b. The duration of behavioral physical restraint is prespecified whereas the duration of custodial physical restraint is not specified.
   c. The duration of behavioral physical restraint is brief (i.e., never more than 30 minutes) whereas custodial physical restraint can last indefinitely.
3. Larry's teacher could restrain his hands with hers for a prespecified period following each instance of self-abuse.
4. Larry's teacher could restrain his arms by placing a splint-like device over them contingent on self-abuse.
5. Any physical contact associated with the restraint procedure could become reinforcing for a student who has been deprived of physical contact. The use of physical contact to reinforce an appropriate behavior provides the student with a means of obtaining physical contact through acceptable behavior.

Answers to Questions on Pages 194–195

1. Marilyn's mother applied an aversive event (spanking) following the misbehavior (biting little sister).
2. Alice's mother used withdrawal of a positive reinforcer because Alice missed a number of reinforcing events (e.g., playing outside or watching TV) while she was in her room.
3. Always provide reinforcement for an alternative appropriate behavior.
4. The four variables that influence the effectiveness of a punishment procedure are immediacy, intensity, the schedule of punishment, and whether or not an alternative appropriate behavior is reinforced.
5. Sending Robert to the corner is not a punishing consequence because it has not decreased his hitting behavior. Ms. Ryland has learned that you specify a consequence

by its effect on the behavior. In this case, sending Robert to the corner may even be a reinforcing consequence that is maintaining his hitting.

6. Advantages of punishment:
   a. Immediately suppresses behavior
   b. Produces an enduring effect
   c. May produce complete suppression of the behavior
   d. May produce an irreversible effect
   e. May be instructive to other students
7. Disadvantages of punishment:
   a. May produce emotional behavior
   b. May cause the student to become aggressive
   c. May produce negative modeling
   d. May cause the student to avoid or escape interactions with his or her instructor
8. Operant, elicited
9. A conditioned aversive stimulus

Answers to Questions on Pages 197–198

1. Exclusionary timeout involves removing the student from the reinforcers (reinforcing environment) whereas nonexclusionary timeout involves removing the reinforcers from the student.
2. exclusionary timeout
3. in the classroom
4. timeout
5. brief
6. misbehaving
7. misbehavior
8. brief, point, No
9. bootleg reinforcement
10. data

Answers to Questions on Page 200

1. a. Timeout room
   b. Timeout behind a partition
   c. Timeout in the hallway
2. a. The student is removed from the reinforcing environment.
   b. The timeout room is devoid of any reinforcing stimuli.
   c. There is no possibility of bootleg reinforcement.
   d. The student's presence in the room serves as a clear signal that timeout is in effect.
   e. The timeout room provides a safe place to take highly agitated students.
3. a. Timeout cannot be implemented immediately.
   b. A special room is required.
   c. Attention may be given to the misbehaving student on the way to the timeout room.
   d. The continuity of classroom educational tasks is interrupted when the instructor leaves to implement timeout.
   e. It is difficult to program for generalization because success of this procedure depends on the availability of a timeout room.
   f. It may not be effective for self-isolates, high rate self-stimulators, or frequent masturbators.
   g. The student's misbehavior in timeout could force the instructor to intervene and thereby nullify the timeout procedure.

4. The disadvantage is that the student may receive bootleg reinforcement.
   The advantages include:
   a. It can be implemented fairly quickly.
   b. It does not require a special room.
   c. There is less interruption of continuity of educational activities.
5. a. The student must be under good instructional control.
   b. The timeout duration must be brief, i.e., 5 minutes or less.
   The major disadvantage is that the student can run away.

Answers to Questions on Pages 204–205

1. a. Withdrawing a specific reinforcer
   b. Requiring student to sit in a corner of the classroom
   c. Using the timeout ribbon procedure
2. a. Timeout can be implemented immediately.
   b. The student sees what he or she is missing.
   c. The presence or absence of the reinforcer provides a clear signal of when timeout is in effect.
   d. No special room or area is required.
   e. There is little chance of bootleg reinforcement.
   f. There is little interruption of classroom routine.
   g. The procedure can be used in a variety of locations.
   h. There is less chance a student will misbehave during timeout.
   i. It is effective with self-isolates, self-stimulators, and masturbators.
3. a. The student may become combative or agitated.
   b. The student may disturb classmates.
   c. There is a slight chance of bootleg reinforcement.
   d. The specific reinforcer must be powerful and the student must be in a state of deprivation.
4. a. A variety of misbehaviors can be treated.
   b. Positive modeling may occur.
   c. The student does not miss any ongoing educational activities.
5. a. The student may not stay in the timeout area.
   b. There is a greater chance of bootleg reinforcement, and the procedure is less effective for self-isolates, self-stimulators, and masturbators.
6. a. Group treatment is possible.
   b. Bootleg reinforcement can be terminated quickly.
   c. Bizarre behavior in timeout can be interrupted and stopped.
   d. The presence or absence of the ribbon provides a clear signal to visitors as to when it is appropriate for them to interact with a student.
   e. The ribbon reminds the teacher to reinforce and to let the student out of timeout.
   f. It can be used across settings.
   g. The timed out student does not have to be kept in one location.
7. The student could more easily disturb classmates or destroy property.

Answers to Review Questions on Pages 206–208

1. physical restraint
2. self-abusive
3. it is often applied noncontingently and arbitrarily
4. the procedure may have long-lasting effects
5. aversive, reinforcing, isometric exercise, arbitrary or punitive, staff person, physically intrusive

6. punishment
7. misbehavior
8. positive reinforcer, misbehavior
9. alternative appropriate
10. effect, behavior
11. enduring, complete, irreversible
12. emotional, aggression, negative modeling, escape, avoid
13. conditioned aversive stimulus
14. timeout
15. exclusionary timeout
16. nonexclusionary timeout
17. when he or she is behaving appropriately
18. minute
19. timeout, partition, hallway
20. classroom, lighting, ventilation, window, mirror
21. specific, corner, classroom, timeout ribbon
22. timeout chair
23. contingent observation
24. timeout interval
25. physical restraint, exclusionary timeout, nonexclusionary timeout, 3
26. parents, school administrators

Chapter 13

DECREASING INAPPROPRIATE BEHAVIORS
Overcorrection

After reading this chapter, you will be able to:

1. Define overcorrection and list its two components.

2. Define and give an example of restitutional overcorrection.

3. Define and give an example of positive practice overcorrection.

4. List the four characteristics of overcorrection.

5. Define graduated guidance.

6. List the four common elements of all overcorrection programs.

7. Define and give an example of quiet training, social reassurance training, household orderliness training, oral hygiene training, medical assistance training, personal hygiene training, personal appearance training, and functional movement training.

8. Select the appropriate overcorrection program for a given misbehavior.

9. List the advantages and disadvantages of overcorrection.

Overcorrection is a recently developed punishment procedure that has been widely used with retarded and autistic students.

> OVERCORRECTION IS A PROCEDURE IN WHICH THE MISBEHAVING STUDENT IS REQUIRED TO DO MORE THAN IS NECESSARY TO CORRECT THE ENVIRONMENTAL EFFECTS OF HIS OR HER MISBEHAVIOR AND TO PRACTICE APPROPRIATE FORMS OF BEHAVIOR IN THOSE SITUATIONS WHERE THE MISBEHAVIOR COMMONLY OCCURS.

The general rationale of overcorrection is to require the misbehaving student: 1) to restore the disturbed situation to a state vastly improved, and 2) to practice overly correct forms of relevant behavior in those situations where the misbehavior commonly occurs. The first objective is accomplished by a component of overcorrection called *restitutional overcorrection* and the second objective by a component called *positive practice overcorrection*.

RESTITUTIONAL OVERCORRECTION

In restitutional overcorrection, the student is required to correct the consequences of his or her misbehavior by restoring the disturbed situation to a state vastly improved from that which existed prior to the disruption. To determine what the student should be required to do, first *identify the specific and general disturbances that resulted from the misbehavior and then identify the related behaviors needed to vastly improve the environment.* Once you have determined those corrective actions, you must require the misbehaving student to perform them whenever he or she misbehaves. For example, a student who overturned a desk would first be required to return the desk to its correct position and then to dust and wax it. After that, he would be required to straighten and dust all other desks in the room.

POSITIVE PRACTICE OVERCORRECTION

In positive practice overcorrection, the student is required to repeatedly practice appropriate behaviors in the situation in which he or she normally misbehaves. Thus, the positive practice overcorrection can serve an educative function because it may teach the student alternative, appropriate ways of responding. (*Note:* No reinforcement is delivered during positive practice or restitutional overcorrection; otherwise, the student might behave in order to receive the overcorrection punishment procedure.) To determine what the misbehaving student should be required to do in the positive practice overcorrection consequence, you must *identify appropriate behaviors that should be practiced* and then require the student to perform them whenever he or she misbehaves. The positive practice for overturning a desk would be to perform an appropriate behavior while seated at the desk, e.g., coloring or working a puzzle. Thus, the purpose of the positive practice would be to teach the student the appropriate behaviors associated with a desk.

Generally, the two overcorrection components are combined and applied as one procedure. In such cases, the restitutional overcorrection component is presented first followed by the positive practice component. There are, however, misbehaviors for which only one of the components is used (discussed below). At this point, let's look at an example of overcorrection in use.

Ms. Santos has decided to design an overcorrection procedure to treat Bobby's self-abusive behavior. She first identifies the specific and general disturbances that result from the self-abuse. Bobby abuses himself by striking the sides of his head with his fists. The specific disturbance or consequence of his self-abuse is that the sides of his head are covered with large, swollen red welts. The general environmental disturbance is that Bobby becomes agitated when he hits himself and this agitation prevents him from attending to educational activities and disturbs his classmates and his instructors. Ms. Santos then identifies the behaviors to be required of Bobby in order to vastly improve the situation. She decides to treat the specific problem of the swelling caused by the blows by using an ice pack. Whenever Bobby hits himself, she will require him to hold an ice pack to his head where the blow was delivered. The use of the ice pack will accomplish two purposes: 1) it will reduce the swelling caused by the blow, and 2) it will serve as an aversive or negative consequence for self-abuse since feeling cold is aversive to most people. To treat the general problem of Bobby's agitation, Ms. Santos decides that whenever Bobby hits himself, she will require him to lie quietly on a mat until he becomes calm. While lying on the mat, he will also be required to hold the ice pack to his head. This "quiet training" will accomplish two purposes: 1) it will reduce Bobby's agitation and, it is hoped, will teach him how to relax, and 2) it will serve as an aversive consequence because it constitutes a timeout from reinforcement (how the quiet training serves as a timeout period is discussed below).

Having designed the restitutional overcorrection component, Ms. Santos is ready to design the positive practice component by identifying the alternative, appropriate behaviors that Bobby will be required to repeatedly practice. Because Bobby hits himself with his fists, it is apparent to Ms. Santos that he must be required to use his hands for appropriate activities. She decides that she wants to bring Bobby's use of his hands under external control. In other words, she wants Bobby to use his hands in a manner that she dictates rather than to hit himself as he usually chooses to do. To gain this external control, Ms. Santos decides that she will require him to move his arms in one of three positions when she instructs him to do so. Specifically, she will require Bobby to lift his arms above his head, out from his sides, and directly in front of him. Bobby will be required to sustain each position for 15 seconds and the entire sequence of positions will be repeated for a period of 10 minutes.

Ms. Santos had designed an overcorrection program to treat Bobby's self-abuse. However, before she began using the program, she needed to first take a baseline and also ensure that there would be a high density of reinforcement available to Bobby when he behaved appropriately, e.g., by working at an educational task. Because of the nature and severity of Bobby's misbehavior, Ms. Santos conducted a brief 1-day baseline that consisted of time sampling Bobby's hitting every 5 minutes. Bobby had been wearing a football helmet up until the time Ms. Santos began the baseline. During the baseline, she removed Bobby's helmet for 1 minute every 5 minutes. Following this 1-minute observation interval, she replaced the helmet until she was ready for the next observation interval 4 minutes later. Ms. Santos's baseline revealed that Bobby hit himself 92% of the time.

The first day of overcorrection, Ms. Santos removed Bobby's helmet and prepared to punish his self-abuse with the overcorrection program. The first time Bobby hit himself, Ms. Santos said, "No, Bobby, don't hit yourself," and restrained his hands with hers. She quickly guided him to a mat, located beside his desk, and then guided him in lying flat on his back (she held his hands throughout in order to prevent him from hitting himself). While Ms. Santos held Bobby on the mat, her aide, Ms. Lee, brought over an ice pack from the refrigerator. Ms. Lee placed the ice pack in Bobby's right hand which Ms. Santos guided to his head. Ms. Santos held Bobby's hand so that he could not drop the ice pack. Meanwhile, Ms. Lee held Bobby's ankles because he had begun kicking in an attempt to get up from the mat. Both Ms. Santos and Ms. Lee avoided looking directly at Bobby's eyes so that they would not be giving him any eye contact and hence any attention. Neither spoke. Whenever Bobby ceased resisting and became relaxed, the instructors relaxed their grips on his hands and ankles. When he resumed struggling, they both once again held him firmly. After 10 minutes, they let Bobby get up. (They did not let him up, however, until he was relaxed.) Holding Bobby's hands, Ms. Santos escorted him back to his chair and guided him in sitting down. She then began giving him the positive practice.

Standing behind Bobby, Ms. Santos instructed him to raise his arms above his head by stating in a neutral tone of voice, "Hands up." Because Bobby did not react to the instruction after a few seconds, she guided his arms above his head and required him to hold that position for 15 seconds. At the end of the 15 seconds, she said, "Hands front," and since he did not respond, she gently guided his arms out in front of him. He was required to hold this position for 15 seconds after which she said, "Hands to the side." Again, she had to guide Bobby's arms into the position since he would not respond to the instruction.

Ms. Santos continued to require Bobby to move his arms into one of the three positions every 15 seconds. She presented the instructions randomly so that he would have to attend to each specific instruction, rather than simply learning a set sequence of movements. Whenever he struggled, she prevented him from moving his arms. Whenever he relaxed his arms, she relaxed her hands but kept them in contact with his arms. She never instructed him to move his arms to another position if he was struggling at the end of the 15-second interval. Rather, she waited until he had ceased struggling before she gave the instruction. (She did not want to pair his struggling with being allowed to move; rather, she wanted Bobby to learn that he could only move when he was instructed to do so and not when he was struggling.) Ms. Santos had Bobby move through the various arm positions until 10 minutes had elapsed.

The complete overcorrection program lasted 20 minutes: 10 minutes of quiet training and the ice pack, and 10 minutes of functional movement training with

Bobby's arms. At the end of the 20 minutes, Ms. Santos released Bobby's arms and said, "Now, do not hit yourself." She then guided his hands to a puzzle, released them, waited 10 seconds, and then reinforced him with a carrot stick.

Ms. Santos used the complete overcorrection program immediately following each instance of self-abuse. After 2 weeks, Bobby's self-abusive behavior had been reduced to a near zero level. At that point, Ms. Santos reduced the duration of the overcorrection to 5 minutes (2 minutes of quiet training and the ice pack, 3 minutes of arm movements). When Bobby's self-abuse was ultimately reduced to zero during the next week, she instituted a verbal warning procedure. In that procedure, Bobby was warned, each day, the first time he hit himself. "Bobby, don't hit yourself." If he did not hit himself again, no overcorrection was given. However, if he did hit himself a second time, he received the 5-minute overcorrection procedure. Eventually, Bobby ceased hitting himself in the classroom.

Ms. Santos noticed several changes in Bobby's behavior over the course of the overcorrection program. The first was that he ultimately learned to move his arms in the instructed direction during the functional movement training. The second was that he stopped struggling during both the quiet training and the functional movement training. The third was that he became more attentive in the classroom both to her and Ms. Lee and to the classroom stimulus materials. Because of these changes and the elimination of Bobby's self-abuse, Ms. Santos felt that the enormous amount of time she had invested in the overcorrection program had been worthwhile.

Now, let us find out why Mrs. Santos's overcorrection program was successful. The following sections discuss the nature of overcorrection and how it can be effectively used.

Before continuing this chapter, answer the following questions:

1. _____ is a procedure in which the misbehaving student is required to correct the environmental effects of his misbehavior and to practice appropriate forms of behavior in those situations where the misbehavior commonly occurs.
2. _____ _____ is the component of overcorrection in which the student is required to restore the disturbed environment to a vastly improved state.
3. The two steps to follow in using restitutional overcorrection are: 1) identify the s_____ and g_____ disturbances that resulted from the misbehavior, and 2) identify the b_____ needed to vastly improve the results of the misbehaviors.
4. _____ _____ is the component of overcorrection in which the student is required to repeatedly practice appropriate behaviors in the situation in which he normally misbehaves.
5. To use positive practice correctly, the instructor must identify the _____ behaviors to be practiced.

Turn to page 230 for the answers.

CHARACTERISTICS OF OVERCORRECTION

Any overcorrection acts the student must perform are designed to have the following characteristics:

1. *The overcorrection acts are directly related to the student's misbehavior.* As a result, there is less chance that an instructor will use overcorrection in an arbitrary or punitive way. For example, it is easy for an instructor to place a student in a timeout room if the student is "getting on her nerves." This same instructor, however, is much less likely to use overcorrection out of frustration because she must spend the overcorrection time ensuring that the student performs the required overcorrection acts. Furthermore, the fact that the overcorrection acts are related to the misbehavior means that the misbehaving student directly experiences the effort that the instructors have had to expend in the past in order to correct the results of his or her misbehavior. Care must be taken not to make the initial teacher's response reinforcing. The least amount of teacher attention possible should be given to the student until the student is involved in appropriate activities. In this case, teacher attention should be slightly aversive, even though aggressive behaviors may be emitted. For example, a student who throws a cup of milk on the floor would be required as part of overcorrection to mop up not only the spill, but also to mop a portion of the floor. This would not happen using any other inhibitory procedure since the instructors would probably implement the consequence (e.g., take the student to the timeout room) and then clean up the spill themselves.

2. *Like all effective punishment procedures, the overcorrection is implemented immediately following the misbehavior.* This immediate application leaves the student with little time to enjoy (be reinforced by) the results of the misbehavior and thus the overcorrection constitutes an extinction trial. For example, many theorists believe that one of the reinforcers for aggression toward another person is the aggressor's seeing the pain and discomfort caused to the victim. Thus, the victim's eyes welling with tears or his face contorting in pain would serve as reinforcers for the attacker's aggression. However, if the attacker is immediately required to comfort and administer to his or her victim through an overcorrection procedure, the reinforcing aspects associated with the aggressive act would be greatly diminished.

3. *The duration of the overcorrection is lengthy.* Because overcorrection is a relatively mild form of punishment, it must be extended in duration in order to be effective. This is because research has shown that a mildly aversive event (punisher) can suppress a behavior as effectively as a highly aversive event provided that the mildly aversive event is applied for a sufficient amount of time for it to become highly aversive. For example, 20 to 30 minutes of constant overcorrection is as aversive or more aversive than a painful slap. (This mention of slaps is purely for the purpose of comparison. We do not

advocate or condone the slapping of students.) There is another advantage associated with the requirement that the overcorrection be lengthy. During the student's performance of the overcorrective acts, little if any time is available to engage in any other activities that may be reinforcing. As a result, the time the student spends in overcorrection is also a period of timeout from positive reinforcement.

4. *The student must perform the overcorrection acts rapidly.* This rapid performance also contributes to the aversiveness of overcorrection, because most people dislike being required to work rapidly. Your use of physical guidance permits you to minimize the use of verbal instructions since you use the physical guidance to ensure that the instructions are completed. This is accomplished manually by guiding the student's limbs through the requested movements, with only enough guidance to ensure that the desired act is completed. The manual guidance is reduced whenever the student begins to perform the overcorrection act voluntarily. If the student is performing the overcorrection act at an appropriate rate, cease all physical contact with the student's limbs but continues to "shadow" them by keeping your hands within 1 inch of the student's hands or limbs. By doing so, you are prepared to immediately reapply physical guidance should the student's corrective act slow down or stop. Over time, the student will learn that your manual guidance can be avoided by performing the desired movements when instructed to do so.

COMMON ELEMENTS IN OVERCORRECTION PROGRAMS

Although a specific overcorrection program is designed for each specific misbehavior, there are several elements common to all overcorrection programs. They are:

1. *The use of a verbal reprimand.* Immediately following the misbehavior, the student is told, "No," and what he or she did wrong, e.g., "No, you hit Rita!" The word "No" is used because it is a conditioned aversive stimulus—a neutral event that has been repeatedly paired with aversive stimuli throughout a person's learning history such that it eventually acquires negative properties. This use of the word "No" facilitates generalization across settings and may temporarily suppress or interrupt any ongoing behavior. The description of the misbehavior, e.g., "You hit Rita," serves as negative feedback to the misbehaving student.

2. *A period of timeout from positive reinforcement.* The misbehaving student's ongoing activities are terminated.

3. *Verbal instructions delivered in a neutral tone of voice.* The instructions you give that inform the student of the various corrective actions he or she is to perform and your mere presence during the overcorrection (you are with the

student the entire time) could be sources of attention. As a result, there are several steps you must take in order to minimize this attention: 1) give each instruction only once and if the student does not respond within a few seconds, use manual guidance to carry out the instructed response, 2) make each instruction as brief as possible, and 3) most importantly, deliver each instruction in a neutral tone of voice in order to minimize its reinforcement value. Many retarded students respond to a stern, loud tone of voice as if it were reinforcing, possibly because many of their previous interactions with people have consisted of people shouting or becoming angry with them. Because our voice inflection appears to play a major role in determining how reinforcing our voices are, giving instructions in a robot-like manner during overcorrection (no inflection or affect) will minimize their social reinforcement value.

4. *Compliance training through the use of verbal instruction and graduated guidance.* The student is motivated to perform the various individual overcorrection acts via verbal instructions and physical guidance. The verbal instructions are given once and in a neutral tone of voice. (How and why this is done is described below.)

TYPES OF OVERCORRECTION

There are several types of overcorrection that have been developed to deal with general classes of misbehavior.

Quiet training is the most common type of overcorrection. It is used whenever a student is agitated (for example, acting aggressively toward others or property), self-abuses, or creates a general commotion, for example by screaming. Following the overcorrection rationale, the agitated student must compensate (overcorrect) by remaining quiet and relaxed for a prespecified period of time. As described previously, the quiet training procedure consists of requiring the student to lie quietly on a mat or bed until all signs of agitation have disappeared. Once the student is quiet, the student is required to complete any other overcorrection acts that were necessitated by the misbehavior. If the student becomes agitated or combative while performing these other overcorrection acts, he or she would once again receive quiet training. Thus, the consistent use of quiet training deters the student from using agitation as a means of escaping the overcorrection. *Quiet training is always the first overcorrection procedure delivered to agitated or disruptive students.* On some occasions you will have to combine quiet learning with some other procedure (DRO) to keep the student from escaping and receiving reinforcement for doing so, or from engaging in other inappropriate behaviors that may be reinforced by attention.

Social reassurance (apology) training is given whenever the student's misbehavior has frightened or annoyed others. The overcorrection rationale dictates that the student reassure everyone in the immediate environment that the misbehavior will not be repeated. Students who have expressive language are required to apologize verbally. Students without speech are required to use gestures, e.g., nodding their heads when asked if they are sorry they misbehaved. It is often necessary to use graduated guidance to motivate the student to perform the gesture.

Household orderliness training is given whenever the misbehaving student has disturbed property. The example cited earlier of turning over a desk and the overcorrection consequences that were applied illustrates this type of training.

Oral hygiene training is given whenever the student's mouth comes into contact with potentially harmful microorganisms. Such misbehavior might include biting oneself or others, chewing or mouthing objects, or eating inedible (non-nutritive) substances such as trash. The logic of the overcorrection rationale dictates that this unhygienic oral contact be corrected by cleansing the student's mouth and lips with an oral antiseptic.

Medical assistance training is given whenever the student's misbehavior results in injury to another person or to the student. In line with the overcorrection rationale, the student is required to assist in the medical treatment that is given.

Personal hygiene training is given whenever the student's misbehavior is a threat to his or her welfare and results in a degrading appearance. Misbehaviors that would qualify for personal hygiene training include handling feces or trash and rumination (vomiting on oneself). The overcorrection rationale dictates that the student restore personal appearance or condition to a vastly improved state.

Personal appearance training is closely related to personal hygiene training. The difference is that personal appearance training is given whenever the student's misbehavior is degrading but not a threat to physical welfare. A misbehavior that would receive personal appearance training is public disrobing (stripping). The overcorrection would consist of the student vastly improving personal appearance.

Functional movement training is given whenever the student's misbehavior consists of stereotyped, repetitive acts such as self-stimulatory or self-abusive behaviors. The overcorrection rationale dictates that the student be required to move the body part used in the misbehavior only when instructed to do so rather than as a part of the repetitive act.

A list of scientific studies that have employed these various types of overcorrection can be found in the reference section at the end of this chapter. Any of these types of overcorrection may contain reinforcing activities. You must be careful not to provide reinforcement as a consequence for inappropriate behaviors.

EXAMPLES OF OVERCORRECTION PROGRAMS

In all instances where the student's misbehavior results in a disruption of the environment, the overcorrection program includes both restitutional overcorrection and positive practice overcorrection. The following examples illustrate misbehaviors that would receive the full overcorrection program (both restitutional and positive practice overcorrection).

Scavenging. This behavior involves pica (the ingestion of non-nutritive substances such as trash, garbage, or cigarette butts) and coprophagy (the ingestion of fecal matter). The restitutional overcorrection procedure for coprophagy would consist of oral hygiene training (cleansing the mouth to remove the fecal matter) and personal hygiene training (handwashing to remove the fecal matter). The positive practice overcorrection would consist of requiring the student to flush toilets and mop the area where the fecal matter was obtained. The same restitutional procedures would be used for pica; however, the positive practice would consist of requiring the scavenger to pick up and throw away trash (if trash had been eaten) or empty and clean ash trays (if cigarette butts had been eaten).

Stripping (public disrobing). Let us say that an adolescent female removed her clothing in class. The restitutional overcorrection would require her to wear extra clothing. If her normal attire consisted simply of a dress, bra, panties, and shoes, the restitutional overcorrection would require her to dress in panties, panty hose, a bra, a slip, a dress, and shoes. This would be personal appearance training. The positive practice would consist of requiring her to improve the appearance of her classmates by buttoning or zipping unfastened clothing and/or combing their hair.

Biting others. The restitutional overcorrection would consist of quiet training (a period of required relaxation on a mat), oral hygiene training (brushing the biter's teeth with an oral antiseptic), and medical assistance training (the biter would be required to cleanse and medicate the victim's wound). The positive practice would consist of social reassurance training (the biter would be required to apologize to everyone in the classroom and practice appropriate interactions).

Screaming and throwing objects. The restitutional overcorrection would consist of quiet training and household orderliness training (the student would be required to straighten, pick up, and clean various objects in the classroom especially those that were similar to the thrown object). The positive practice overcorrection would consist of social reassurance training.

Toileting accidents. The restitutional overcorrection for wetting pants would consist of requiring the student to mop the floor where the accident occurred, wash the soiled clothing, and get dressed in clean clothing. The positive practice procedure would consist of requiring the student to repeatedly walk to the toilet or potty chair and rapidly engage in the entire chain of behaviors involved in properly toileting oneself. The chain would be rapidly lowering the pants, sitting briefly on the toilet, and then rapidly raising the pants.

The overcorrection time required for each of the above examples is 30 minutes with equal amounts of time spent on each type of training.

When no environmental disruption is created by the misbehavior, restitutional overcorrection procedures are not applicable and only positive practice is used. Since self-stimulatory behaviors usually have no effect in the environment (the exceptions are mouthing and self-abuse, if they are included under the general class of self-stimulatory behaviors), only positive practice is used to treat them. It is important to note that although self-stimulating students are not harming themselves or disturbing the environment, scientific studies have shown that they cannot learn while they are self-stimulating. This is why we must take steps to reduce high rates of self-stimulatory behavior. The specific type of positive practice used to reduce self-stimulatory behavior is functional movement training. The following examples illustrate its use.

Head weaving. When a student randomly moves his or her head from side to side, functional movement training for this head weaving would be conducted as follows. Immediately following a head weave, the student's head would be gently restrained by the teacher. Once the student's head was still, the teacher would instruct the student to move his head in one of three positions, up, down, or straight. If the student did not immediately move his head in the instructed direction, the teacher would use graduated guidance to guide the student's head in that direction. The student would be required to hold each position for 15 seconds after which another instruction would be given. Shadowing would be used whenever the student voluntarily moved his head in the instructed direction. The entire sequence would last 15 to 20 minutes. (The length of functional movement training would ultimately be faded as was done with Bobby, the self-abuser.)

Rocking while seated in a chair. Body rocking would be treated by functional movement training as follows. The rocker would be required to move his upper torso forward in the chair and to hold that position for 15 seconds and then to move his torso back in contact with the chair for 15 seconds. These alternating movements would be conducted until 20 minutes had elapsed since the student rocked. The rocker's shoulders would be guided whenever he did not respond within 1 to 2 seconds to the instruction to move his torso.

Hand clapping, hand gazing, and paper flipping. The student would be given the same functional movement training that was used with Bobby, the self-abuser.

It is appropriate at this time to address three common misconceptions about positive practice. The first is that it involves the delivery of positive reinforcement, since the behaviors being practiced are appropriate. As mentioned previously, positive reinforcement *is never* given during positive practice; otherwise the student might begin misbehaving in order to receive overcorrection. The second misconception is that positive practice is similar to negative practice (Chapter 11). Actually, the two procedures are completely dissimilar. As you recall, in negative practice the student repeatedly practices the inappropriate behavior rather than the appropriate behavior as is the case in positive practice. Positive practice should never be practice of a misbehavior. It should be practice of an appropriate behavior to be reinforced. However, reinforcement should not be available as a consequence of the inappropriate behavior.

Before continuing this chapter, answer the following questions.

1. List the types of overcorrection training that you would use for each of the misbehaviors listed below:
   a. Spitting
   b. Breaking windows
   c. Rumination
   d. Eating mucus from the nose
   e. Clothes ripping
   f. Self-abusive biting
   g. Self-stimulatory clapping
   h. Self-stimulatory object mouthing
2. How long should a complete overcorrection program generally last?
3. How long should a functional movement training program last when it is used solely to treat self-stimulation?

Answers are on page 230.

OVERCORRECTION: A STEP TOWARD NORMALIZATION

The rationale behind the development of the procedure of overcorrection was that the use of natural negative consequences would promote normalization because it would help close the gap between the behavior of retarded persons and others. While traditional behavioral punishment procedures are effective, they employ artificial consequences and only teach the student what not to do. The overcorrection procedure was developed as a realistic punishment consequence (restitutional overcorrection) and as a means of teaching the student what should have been done (positive practice overcorrection).

Perhaps the best way of illustrating how normalization is enhanced by overcorrection (the use of realistic, natural negative consequences) is the following real-world example. It illustrates how we generally correct the specific effects of our own misbehavior. In other words, we use the same procedures with each other that we use with our retarded students.

Suppose that you come to my house for a visit. I invite you in and we go into my living room and sit on the couch. After a while, I go to the kitchen and prepare something to drink. I return with the drinks and we resume our conversation. For some reason, you act carelessly and spill your drink on my couch. Your behavior of spilling your drink on my couch is inappropriate. There are several rationales I could use in providing a consequence for your spilling behavior. If I followed a physical punishment rationale, I would move toward you and either shock you with a cattle prod or slap you. If I followed a timeout rationale, I would immediately escort you to another room. If I followed a physical restraint rationale, I would somehow restrict your movements either by tying you up or holding you down on the floor. If I followed a differential reinforcement of other behavior rationale, I would wait for a period of time to elapse during which you did not spill any more of the drink and then I would deliver a reinforcer to you. If I followed an extinction rationale, I would ignore the liquid seeping into my couch. Following a negative practice rationale, I would require you to repeatedly spill more cups on my couch.

Obviously, I would not use any of the above procedures because you are a "normal" individual. You probably would not have waited for me to provide a consequence, since as soon as you spilled the liquid you would have made a mad dash into the kitchen or bathroom, obtained a damp cloth, and returned to the couch where you would begin wiping up the spill. After you have soaked up as much of the spill as possible, you would have offered to have the couch cleaned since some of the spill would probably have already stained the couch. It would not be feasible just to clean the one cushion that had been stained because it would then be much cleaner than the rest of the couch. You would offer to have the entire couch cleaned. In a way, you would be overcorrecting for having spilled a drink on one cushion, since the entire couch would be cleaned as a result of your accident. The reinforcing consequences for the individual behavior would be the approval and admiration of those people present. If there were no reinforcing consequences for these behaviors, you would have probably just asked for another drink.

In the above example, we see that normal people can and do engage in forms of overcorrection. In fact, this overcorrection often seems the most natural and normal way to correct our mistakes. If this is the way "normal" people behave, then that same rationale fits nicely within any program designed to promote the normalization of retarded students.

ADVANTAGES AND DISADVANTAGES OF OVERCORRECTION

Overcorrection offers several advantages and disadvantages in treating misbehaviors. As a punishment procedure, it has the general advantages associated with all punishment procedures:

1. It will suppress the misbehavior immediately.
2. It produces long-lasting suppression.
3. It has the potential to eliminate the misbehavior.
4. The misbehavior may remain at a zero level forever even after overcorrection has been discontinued.

The specific advantages of overcorrection have been described in detail in the section of this chapter on the characteristics of overcorrection. Briefly, these advantages are:

1. The procedure is directly related to the misbehavior.
2. The student directly experiences the effort normally required of others to correct the effects of the misbehavior.
3. The procedure constitutes an extinction trial because the student has little time to enjoy or be reinforced by the effects of the misbehavior.
4. It represents an extended timeout from positive reinforcement.
5. The procedure consists of an annoying effort requirement.

There are disadvantages associated with overcorrection that are shared with all forms of punishment (see Chapter 12) and some disadvantages that are unique to it:

1. Overcorrection is a complex procedure. The subtlety of several of the procedural components, e.g., graduated guidance, and the fact that each overcorrection program is uniquely designed to treat a specific misbehavior increases the chances that overcorrection will be conducted incorrectly. Unlike some programs that can be implemented successfully by simply giving written instructions to staff members (e.g., timeout), a successful overcorrection program requires that all staff be individually trained in the procedures. (A model for a staff training and certification procedure can be found in *Toilet Training the Retarded* (see the Suggested Readings at the end of this chapter).) The complexity of overcorrection also requires that staff performance be monitored more frequently than in most other programs. As a result, not only is more staff time spent on the overcorrection program, but more of the professional's, consultant's, or administrator's time is taken as well.
2. The length of time required and the fact that an instructor has to be present throughout the procedure can be counterproductive when the student's misbehavior occurs at high rates and/or when only a few instructors are available to provide programming for several students. In such cases, either additional staffing must be sought or an alternative inhibitory procedure chosen.
3. Its physically intrusive nature makes it inappropriate for physically strong students who may react to the use of graduated guidance by becoming combative. In general, when more than two instructors are involved at one time in overcorrecting a student, the chances of injury to someone are greatly increased.

However, as mentioned previously, the amount of time that overcorrection requires and the requirement that an instructor be present to give overcorrection can be viewed as advantages, since these requirements reduce or eliminate arbitrary or punitive applications of the procedure. A major problem in some schools is the fact that many inhibitory procedures require little of the instructor. For example, timeout requires few response requirements from the instructor and therefore is sometimes used when no misbehavior has occurred. Overcorrection, however, requires a great deal of time and effort by the instructor. As a result, the instructor is not likely to use overcorrection unless the misbehavior has indeed occurred.

Overcorrection procedures can be used to decrease a wide range of misbehaviors. Part of the appeal of using overcorrection is that it permits individualized treatment because the instructor must design the overcorrection procedure to fit the specific misbehavior. This, of course, permits the instructor to be creative in his or her behavioral programming. As is true for all inhibitory procedures, there will be situations and students for whom overcorrection will not be appropriate or useful. However, when applicable, overcorrection can be regarded as an effective, humane, and enduring method of reducing problem behaviors.

THE LEAST RESTRICTIVE TREATMENT MODEL

We have now concluded our discussion of the three levels of procedures to decrease behavior in the Least Restrictive Treatment Model. To review, level 1 procedures contain no aversive properties. Level 2 procedures do contain some aversive properties. Procedures at level 3 are aversive and thus parental and administrative approval should be sought before using them (under ideal circumstances, it should be mandatory that you seek such approval).

Level 1 procedures	Level 2 procedures	Level 3 procedures
DRO (differential reinforcement of other behavior)	Negative practice Extinction	Physical restraint Nonexclusionary timeout Exclusionary timeout Overcorrection
DRA (differential reinforcement of appropriate behavior)		
DRI (differential reinforcement of incompatible behavior)		
Satiation		

SUMMARY

Overcorrection is a punishment procedure in which misbehaving students are required to overcorrect the environmental effects of their misbehavior and to practice appropriate forms of behavior in those situations in which the misbehavior commonly occurs. Overcorrection has two parts: restitutional overcorrection, and positive practice overcorrection. In restitutional overcorrection, students are required to correct the consequences of their misbehavior by restoring the disturbed situation to a vastly improved state. In positive practice overcorrection, students are required to repeatedly practice appropriate behaviors in the situation in which they normally misbehave.

Overcorrection acts are designed to have the following characteristics: 1) they are directly related to the misbehavior and the student directly experiences the effort normally required of others to correct the effects of the misbehavior, 2) they are implemented immediately, 3) they are lengthy, and 4) they are performed rapidly.

There are four common elements in all overcorrection programs: 1) the use of verbal reprimands, 2) a period of timeout from positive reinforcement, 3) verbal instructions delivered only once and in a neutral tone of voice, and 4) compliance training through the use of verbal instructions and graduated guidance.

Types of overcorrection training for general classes of misbehavior include quiet training, social reassurance training, household orderliness training, oral hygiene training, medical assistance training, personal hygiene training, personal appearance training, and functional movement training. Although most misbehaviors are treated by both restitutional and positive practice overcorrection, most forms of self-stimulation that have no disruptive effect on the environment are treated by positive practice alone.

The general advantages of overcorrection that it shares with all punishment procedures are: 1) it may suppress the misbehavior immediately, 2) it may produce long-lasting suppression, 3) it may eliminate the misbehavior, and 4) the misbehavior may remain at zero after the overcorrection is discontinued. The specific advantages of overcorrection are the same as its four characteristics listed above. The general disadvantages of overcorrection are those that it shares with all punishment procedures (see Chapter 12). The specific disadvantages of overcorrection are: 1) its complexity, 2) the length of time it requires, and 3) its physically intrusive nature.

Overcorrection is a level 3 procedure in the Least Restrictive Model of Treatment because it is a punishment procedure.

REVIEW QUESTIONS

1. Overcorrection is a punishment procedure because it reduces _____
_____.

2. There are two parts of overcorrection: _____ overcorrection, and
____ _____ overcorrection.

3. Overcorrection acts are designed to have the following characteristics and

hence advantages: 1) they are _____ related to the misbehavior, 2) they are implemented _____, 3) their duration is _____, 4) they are performed _____, and 5) there is an e_____ requirement.

4. During overcorrection, the instructor's verbal instructions are given in a tone of voice that is _____.

5. The manual guidance procedure that is used to ensure that the student will perform the overcorrection acts is _____ _____.

6. The common elements in all overcorrection procedures are: 1) the use of a v_____ r_____, 2) a period of _____ from positive reinforcement, 3) v_____ i_____ delivered in a neutral tone of voice, and 4) c_____ training.

7. Whenever a student is agitated, you may want to use q_____ t_____.

8. Whenever the student has annoyed or frightened others, you can use _____ _____ _____.

9. Whenever the student has disturbed property, you can use _____ _____ _____.

10. Whenever the student's misbehavior results in unhygienic oral contact, you can use _____ _____ _____.

11. Whenever the misbehavior results in an injury, you can use _____ _____ _____.

12. Whenever the misbehavior is a threat to the student's welfare and makes the student's appearance degrading, you can use _____ _____ _____.

13. Whenever the student's misbehavior is degrading but not a threat to physical welfare, you can use _____ _____ _____.

14. Whenever the misbehavior consists of stereotyped, repetitive acts such as self-stimulation or self-abuse, you can use _____ _____ _____.

15. Positive practice differs from negative practice in that the student is required to practice appropriate rather than _____ _____.

16. No reinforcement is given during p_____ p_____.

17. The general advantages of overcorrection that it shares with all punishment procedures are: 1) immediate s_____ of the behavior, 2) l_____-l_____ suppression, 3) e_____ of the misbehavior, and 4) the behavior may remain at z_____ after the overcorrection has been discontinued.

18. The specific disadvantages of overcorrection are: 1) its _____, 2) the length of _____ it requires, and 3) its physically i_____ nature.

19. Overcorrection is a level _____ procedure in the Least Restrictive Treatment Model.

Turn to page 231 for the answers.

SUGGESTED READINGS

Barnard, J. D., Christopherson, E. R., & Wolf, M. M. Parent mediated treatment of children's self-injurious behavior using overcorrection. *Journal of Pediatric Psychology*, 1977, 2, 56–61.

Epstein, L. H., Doke, L. A., Sajwaj, T. E., Sorrell, S., & Rimmer, B. Generality and side effects of overcorrection. *Journal of Applied Behavior Analysis,* 1974, *7,* 385–390.

Foxx, R. M. The use of overcorrection to eliminate the public disrobing (stripping) of retarded women. *Behaviour Research and Therapy,* 1976, *14,* 53–61.

Foxx, R. M. Attention training: The use of overcorrection avoidance to increase eye contact of autistic and retarded children. *Journal of Applied Behavior Analysis,* 1977, *10,* 489–499.

Foxx, R. M., & Azrin, N. H. Rapid method of toilet training children. *Proceedings of the 81st Annual Convention of the American Psychological Association,* 1973.

Foxx, R. M., & Azrin, N. H. *Toilet training the retarded: A rapid program for day and nighttime independent toileting.* Champaign, IL: Research Press, 1973.

Foxx, R. M., & Azrin, N. H. Restitution: A method of eliminating aggressive-disruptive behaviors of retarded and brain damaged patients. *Behaviour Research and Therapy,* 1972, *10,* 15–27.

Foxx, R. M., & Azrin, N. H. The elimination of autistic, self-stimulatory behavior by overcorrection. *Journal of Applied Behavior Analysis,* 1973, *6,* 1–14.

Foxx, R. M., & Martin, E. D. Treatment of scavenging behavior (coprophagy and pica) by overcorrection. *Behaviour Research and Therapy,* 1975, *13,* 153–162.

ANSWERS TO CHAPTER QUESTIONS

Answers to Questions on Page 217

1. Overcorrection
2. Restitutional overcorrection
3. specific, general, behaviors
4. Positive practice
5. appropriate

Answers to Questions on Page 224

1. a. Social reassurance training (spitting is annoying), household orderliness training (cleaning the spat upon object or person), and personal appearance training (spittle around the mouth is degrading). *Note:* No oral hygiene training would be used because no unhygienic oral contact would have occurred.
    b. Social reassurance training (others were annoyed or frightened), quiet training for agitation, household orderliness training (repairing and cleaning windows), and medical assistance training if someone was injured by the broken glasses.
    c. Oral hygiene training (although no unhygienic oral contact occurred, the oral antiseptic would clean the vomitus from the mouth and freshen the ruminator's breath) and personal appearance training.
    d. Oral hygiene training (unhygienic oral contact) and personal hygiene training.
    e. Quiet training (agitation), personal appearance training, and functional movement training (inappropriate use of the hands).
    f. Quiet training, medical assistance training, and oral hygiene training.
    g. Functional movement training (no restitutional overcorrection would be given since there was no environmental disruption).
    h. Oral hygiene training because of unhygienic oral contact.
2. 30 minutes
3. 15 to 20 minutes

Answers to Review Questions on Pages 228–229

1. the future probability of occurrence of the misbehavior it follows.
2. restitutional, positive practice
3. directly, immediately, lengthy, rapidly, effort
4. neutral
5. graduated guidance
6. verbal reprimand, timeout, verbal instructions, compliance
7. quiet training
8. social reassurance training
9. household orderliness training
10. oral hygiene training
11. medical assistance training
12. personal hygiene training
13. personal appearance training
14. functional movement training
15. inappropriate behaviors
16. positive practice
17. suppression, long-lasting, elimination, zero
18. complexity, time, intrusive
19. 3

Part III

Maintaining Appropriate Behaviors

Chapter 14

GENERALIZATION, MAINTENANCE, AVOIDING PROGRAM PROBLEMS, AND GUIDELINES FOR ESTABLISHING BEHAVIORAL PROGRAMS

After reading this chapter, you will be able to:

1. Define generalization training.

2. List five ways of facilitating generalization training.

3. Explain why behavior maintenance is so important.

4. List six procedures or ways to increase behavior maintenance.

5. List three pitfalls to avoid in behavioral programs.

6. List five factors to consider when analyzing why a program is not working.

7. List five guidelines to follow when establishing a behavioral program.

Four important concerns regarding behavioral or educational programs are considered in this chapter. Generalization training and the maintenance of behavior change are discussed first. The available scientific evidence indicates that students' newly learned skills or behaviors do not automatically transfer to new settings or situations or occur after the termination of the behavioral program. Thus, because your students' performance is likely to be situation specific, you need to know how to program for generalization and the maintenance of the educational or therapeutic effect.

Some of the pitfalls that you must avoid in order to make your behavioral programs successful are also considered in a section of this chapter. The chapter then concludes with a discussion of several useful guidelines to follow to ensure that your behavioral programs will be humane, ethical, beneficial, enduring, and successful.

GENERALIZATION TRAINING

GENERALIZATION TRAINING IS A PROCEDURE DE-
SIGNED TO TRANSFER THE CONTROL OVER BE-
HAVIOR FROM ONE STIMULUS TO OTHER STIMULI.

We want our students to display their newly learned skills or absence of mis-behaviors in a variety of situations or environments. When they do, we say that their behavior has generalized or that generalization has taken place. Unfortunately, there are very few instances where students spontaneously display learn-ing or therapy gains in a new setting. Thus, skills learned in the classroom do not automatically transfer to the home, skills learned in a one-to-one session do not automatically transfer to the classroom, and skills learned from one instructor do not automatically transfer to another instructor. The same holds true for mis-behaviors that have been eliminated in the classroom, in a one-to-one session, or by one instructor; there is rarely any generalization to home, to the classroom, or to other instructors. The reason generalization rarely occurs is that all students, even the most severely intellectually impaired, can *discriminate* between home and the classroom, between one-to-one sessions and the classroom, and among instructors. As a result, if we want generalization to occur, we must program for it. The means by which we do this is called generalization training.

Generalization training can be accomplished either during or after a be-havioral program. You can implement generalization training while the student is in the process of achieving a behavioral objective or reducing misbehavior or you can implement it after the objective has been achieved or the misbehavior has been eliminated.

Several ways of facilitating generalization training are listed below.

Emphasize common elements that the new settings or situations share with the original training setting. You can help your students learn to generalize by ensuring that the discriminative stimuli and reinforcing or aversive conse-quences from the original setting are present in the new settings. For exam-ple, if you want a student to give eye contact to his mother or another instructor, make sure that they use the same verbal prompt and edible reinforcer that you used. Or, if you want a student to not disrobe at home, make sure that her parents have set up a timeout area in the home and that they use "No" and place their child in timeout in the same manner as you have done at school.

Use an intermittent reinforcement schedule in the original training situation before you institute generalization training. Using an intermittent reinforcement schedule helps to ensure that the desired behavior is maintained (response or behavior maintenance is described below) and will facilitate generalization in any new settings. Research has shown that intermittently reinforced behaviors are more likely to generalize than continuously reinforced behaviors.

Teach the student the behavior under a variety of conditions. The more conditions in which a student performs the behavior, the more likely it is that his or her behavior will generalize to new situations. For example, if you want to increase the likelihood that the student will eat with a spoon at home, have several different classroom instructors train him to eat with a spoon in several different situations at school, e.g., alone, sitting at a table with others, etc. Research has indicated that generalization is more likely to occur when several different instructors train the student in several different situations or settings.

Add supplemental discriminative stimuli to the new situation. After you have been successfully using behavioral programs with your students, there may be some discriminative stimuli that exercise a great deal of control over several of a student's other behaviors. For example, a verbal prompt "Do this" or a gestural prompt (e.g., pointing to an object) may have been used to teach several different behaviors in the past. By adding these S^Ds to the original training session and the new training situations, you will be increasing the prospects for generalization to occur. Or, you can simply add them to the new situations or settings. Bear in mind, however, that these supplemental discriminative stimuli must be faded once the student's behavior has generalized.

Change the reinforcement conditions in the original training situation so that natural reinforcers, rather than artificial reinforcers, are controlling the student's behavior. By doing this, you can greatly facilitate the generalization process and, for that matter, response or behavior maintenance. For example, you should endeavor to eliminate reliance on edibles whenever possible and switch instead to social reinforcers such as praise, since it is much more likely that the student will receive praise for successful efforts in a variety of situations than that he or she will receive edibles.

BEHAVIOR OR RESPONSE MAINTENANCE

No matter how spectacular your behavioral procedure has been in increasing an appropriate behavior or decreasing an undesirable behavior, its significance is meaningless if the appropriate behavior disappears or the undesirable behavior returns once the procedure is discontinued. To ensure that this does not happen, we must be concerned about maintaining the effect of our intervention. We can never assume that the effect will be maintained after the program is withdrawn; consequently, we must program for the maintenance of the behavior or effect.

There are several procedures that can be used to increase the likelihood that the behavior will be maintained. You will note that there is not much difference between these procedures and the procedures that facilitate generalization training. (In fact, some of the same procedures are used in both cases.) This is because our concerns regarding behavior maintenance and generalization training are so closely related.

Substitute naturally occurring reinforcers for the artificial or programmed reinforcers that were used to produce the therapeutic effect. Although artificial reinforcers are often necessary to effectively change the behavior, they should be phased out once the behavior is occurring at the desired level and a more natural reinforcer should be substituted. Furthermore, the use of artificial reinforcers together with the natural reinforcer may, in fact, enhance the subsequent effectiveness of the natural reinforcer. For example, the simultaneous use of an edible and praise during eye contact training sessions increases the likelihood that the praise (or attention) alone will maintain eye contact after the student has learned to give eye contact. Or, praise can be used to reinforce eating with a spoon and then gradually eliminated as the student begins eating properly. At that point, the natural reinforcer (a bite of food) that follows the correct eating response should be sufficient to maintain proper eating.

Train other individuals in the student's life, such as relatives or residential caregivers, to carry out your behavioral program. You want to ensure that the student's newly learned behaviors will be maintained at home, over the summer, or in the new classroom during the coming school year. To do so, you should train "significant others" to carry out your successful behavioral program in other settings. We cannot stress this point enough, since research has shown that autistic children whose parents were trained in behavioral techniques actually improved slightly after training, whereas those children who were institutionalized in facilities where the staff were untrained in the treatment techniques regressed and lost the skills they had been taught.

Gradually remove or fade the behavioral consequences so that the student becomes less and less dependent on them. The less dependent a student is on structured behavioral consequences, the more he or she will be prepared for normalization, that is, functioning under the same types of contingencies and consequences as normal persons. This is important because the real world provides much less structure and fewer immediate behavioral consequences. With severely and profoundly retarded students, it is not probable that you would be fading or gradually removing the behavioral consequences for some time, since this technique works best when the student is capable of performing a variety of complex behaviors. For example, you could fade the behavioral consequences with a student who is being phased into a "more normal classroom." It would be important for this student to learn to perform a variety of complex behaviors in a variety of situations for varying lengths of time before the student was reinforced if he or she were to function in his or her new environment. Gradually fading the structured behavioral consequences that the student received in the old classroom environment would be the means by which the student would be prepared for a new "life-style." Although it is doubtful that you will be using this technique in the near future, you should be aware of it so that you can utilize it when it is needed. Remember, you will never fade all the consequences. If all the consequences are faded, the behavior probably will be extinguished. So, fading to normal specified consequences is appropriate.

Vary the training conditions so that the student cannot discriminate as to when a consequence is likely to occur. The best way to prevent the student from discriminating, that is, picking up cues regarding when and where the consequences will be delivered and by whom, is to train the behavior in a variety of settings with several individuals delivering the consequences. This, of course, constitutes generalization training. It is especially important in punishment or aversive programs that you ensure that a number of individuals are associated with the program. Otherwise, the misbehavior will be reduced or eliminated only in the presence of those few individuals who participated in the program.

Use intermittent schedules of reinforcement to make the student's behavior more resistant to extinction. As mentioned previously in the section on generalization training, intermittent reinforcement schedules are ideal for maintaining a desirable behavior. You should make every effort to ensure that the schedule of reinforcement becomes more and more intermittent. This, of course, also prepares the student for a "normal way of life" because many of the reinforcers that normal individuals receive are on an extremely intermittent schedule (for example, being complimented by your boss).

Delay the delivery of reinforcers so that the student will not expect to be reinforced immediately following performance of an appropriate behavior. Although it is crucial that behavior be established via immediate reinforcement, it is unrealistic and unwieldy to continue to immediately reinforce the student each time he or she behaves appropriately. Furthermore, immediate reinforcement is counter to the spirit of normalization since most of our reinforcers, especially social and monetary ones, are delivered only after the passage of greater lengths of time. A good example of when it is especially important for you to have built-in reinforcement delays is when you move a student from one-to-one training situations to a group instructional setting with several students seated around a table. Any student who is to succeed in such a situation must have learned to accept a delay in the delivery of reinforcers. Accordingly, you would begin delaying the delivery of reinforcers while the student was still in the one-to-one training situation and only transfer the student to a group instructional situation when the student could tolerate reinforcement delays.

AVOIDING PROBLEMS IN ESTABLISHING AND CARRYING OUT BEHAVIORAL PROGRAMS

There are several pitfalls that you should avoid as you establish and carry out your behavioral programs. The suggestions below will help you avoid these pitfalls.

1. *Do not attempt to modify complex or highly disruptive behaviors until you become thoroughly proficient as a behavior change agent.* Rather, work with simple behaviors and problems until you have achieved a sufficient amount of expertise.

2. *Do not expect too much, too soon from the student.* Even though behavioral techniques are highly effective in changing behavior, the speed with which they will work depends on a multitude of factors, including your expertise, characteristics of the student, and the learning environment. There are no hard and fast rules on how rapidly a behavior should change. The best advice we can give is to continuously evaluate all the factors in your program and in the learning environment.

3. *Do not change a program or drop it until you have thoroughly analyzed why it may not be working.* Some factors to consider in your analysis are: a) Does the student know what is expected of him? You can answer this question for nonverbal students by making sure that your behavioral objectives are reasonable, clear-cut, and have appropriate criterion levels. For verbal students, simply tell them what you expect. b) Do all of the change agents in the environment, i.e., all instructors and volunteers, understand the program that you are using? You should make sure that everyone is very familiar with the program. Never set up a program without informing everyone of what you are doing and gaining their cooperation to help you with the program. c) Are all of the change agents motivated to participate in the program and help make it work? Oftentimes, other change agents are unmotivated to participate or to agree to participate in a program because they do not feel adequately informed or involved. By involving them early in the design of the intervention, you will avoid the problems of apathy and sabotage and will gain their willingness to make the necessary sacrifices to ensure the success of your program. d) Are the reinforcers working as they should? If it appears that the student is not under the control of the reinforcers, you should evaluate and possibly change the following variables: the type of reinforcer being used, the schedule of reinforcement, the amount of reinforcer being given, the immediacy of deliv-

ering the reinforcer, and the actual reinforcing quality of the reinforcer for the student. e) Is the program being applied consistently and correctly? Failure to consistently apply the program is probably the most common reason why programs fail to change behavior.

SOME GUIDELINES FOR ESTABLISHING PROGRAMS

You have now learned the behavioral and educational principles in this book and are ready to apply them in the classroom. Before you do, we suggest that you carefully consider the following suggestions and guidelines. Once you have, you should be ready to begin effectively changing the behavior of your students.

Know yourself. Do not consider changing the behavior of others until you have gained some insight into your own behavior. Understanding why you behave as you do will help you become a proficient and humane behavior modifier.

Know the student. You should always strive to learn as much about your students as possible. And the only way to learn about them is to work directly with them. Knowing your students' strengths and weaknesses will ensure that your students are developmentally ready to benefit from whatever intervention you have selected for them.

Know that the program will be beneficial for the student. No program should be used simply because it will make the student less annoying or easier to work with. Rather, a program should only be used if it will further the student's progress toward a normal, productive life.

Develop an educational value system that respects the dignity of the student and that operates on the principle of fairness to the student. Our students deserve fairness and respect just as do all people. You will be demonstrating that you are fair and respect the student if you: 1) do not apply procedures arbitrarily, 2) do not refuse to use a procedure simply because of a personal bias (for example, refusing to use edible reinforcers simply because you do not believe in using them), 3) always attempt to use a systematic approach in modifying the student's behavior and evaluate that approach, 4) do not refuse to seek help from other teachers or consultants because you think that such assistance would make you appear incompetent, and 5) systematically evaluate your own teaching performance from time to time to ensure that you are correctly carrying out the various procedures you are using with your students.

Keep everyone informed about your programs. If your program is well designed and based on sound behavioral and educational principles, then there is no need to be concerned about informing a student's parents and the school administration about what you are doing. It is imperative that you seek informed consent when you are considering the use of aversive procedures to decrease a student's undesirable behaviors. However, it also is a good idea to keep all concerned parties abreast of all your various programs. By doing so, you will be demonstrating your competence and concern for your students.

Any system can be misused and abused by the individuals who are responsible for implementing it. Knowledge is power, and people with power must take responsibility to use that power in beneficial ways. Behavioral techniques are powerful procedures that can be beneficial or damaging depending on how they are used. You now have the power to change behavior with behavioral techniques and the responsibility to use that power wisely.

SUMMARY

We want our students to display their newly learned behaviors or skills in a variety of situations and settings and also after their training program has been terminated. Unfortunately, neither of these events happens automatically. As a result, we cannot leave them to chance. To ensure that students generalize their behavior to a variety of situations and settings, we use a procedure called generalization training.

A related concern is to ensure the maintenance of the behavioral effect after the original program has been terminated. This is very important because the true measure of a program's success is whether or not the educational or therapeutic effect on the student's behavior persists. Fortunately, there are several procedures that can be used to increase the likelihood that the student's behavior will be maintained.

Educational programs fail because the behavior change agents fail to avoid certain pitfalls or ignore certain crucial programmatic guidelines. The major pitfalls are: attempting to modify complex or highly disruptive behaviors without having sufficient expertise, expecting too much of the student too soon, and dropping or changing a program before thoroughly analyzing why it is not working.

There are several important guidelines to follow when establishing a behavioral program. These guidelines deal not only with programmatic considerations but with the rights of the students as well. And, finally, the instructor must accept the responsibility that comes with the power to change behavior.

REVIEW QUESTIONS

1. A procedure designed to transfer the control over behavior from one situation to other situations is called _____ _____.
2. The reason why generalization rarely occurs spontaneously is that students can d_____ between situations.
3. There are several ways of facilitating generalization training: 1) emphasize common elements in the new setting that are shared with the original training setting, 2) use an i_____ r_____ s_____ in the original training situation before you institute generalization training, 3) teach the student the behavior under a v_____ of c_____, 4) add supplemental d_____

s_____ to the new situation, and 5) change the r_____ c_____ in the original training situation.

4. Behavior maintenance and generalization training are closely related because both are concerned with the _____.

5. There are several procedures that can be used to facilitate behavior maintenance: 1) substitute n_____ o_____ reinforcers, 2) t_____ other people in the student's life, 3) gradually r_____ or f_____ the behavioral consequences, 4) vary the t_____ c_____, 5) use i_____ s_____ of r_____ and 6) d_____ the delivery of r_____.

6. Three pitfalls to avoid when you attempt to establish or carry out a behavioral program are: 1) attempting to modify c_____ or highly d_____ behaviors before you have become thoroughly proficient as a behavior change agent, 2) expecting too much, too soon from the s_____, and 3) changing or dropping a program before you have thoroughly a_____ it.

7. Some factors to consider when you analyze why a program is not working are: 1) Does the student know what is e_____ of him? 2) Do all of the c_____ a_____ understand the program? 3) Are all of the change agents m_____ to participate in the program? 4) Are the r_____ working as they should? and 5) Is the program being applied c_____ and c_____?

8. Some guidelines for establishing programs are: know y_____, know the s_____, know that the p_____ will be beneficial for the s_____, develop an educational value system that r_____ the d_____ of the student and that operates on the principle of f_____, and keep everyone i_____ about your programs.

9. You will be demonstrating that you are fair and respect the student if you: 1) do not apply procedures a_____, 2) do not refuse to use a procedure because of a p_____ b_____, 3) always attempt to use a s_____ approach in modifying the student's behavior and e_____ that approach, 4) do not refuse to seek help from other t_____ and c_____, and 5) systematically evaluate your own t_____ p_____ periodically.

Answers are on page 244.

SUGGESTED READINGS

Birnbrauer, J. S. Mental retardation. In: H. Leitenberg (ed.), *Handbook of behavior modification*. New York: Appleton-Century-Crofts. In press.

Bricker, W. A., Morgan, D. G., & Grabowski, J. G. Development of maintenance of a behavior modification repertoire of cottage attendants through T.V. feedback. *American Journal of Mental Deficiency*, 1972, 77(2), 128–136.

Frisch, S. A., & Schumaker, J. B. Training generalized receptive prepositions in retarded children. *Journal of Applied Behavior Analysis*, 1974, 7, 611–621.

Garcia, E. The training and generalization of a conversational speech form in nonverbal retardates. *Journal of Applied Behavior Analysis*, 1974, 7, 137–149.

Jeffrey, B. D. Increase and maintenance of verbal behavior of a mentally retarded child. *Mental Retardation,* 1972, *10*(2), 35–40.

Murdock, J. Y., Garcia, E. E., & Hardman, M. L. Generalizing articulation training with trainable mentally retarded subjects. *Journal of Applied Behavior Analysis,* 1977, *10*(4), 717–733.

Nowas, M. M., & Braun, S. H. An overview of behavior modification with severely and profoundly retarded: Part III, Maintenance of change and epilogue. *Mental Retardation,* 1970, *8*(4), 4–12.

Spradlin, J. E., & Girardeau, F. L. The behavior of moderately and severely retarded persons. In: N. R. Ellis (ed.), *International review of research in mental retardation* (Vol. 1). New York: Academic Press, 1966.

Stokes, T. F., Baer, D. M., & Jackson, R. L. Programming the generalization of a greeting response in four retarded children. *Journal of Applied Behavior Analysis,* 1974, *7,* 599–610.

Whelan, R. J., & Harding, N. G. Modification and maintenance of behavior through systematic application of consequences. *Exceptional Children,* 1966, *32,* 281–289.

Answers to Review Questions on Pages 242–243

1. generalization training
2. discriminate
3. intermittent reinforcement schedule; variety, conditions; discriminative stimuli; reinforcement conditions
4. occurrence of the behavior in a new situation
5. naturally occurring; train; remove, fade; training conditions; intermittent schedules, reinforcement; delay, reinforcers
6. complex, disruptive; student; analyzed
7. expected; change agents; motivated; reinforcers; consistently, correctly
8. yourself; student; program, student; respects, dignity, fairness; informed
9. arbitrarily; personal bias; systematic, evaluate; teachers, consultants; teaching performance

APPENDIX A

Potential Reinforcers to Use in the Classroom with Retarded Students

1. **Edibles**
   Snacks (give very small pieces when shaping behavior)

   corn chips
   pretzel pieces
   cookies
   sugared cereals
   candy
   ice cream (spoonful from a cup)
   raisins
   peanuts
   pudding (spoonful from a cup)

   gelatin (spoonful from a cup)
   marshmallows
   potato chips
   fruit (cherries, grapes, orange slices, apples)
   vegetable bits (carrot sticks, celery sticks)
   cheese

2. **Liquids**
   Drinks (give in small sips or a squirt from a squirt bottle)

   colas, soft drinks
   orange drink, grape drink, cranberry drink
   fruit juices

   milk
   Kool-Aid
   water

3. **Objects**

   dolls
   mechanical toys
   whistles
   stuffed animals
   small rubber toys
   rattles
   noise makers
   musical toys
   toys used in post-learning experiences

   trucks
   bubble blower
   balloons
   sweatshirt
   ribbon
   key chain
   decals
   colored chips

4. **Activities**

   playing catch with instructor
   playing on swings

   playing on jungle gym
   going on merry-go-round

245

running
playing tag or hide-and-go-seek with instructor
going for a walk with instructor
playing with a pet
automobile ride
hike
trip to zoo, carnival, or circus
swimming

visiting instructor's home
looking through a book or magazine
playing in the gym (unstructured play)
hearing music
riding on rocking horse
finger painting
ride on a wheeled chair
lying on a water bed or moon walk
smelling different fragrances

5. **Social Praise**

Statements

"Good." "Good boy (girl)."
"Very good."
"Good eating."
"Good dressing."
"Good _____."
"I like that."
"That's good."
"I'm glad you did that."
"I appreciate what you have done."

"That's right."
"You did a good job."
"Mmm-hmm."
"Fine."
"You did it. Very good."
"Thank you." "Thank you very much."
"I'm so happy with you."
"I'm proud of you."

6. **Nonverbal Messages and Movements**

Facial expressions

smiling
showing surprise and delight
nodding head in an approving manner

laughing
winking

Being near to the child

standing near child

sitting near child

Physical contact

hugging
patting
touching arm
rubbing back
kissing
picking up child
wrestling

tickling
bouncing child on knees
playing patty-cake
holding child
slow rolling
slow stroking

APPENDIX B

Journals Publishing Behavior Modification Articles on Research with Retarded Students

---

American Journal of Mental Deficiency. Albany, NY: American Association on Mental Deficiency.

Analysis and Modification of Severe Developmental Disorders. New York, NY: Pergamon Press.

Behavior Modification. Beverly Hills, CA: Sage Publications.

Behavior Research and Therapy. Elmsford, NY: Pergamon Press.

Behavior Therapy. New York, NY: Academic Press, Inc.

Child Behavior Therapy. New York, NY: The Haworth Press, Inc.

Education and Training of the Mentally Retarded. Montpelier, VT: Capital City Press.

Education and Treatment of Children. Pittsburgh, PA: Pressley Ridge School.

Exceptional Children. Reston, VA: The Council for Exceptional Children.

Journal of Applied Behavior Analysis. Lawrence, KS: Department of Human Development, University of Kansas.

Journal of Autism and Developmental Disabilities. New York, NY: Plenum Press.

Journal of Consulting and Clinical Psychology. Washington, DC: American Psychological Association.

Journal of Educational Research. Madison, WI: Dembar Educational Research Services, Inc.

Journal of Learning Disabilities. Chicago, IL: The Professional Press, Inc.

Journal of School Psychology. Provincetown, MA: The Journal Press.

Journal of Special Education. Philadelphia, PA: Buttonwood Farms, Inc.

Mental Retardation. Albany, NY: American Association on Mental Deficiency.

Teaching Exceptional Children. Reston, VA: The Council for Exceptional Children.

APPENDIX C

Data Collection Sheet for
Observing and Recording Behaviors

The data collection sheet presented in this appendix will help you isolate variables that may be contributing to a student's inappropriate behavior. Data should be collected for a minimum of 5 days to determine whether or not any one variable is cuing or maintaining the inappropriate behavior.

Susan, a profoundly retarded 8-year-old, would scream throughout the day. According to the completed chart on pages 250 and 251, the data collected on Susan's screaming behavior indicate that the staff response was maintaining the inappropriate behavior of screaming. There were no consistent patterns within the other categories of behavior (location, time, ongoing activity) except for individuals involved. Here it was discovered that Susan was alone most of the time when her screaming occurred; staff response, however, was always the same.

An appropriate behavioral intervention would be the elimination of shouting, "Stop it, Susan." This staff response gives Susan the attention she is seeking and maintains the inappropriate behavior.

Another response must be planned for Susan's screaming behavior. Once you have decided upon a new consequence for Susan's screaming (based on Chapters 11–14), you will continue to collect data. These intervention data will determine the effectiveness of your program.

This data collection sheet can be helpful in planning educational programs. It isolates problems in the environment, with other individuals, or with activities, and it helps you to become aware of your own responses to student behavior.

The data collection will be easily implemented after you have completed this text. A blank copy of the data collection sheet is included on page 252 for your reference.

DATA COLLECTION SHEET

Child's name: Susan

Behavior: screaming

Date	What time did the behavior start?	What time did the behavior stop?	Location of the behavior	Ongoing activity	Individuals involved	Staff response
2/9/81	12:05 p.m.	12:30 p.m.	lunchroom	lunch	Mary (aide)	Mary shouting, "Stop it, Susan."
	2:10 p.m.	2:15 p.m.	day room	free time	Douglas (student)	aide shouting, "Stop it, Susan."
	2:30 p.m.	2:45 p.m.	day room	free time	no one	aide shouting, "Stop it, Susan."
2/10/81	8:00 a.m.	8:30 a.m.	classroom	unloading buses	Kathy (student)	teacher shouting, "Stop it, Susan."
	9:15 a.m.	9:40 a.m.	classroom	toileting	no one	teacher shouting, "Stop it, Susan."
	11:20 a.m.	12:20 p.m.	classroom lunchroom	lunch	no one	aide shouting, "Stop it, Susan."
	1:45 p.m.	1:50 p.m.	playground	walking	no one	aide shouting, "Stop it, Susan."
2/11/81	3:00 p.m.	3:05 p.m.	hallway	walking to bus	no one	teacher shouting, "Stop it, Susan," and took Susan's hand
2/12/81	8:00 a.m.	8:30 a.m.	classroom	unloading buses	David (student)	aide shouting, "Stop it, Susan."

Date						
	10:10 a.m.	10:20 a.m.	gym	walking	no one	gym teacher shouting, "Stop it, Susan," and holding her hand as she walked
	2:25 p.m.	2:30 p.m.	day room	free time	no one	aide shouting, "Stop it, Susan."
2/13/81	9:15 a.m.	9:45 a.m.	classroom	waiting turn self-help	no one	aide shouting, "Stop it, Susan."
	10:10 a.m.	10:20 a.m.	classroom	self-help	no one	aide and teacher left room with principal in charge; principal shouted, "Stop it."
	12:00 noon	12:05 p.m.	lunchroom	cleaning up	Jennifer (student)	teacher shouting, "Stop it, Susan."

DATA COLLECTION SHEET

Child's name: _____

Behavior: _____

Starting date of log: _____

Date	What time did the behavior start?	What time did the behavior stop?	Location of the behavior	Ongoing activity	Individuals involved	Staff response

GLOSSARY

Adaptation: The phase in a behavioral program during which the student is allowed to adjust to novel stimuli in the new learning environment.

Aversive stimulus: A stimulus that has the effect of decreasing a behavior when it is presented as a consequence of (contingent upon) that behavior. A stimulus that the individual will actively work to avoid.

Avoidance learning: When someone responds in order to avoid or escape something that is unpleasant to him or her.

Backward chaining procedure: A teaching procedure in which instruction begins with the last step in the chain and proceeds toward the first step in the chain.

Baseline: The period of time during which a behavior is observed and measured without any therapeutic or instructional intervention.

Baseline data: Data that are used to determine the effectiveness of an intervention by comparing the occurrence of the behavior during baseline versus its occurrence during intervention.

Behavior: Any observable and measurable act of a student. A response. (See also *Response.*)

Behavior chain: A sequence of stimuli and responses that end with a terminal reinforcer.

Behavior frequency: The number of times a behavior occurs during a specific period of time.

Behavior modification: Changing behavior through the systematic application of the methods and experimental findings of behavioral science.

Behavioral objective: A description of the performance the student must exhibit.

Behavioral physical restraint: A procedure in which the student is prevented from moving his or her limbs and/or body for a prespecified period following performance of a misbehavior.

Behavioral repertoire: The behaviors that a particular student, at a particular time, is capable of performing.

Chain: Two or more performances combined into a more complex behavioral sequence, occurring in a sequence.

Conditioned aversive stimulus: A neutral stimulus that has acquired aversive properties because it has been repeatedly paired with a primary aversive stimulus.

Conditioned reinforcer: A stimulus, initially having no reinforcing properties, that has been repeatedly paired with the delivery of strong reinforcers so that it becomes a reinforcer.

Consequence: The environmental change that follows the occurrence of the behavior is the consequence.

Contingency: The relation between the response (the target behavior) and the reinforcer.

Contingent reinforcement: Reinforcement that depends upon a specific response.

Continuous recording: Recording each behavior every time it occurs for a given time period.

Continuous reinforcement: Delivery of a reinforcer each time the desired behavior occurs.

Criterion: A specification of an acceptable level of performance that the student is to achieve. Criteria are used to evaluate the success of a behavioral or educational program.

Deprivation: When a reinforcer has not been presented for a while. As a result, the student usually will respond eagerly to obtain that reinforcer.

Differential reinforcement of appropriate behavior (DRA): A procedure in which a reinforcer is given following the performance of one specified appropriate behavior.

Differential reinforcement of incompatible behavior (DRI): A procedure in which a reinforcer is given following the performance of a prespecified behavior that is physically and functionally incompatible with the targeted inappropriate behavior.

Differential reinforcement of other behavior (DRO): A procedure in which a reinforcer is given at the end of a specified period of time provided that a particular misbehavior has not occurred during the specified interval.

Discrimination: The process of behaving one way in one situation and a different way in another situation.

Discriminative stimulus: A stimulus associated with reinforcement.

Duration recording: Measuring the total amount of time a student spends engaging in a prespecified behavior.

Edible reinforcer: Foods preferred by a student.

Entering behaviors: Those behaviors the student possesses before instruction begins. Data on these behaviors tell you where to begin your instruction.

Exclusionary timeout: A procedure in which the misbehaving student is removed from the reinforcing environment for a specified period of time.

Extinction: Withholding the reinforcer that has been sustaining or increasing an undesirable behavior.

Extinction-induced aggression: Aggressive behavior that accompanies the early phases of an extinction program.

Fading: The gradual change of the stimulus control.

FI: Fixed interval.

Fixed interval (FI) schedule: Reinforcing the first prespecified response that occurs after a specified amount of time has elapsed.

FR: Fixed ratio.

Fixed ratio (FR) schedule: Reinforcing a response after a prespecified number of responses have occurred.

Forward chaining: A procedure in which instruction begins with the first step in the chain and proceeds toward the last step in the chain.

Frequency recording: A recording procedure that measures the number of times a student engages in a specific behavior within a set period of time.

Generalization training: A procedure designed to transfer the control over behavior in one situation to other situations.

Graduated guidance: A technique in which physical guidance and fading are combined such that the physical guidance is systematically and gradually reduced and then faded completely.

Incompatible behavior: A behavior that cannot be emitted simultaneously with another behavior. A behavior that interferes with the performance of another behavior. (See also *Differential reinforcement of incompatible behavior (DRI).)*

Instructional cycle: The stimulus, response, and consequence.

Intermittent reinforcement: When some, but not all, of the specific responses are reinforced.

Interval recording: Counting the number of times a prespecified behavior occurs within a series of timed intervals.

Interval schedules of reinforcement: A schedule based upon the interval of time between reinforced responses. There are two kinds of interval schedules: fixed interval and variable interval.

Intervention: The action that is taken to change a target behavior.

Learning history: The sum of an individual's behaviors that have been conditioned or modified as a result of environmental events.

Least restrictive model of treatment: A list of the behaviorally based treatment procedures for decreasing the inappropriate behavior of retarded persons in which the procedures are ranked according to their aversiveness, severity, and intrusiveness.

Noncontingent reinforcement: Reinforcement that is not related to any specific behavior.

Nonexclusionary timeout: A procedure in which the student is allowed to remain in the reinforcing environment but not allowed to engage in reinforcing activities for a specified period of time.

Operant behavior: Behavior that is controlled by its consequences.

Operant level: The frequency of the behavior before instruction or intervention begins. Used in this book interchangeably with baseline. (See also *Baseline* and *Baseline data.*)

Overcorrection: A procedure in which the misbehaving student is required to overcorrect the environmental effects of his or her misbehavior and to practice appropriate forms of behavior in those situations where the misbehavior commonly occurs.

Physical reinforcer: Bodily contact that the student likes or enjoys.

Physical restraint: A procedure in which the student is prevented from moving his or her limbs and/or body.

Positive practice overcorrection: The component of overcorrection in which the student is required to repeatedly practice appropriate behaviors in the situation in which he or she normally misbehaves.

Positive reinforcement: The delivery of a positive reinforcer contingent upon a response or behavior.

Positive reinforcer: A stimulus that, when presented as a consequence of a behavior, results in an increase or maintenance of that behavior.

Premack principle: A procedure in which a behavior the student performs frequently is used to reinforce a behavior the student seldom performs.

Prompt: An additional discriminative stimulus that is presented in order to cue the student to perform a specified behavior. Prompts are usually faded before the terminal behavior is judged as having been achieved. There are three types of prompts: verbal, physical, and gestural.

Punisher: Any unpleasant event that decreases the probability of the response it follows. In this book, the term aversive stimulus is used interchangeably with punisher. (See also *Aversive stimulus.*)

Punishment: An event that decreases the frequency of the behavior it follows. One type of punishment involves the application of an aversive event following the misbehavior. A second type of punishment involves the withdrawal of a positive reinforcer following the misbehavior.

Ratio schedules of reinforcement: A schedule based on the number of responses that are performed. There are two kinds of ratio schedules: fixed ratio and variable ratio.

Reinforcement: A procedure that has occurred when a stimulus that follows a response results in an increase or maintenance of that response.

Reinforcement density: Frequency or rate with which responses are reinforced.

Reinforcement history: See *Learning history.*

Reinforcement schedule: See *Schedule of reinforcement.*

Reinforcer: Any event that maintains or increases the probability of the response it follows.

Reinforcing incompatible behaviors: See *Differential reinforcement of incompatible behavior (DRI).*

Reinforcer sampling: A procedure whereby the student tries a potential reinforcer.

Response: The activity or behavior the student performs in the presence of a particular stimulus.

Restitutional overcorrection: The component of overcorrection in which the student is required to correct the consequences of his or her misbehavior by restoring the disturbed situation to a state vastly improved from that which existed before the disruption.

Satiation: When a reinforcer has been presented to the point where it is no longer effective in producing or maintaining a behavior.

Schedule of reinforcement: The specification as to which behaviors will be reinforced on an intermittent schedule.

SD: See *Discriminative stimulus.*

Shaping: A procedure to produce a behavior that is currently not in the student's behavioral repertoire.

Social reinforcer: Praise, a smile, attention, friendly remarks, etc., that a student likes or enjoys.

Spontaneous recovery: The reappearance of a behavior that has been eliminated by means of an extinction procedure.

Stimulus: Any physical object or occurrence in the environment that sets the occasion for the response to occur. Stimuli frequently used in behavioral programs include reinforcing stimuli, aversive stimuli, and discriminative stimuli.

Successive approximations: Behavioral elements (responses) or subsets each of which more and more closely resembles the specified terminal behavior.

Target behavior: A desired behavior that does not occur but which we wish to establish. (See also *Terminal behavior.*)

Task analysis: A detailed description of each behavior needed to accomplish an objective.

Terminal behavior: See *Target behavior.*

Terminal reinforcer: The reinforcer at the end of a behavior (stimulus-response) chain.

Time sampling: An observation or recording method in which you count the number of times a prespecified behavior occurs at the end of a specified interval of time.

Timeout: A punishment procedure in which positive reinforcement is withdrawn for a prespecified period of time following the performance of the misbehavior.

Timeout ribbon procedure: A nonexclusionary timeout procedure in which a student's ribbon (a conditioned reinforcer) is removed following a misbehavior.

Timeout room: A small room that is devoid of any reinforcing stimuli.

Variable interval (VI) schedule: Reinforcing the first prespecified response that occurs after a specified amount of time has elapsed.

Variable ratio (VR) schedule: Reinforcing a different number of responses each time such that over time a specific average number of responses are reinforced.

VI: Variable interval.

VR: Variable ratio.

INDEX